ANCIENT COIN COLLECTING IV

Roman Provincial Coins

WAYNE G. SAYLES

Published by

krause publications

700 E. State Street
Iola, WI 54990-0001
Telephone: 715/445-2214

Please call or write for our free catalog. Our toll-free number to place an order or obtain a free catalog is 800-258-0929 or please use our regular business telephone 715-445-2214 for editorial comment and further information.

Library of Congress Catalog Number: 95-82428
ISBN: 0-87341-552-3

Printed in the United States of America

To

Scott, Steve and Stephanie

PREFACE

This fourth volume of the *Ancient Coin Collecting* series is intended to serve as a road map to the coinage of Roman administration in lands which came within their sphere of influence either by subjugation or by supplication. We tend to think of the Romans as great conquerors, but they were also a great stabilizing force within the ancient world. It was not always the case that nations succumbed to the might of Roman arms. In at least two cases, entire kingdoms were bequeathed to the Roman people on the death of a Hellenistic monarch. In other cases, minor royalty actively sought the allegiance and protection of Rome, voluntarily accepting nominal titles and varying degrees of authority.

In a masterful stroke of diplomacy, the new masters of the Mediterranean (and subsequently lands beyond) catered to local traditions and customs when it came to the style and imagery of provincial coinage. This fostered an acceptance of the coinage which, although controlled by Roman administration, was mainly intended for limited local circulation—at least in the case of bronze coinage. Silver and billon coin types tended moreso to reflect the norms of Imperial mint production, and may in fact have circulated to a wider extent than the bronze. The transfer of wealth from the provinces to Rome did not come in the form of provincial coinage itself. Instead, it appeared in the form of imported goods and services, which could be purchased with provincial coinage from locally generated revenues. The long term result of this system was a fascinating series of coinage, with widely divergent character, circulating for the most part in small geographical regions. For the collector of ancient coins, this provides a numismatic, historical and iconographic cornucopia.

In previous generations, the coinage of this general type was referred to as "Greek Imperial". That is, coinage of Greek lands struck under Roman Imperial domination. This term is inadequate in many respects, and it is generally accepted now that Roman Provincial is a more accurate and appropriate description. In fact, some provincial coins were struck in regions that had no Greek traditions at all. The scholarship of this series has suffered somewhat due to its vagueness. Historically, Roman specialists have avoided it because of the Greek legends, and Greek specialists have seen it as a product of the Roman world. Only in the past 50 years or so has there been any serious study of provincial coinage. Consequently, it is still a field very much open to discovery and analysis.

The distinction between "Imperial" coins and "provincial" coins is not entirely one of geography. For example, great quantities of Imperial coinage were struck at the mint of Lugdunum (Lyon) in southern Gaul, as well as in Eastern mints and travelling mints. It also seems clear that there was interaction between the Imperial mint at Rome and mints in the provinces—especially in regard to official portraits and titulature. In fact, some provincial mints even shared obverse dies from time to time. It has also been suggested that there was some centralization among provincial mints. Some scholars have tried to make a distinction between coins issued by the emperor and those issued by a city, but this is fraught with problems. The most acceptable criteria for differentiating between Imperial and provincial coins seems to be a consideration of the purpose for which the coinage was struck. Locally produced and circulated coinage (mostly commonly in bronze) can be considered provincial while that struck specifically for the use of Rome and the emperor (or his army) is more imperial in nature. Unfortunately, even this simple rule has its exceptions—as the more advanced collector will discover. The phenomenon of provincial coinage extends, for our purposes from the proclamation of Octavian as Augustus (27 BC) to the usurpation of Domitius Domitianus (AD 296-297) in Egypt. After that date, all coinage in the empire was issued at imperial mints for use throughout the realm. That this system did in fact become universal is proven by the occasional finding of Alexandria mint coins in the Balkans and London or Gallic mint coins in the Middle East.

In the preceding two volumes, we featured portrait galleries of political leaders. Although this volume will include a small portrait gallery of Roman Client-Kings, it is primarily a book about the cultural and geographic influences in provincial coinage. These coins present a unique blend of Greek idealism and Roman pragmatism. As works of art, they are most often appreciated for their narrative qualities. Narration was a dominant characteristic of Roman coin motifs, and the Roman administrators of these widespread provinces found it easy to accept local traditions in numismatic narrative. It is often the case that a provincial coin will honor both the emperor and the city of issue. This leads to a coin of two faces. The obverse typically pays homage to the incumbent ruler, while the reverse promotes some aspect of the political or social life of the city. Of course there are also coins of a more Imperial flavor in which the emperor or empire is the dominant theme on both sides. In rare cases, the imperial portrait was presented without an accompanying city reference. Conversely, cities or individuals were occasionally granted the authority to issue certain types of coinage in their own name. These issues are referred to as "semiautonomous" and they do not include the name of an emperor. The diversity of types, and no less that of the images, is extraordinary. As we explore the field of Roman provincial Coinage, we are actually exploring the history of Roman military and political policy in the lands that they touched. In a unique mixture, Roman and local influences merge to form a coinage of remarkable interest, relative rarity, and complex symbolism. What better qualifications could a collectible present?

We shall begin our survey of the provincial coinage with a geographical tour. The system of cataloguing Greek coins that was devised by Jan Eckhel in the 18th century is still in use today. Following Eckhel's method of arrangement we will look at the coinage of this period beginning at the western Mediterranean. Starting with Spain, we shall explore the coinage of each Roman province, proceeding to Gaul, Britain and Germany. A few coins of Italy and Sicily may also be considered provincial. From there we shall examine the provinces of Greece and the Balkans, Asia Minor, Syria, the Near East, Arabia and North Africa. Among the regional coinages, none stands out more distinctly than that of Roman Egypt. The fabric, style, denominations, imagery and minting practices are unique. For this reason, we have included a special section about provincial coinage from Egypt. Authoring this section is Kerry K. Wetterstrom, an internationally acknowledged expert and himself a passionate collector of the series.

Following this armchair tour, we will delve into the nature of the coins themselves. That is, we will learn how to recognize and attribute provincial coins. Reading the inscriptions on these coins can be a bit more challenging than those on Roman Imperial coins. The legends are often written in Greek, and the alphabet is somewhat different from that of earlier periods. However, with practice and perserverance these legends can be mastered—even by the amateur. In some ways, the provincial coins are more descriptive than Imperial issues. They often spell out the name of the city, along with a precise date of issue. At the same time, they tend to include enough honorific titles and abbreviations that deciphering the legend can require the virtue of patience. If the process seems difficult at first, hang in there. The reward is that this is a field where the amateur collector can make true and valuable discoveries.

Finally, we will look at the varied and fascinating imagery that appears on provincial coins. From agonistic types heralding festivals and games to architectural designs in complex perspective, from allegory to allusion, the motifs are extraordinary. We will also present a section of "Masterpieces" from this series. By their very nature, these coins are usually scarce or rare in comparison to coins of the Imperial mints. Some major cities, like Antioch, produced great quantities of coinage. Most, however, struck coinage for a relatively small populace. It happens that some personalities whose coins are very rare in the Imperial series are fairly common in the provincial series. In fact, some numismatic portraits are available *only* on provincial coins. Conversely, some emperors, whose Imperial mint issues are common, will be found on very few provincial issues.

In style, this volume of the *Ancient Coin Collecting* series follows the same pattern as its predecessors. Many short chapters deal with a variety of subjects. The scope of provincial coinage is immense, and it is impossible for a book of this size to deal with it in any really substantial way. Therefore, we have attempted to present a "road map" for the collector. This, we hope, will save time and effort by synthesizing and distilling much of the information that he or she needs to learn. Where broader resources are available, we shall direct the reader to them.

All of the books in this series forego footnoting in favor of textual and bibliographic references. In an introductory work, we feel that the beginning collector will find this approach more "user-friendly" than the traditional approach required of scholars. For those who demand greater depth, we have provided bibliographic references throughout. The convention of using Latinized names in catalogues and references may be a bit confusing to the beginner, e.g. Nicaea for Nikaia, but familiarity will eventually make the differences clear. We have tried here to use forms of proper names that the collector will most likely find in modern literature and commercial references.

The illustrations herein are intended to introduce the reader to the beauty and complexity of provincial coins, but it should be understood that some of these represent particularly fine examples of coins which often are difficult to obtain. This should not deter the collector, however, since there are many interesting and beautiful coins in this series which *are* obtainable, even at modest prices. As in the earlier volumes, it is our intention throughout to project visual images rather than to document specific coin types or specimens. Where the illustrated size varies significantly from that of the actual specimen, we have made note. Since this book is neither a catalogue nor attribution guide, we have sometimes illustrated only the obverse or reverse of a coin as appropriate to the purpose at hand.

Once again, we hope that the following pages will serve as a catalyst to further study and foster a deeper appreciation of the hobby. Welcome to the fascinating world of Roman provincial coins!

Gainesville, Missouri 1998 W.G.S.

ACKNOWLEDGMENTS

We are grateful to Kerry K. Wetterstrom, friend and professional numismatist, for sharing his expertise on the coinage of Roman Egypt. We are honored that he would contribute to this effort in such a valuable way. The kind permission of Kevin Ferguson to quote his *Celator* article about the Roman founder motif is much appreciated. We are indebted to Marvin Tameanko for his lucid hypothesis about dimples on coins. Our thanks also go to Dr. William Metcalf of the American Numismatic Society for suggestions which improved the accuracy of information about cistophoric tetradrachms. Since this book is, for the most part, a synthesis of information from many sources, we could not possibly acknowledge all of the numismatists who have made a contribution. Let us simply give our thanks to everyone who has taken the time and made the effort to share their knowledge in print.

Illustrated in this fourth volume of the *Ancient Coin Collecting* series are even more of the finest coins to have come on the ancient coin market in recent decades. We are deeply indebted to Classical Numismatic Group, of Lancaster, Pennsylvania, Leu Numismatik of Zürich, Switzerland, M&M Numismatics Ltd. of Basel Switzerland and Edward J. Waddell of Gaithersburg, Maryland, for permission to reproduce photos from fixed price lists and auction catalogues issued by their firms. For the sake of avoiding tedious repetition, we have not credited each photograph. The great majority of photographs in this book came, however, from these sources. The illustrations of Bedoukian 1 and 2 in the section on Armenia were extracted from Dr. Bedoukian's useful monograph about Roman coins with Armenian references (see bibliography). Line art illustrations were extracted from Duruy's *History of Rome,* 1894 edition. Our thanks to Parnell Nelson, long time illustrator of cartoons in *The Celator,* for permission to reproduce the cartoonist's answer to the dimpling question.

As always, my wife Doris has been a constant encouragement, a source of motivation, a patient companion and an invaluable production assistant.

TABLE OF CONTENTS

What are Provincial Coins?

Commagene, AE dupondius
Tiberius, ca. AD 19-21

The distinction between Roman Imperial and Roman Provincial coinage is not clear-cut by any means, and numismatic cataloguers often struggle with the issue. One view is that provincial coins bear Greek inscriptions and imperial coins bear Latin inscriptions. This is overly simplistic, as one will discover before very long in dealing with these issues. There are colonial coins which bear nothing but Latin inscriptions. Some take the view that imperial coins bear the "SC" indicating senatorial approval, whereas provincial coins do not. This does not work either, because one can easily point to denarii from the Rome mint which are devoid of the letters SC, and to a number of provincial bronzes which *do* have SC in the fields. Another view is that imperial coins were issued by the emperor and provincial coins were issued under authority of the senate or local semi-autonomous city governments. This too has its problems.

For example, Tiberius annexed Commagene in AD 19 and ordered the striking of dupondii bearing his portrait along with a distinctly imperial reverse type. However, the dies were engraved in a decidedly crude style, on planchets with chamfered edges. These are typical provincial mint characteristics. This coin type is published both in *Roman Imperial Coinage* (RIC I, *Tiberius,* 90) and in *Roman Provincial Coinage* (RPC 3868). In the trade, it has been listed along with either imperial or provincial coins, depending on the view of the cataloguer.

What about distinguishing by denominations? No—we find denarii and sestertii with Greek and Latin colonial legends. Neither can one make the distinction based on location of minting, because many rulers struck imperial coins at mints within the provinces. Among the most notable of these are the first century imperial issues from Spain and Gaul and the Severan denarii struck at Eastern mints. So, where do we draw the line? If anything, style seems to be a major factor in the cataloguer's decision as to where a particular type should be placed. Imperial coins tend to have a consistency of size, weight and iconography that provincial coins—for better or worse—lack. The difficulty with this, of course, is that style is a subjective determination. Back to square one! So, where would this cataloguer put the Tiberius bronze from Commagene? Naturally, where it belongs—with the provincials.

The Expanding Roman World

The goddess Roma

During the later days of the Republic, the Romans expanded their interests far beyond their homeland. Through the force of arms, immense tracts of land from Spain to Syria and Britain to North Africa were brought under Roman control. These acquired lands were brought into the Roman system as provinces, and their cities were conferred with one of several hierarchal titles. The Roman civil and military presence in these regions was substantial. Following the Battle of Actium Octavian could count something like 60 widely dispersed legions under his command. Because of this vastness of territory, and the diverse histories of each conquered land, it is easy for us to think of them in isolation. We often read about life in Roman Britain, or on the Parthian frontier, and build a vision of brave garrisons holding on to precarious outposts. In reality, this was the exception rather than the rule. The provincial system was, on the whole, as stable as the government of Rome itself. And, it took on a commonality that forever changed local ways of life in most of the western world.

The great success of this administrative and bureaucratic system may be attributed primarily to the wisdom of its designer. Augustus, although recognized as an extremely successful military leader, must also be credited with implementing the political and social policies that led to Roman Imperial hegemony for a half-millennium. His early reorganization of the army into 28 fully manned legions secured several important benefits. It eliminated units which had been loyal to his adversaries, it provided a ready source of trained veterans for emergency recall, and it improved the stability of provincial settlements by giving land and a vested interest to capable defenders. The settling of veterans in cohesive groups also provided a source of nearby reserves to move into troublesome areas. In times of minor crisis, it was much easier and more effective to mobilize a local force of former legionaries than to move an active legion to the hotspot. The distribution of active legions within the provinces was such that no single provincial leader could muster enough strength to challenge the central authority.

The provincial system was well devised, but required an extensive logistical support capability and a massive bureaucracy to manage its affairs. Toward the end of his lengthy reign, Augustus apparently recognized that the empire had reached its limit, at least in terms of efficient management. His final instruction to Tiberius, his heir, was to avoid further expansion. This admonition seems to have been well received, as Tiberius spent most of his 23 year reign maintaining the status quo.

Later, the temptation to add new lands of opportunity proved too great for the emperors of Rome. Britain was settled during the reign of Claudius, the Danubian and Arabian frontiers were pushed back by Trajan, and under Marcus Aurelius multiple excursions against the Parthians resulted in temporary control of Mesopotamia. In addition to growth through acquisition, the total number of provinces grew through division. The successors of Augustus saw wisdom in reducing a province's size by dividing it. This reduced the power of provincial governors, and increased the influence of central (imperial) authority. It has been estimated that by the time of Constantine the Great there were as many civil servants in the government as there were legionaries in the army. All of this expansion was of course accompanied by the production of coinage—both to pay the legions and civil servants, and to establish new settlements in the conquered lands.

Initially, the Senate retained control of entire provinces, but over time its strength was increasingly weakened. Of the 45 Roman provinces known to exist during the reign of Marcus Aurelius, only six were controlled by the Senate. Also, many cities were refounded under imperial authority and were thereby lost to the Senate, which eventually lost all of its colonial possessions. Provincial cities generally fall into two basic categories, that is, Roman colonies and non-colonial cities or districts. The rights of colonies varied by their individual status, but the most important right for many was the exemption from tribute to Rome.

Colonies were both military and non-military in origin. The military colony was normally settled by the emperor, with soldiers who had been released from active service. The non-military colony was typically established by the Senate, with a settlement of Roman citizens who retained full rights as Romans. Initially, the Senate retained control of entire provinces, but over time its strength was increasingly weakened. Of the 45 Roman provinces known to exist during the reign of Marcus Aurelius, only six were controlled by the Senate. Many cities were refounded under imperial authority and were thereby lost to the Senate, which eventually lost all of its colonial possessions.

A meritorious city, acquired either through conquest or negotiation, was sometimes awarded the rights of a colony—even though its inhabitants were indigenous. The highest level of self-government bestowed on these cities was the *municipium,* with full Roman citizenship and protection of law. Of lesser prestige were the *municipia* with limited citizenship and native law. These new colonies usually retained their original

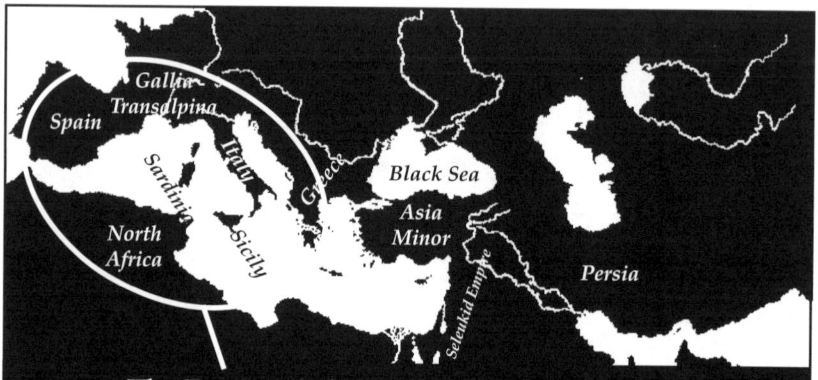

The Roman Sphere of Influence - 2nd c. BC

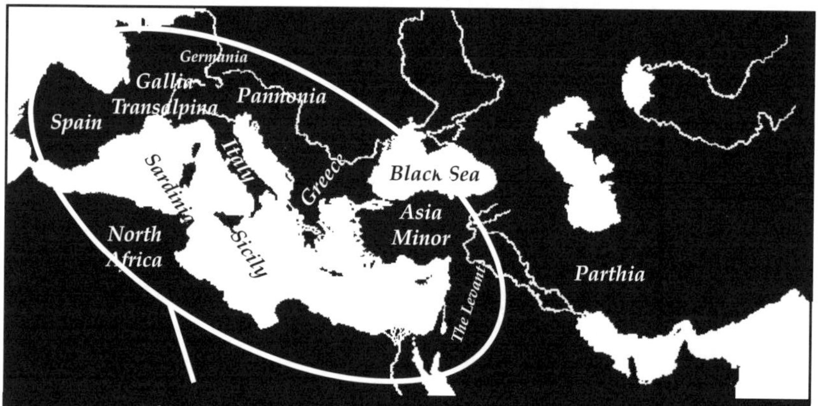

The Roman Sphere of Influence in AD 14

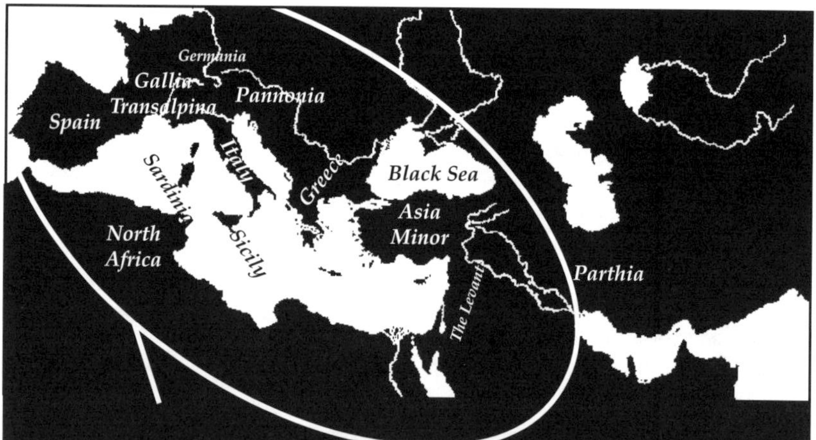

The Roman Sphere of Influence - 2nd c. AD

names, but on occasion were renamed in honor of the Roman founder or his family. Colonial status was a great honor, and normally was reflected within coin inscriptions as COL in Latin or ΚΟΛ in Greek. Julius Caesar bestowed this privilege upon several cities in Spain which had helped him in the war against Pompey. The status was also awarded to honored cities throughout the Roman world by Marc Antony, Augustus and several of his successors. The management of these colonies (cities) was placed in the hands of a bureaucracy not unlike that of Rome itself. It should be understood that most provincial cities were *not* colonies. Still, Eckhel named over 100 of them in his monumental study.

The entire province was ruled by a governor, either a proconsul or praetor in rank. The proconsul exercised power over both civil and military functions, while the praetor had power only over civil affairs. Normally a proconsul was assigned when stability was questionable. The praetor served in more peaceful provinces. As governor, either exercised absolute authority within their province—except that Roman citizens could theoretically appeal any action or decision to the People's Tribune at Rome (not always a practical alternative). Assisting the governor were legates, who assumed control of specified districts. These were normally military leaders. Their civilian counterparts, called quaestors, normally handled the financial affairs of the province. Individual cities within the province were governed by various magistrates. One of the most important magistrates was the aedile. This magistrate was responsible for commerce, provisions and public games, and sometimes for the striking of coins. The monograms of aediles therefore appeared on city coinage. In some cases, more than one aedile served in a given year—hence multiple monograms. Usually, the rank was awarded to not more than two magistrates at a time.

Sardis, Lydia, AE 29mm (x 1.75)
Caracalla, AD 198-217
Lion crouching before city walls

Although there was a consistency of Roman administration, engineering and law throughout the empire, each province stood independent of its neighbors. A governor who possessed virtually unlimited power within his own province, was forbidden to step foot on the soil of a neighboring province without surrendering his insignia. Doing so was considered treason. Each province

Anchialos, Thrace, AE 26mm
Septimius Severus, AD 193-211

was like a small state, and all forms of intercourse between the provinces was controlled by the central administration. This was undoubtedly by design, and part of the mechanism which safeguarded against usurpation of power.

On many provincial coins we see the portrayal of city walls and major fortifications. These conjure up visions of feudal castles where lords and barons held court and directed their domains. Actually, the opposite was true. The walled city was, in Roman times, a place of refuge. The real wealth of the provinces was agricultural, and the landed nobility, along with the working class, lived and worked outside of the city. Within the walled cities were merchants and administrators, meeting places and entertainments, temples and treasuries, and of course the mint. In times of danger, the nobles withdrew to the city—often to an acropolis—for protection.

Mint activity in the provinces seems to have peaked during the Severan dynasty, when virtually every town of any consequence issued their own coinage—especially so in the Balkans, Asia Minor and the Levant. Only 40 years later, the picture had changed dramatically. Most of the cities of Asia Minor stopped producing local coinage by the time of Gallienus, and with the overthrow of Domitius Domitianus in 297, even Egypt stopped producing its own coinage. In our eyes, this marks the end of a monetary system. To the local populaces, it probably did not make a huge difference. By then, imperial coinage had infiltrated so deeply into provincial affairs that it was commonly accepted and in most cases readily available.

Throughout the course of three centuries, the images and inscriptions on provincial coinage recount the expansion of Roman influence, the deeds of Roman authority and the diffusion of Roman culture. In no other series of ancient coinage can we observe such dramatic events and feel such an affinity with the people of a particular region. The expansion of Roman influence brought with it an infrastructure of lasting consequence. Even today, visitors to these lands are inspired by monumental public works, transportation systems, and communications capabilities that are the hallmarks of a massive governmental machine. Many of these administrative accomplishments were portrayed on coinage in truly Roman propagandistic fashion.

It is our good fortune, as collectors and antiquarians, that the system of local coinage in place at that time allowed for such remarkable diversity and captured such wonderful vignettes of the life and times of provincial Rome.

Foundation Iconography

In the vast imagery of ancient coins, few instances occur where the observer can rest more confident in the meaning than in Roman foundation scenes. The depiction of a Roman plow, being pulled behind oxen, is an unmistakable reference to the founding of a colonial city. At first sight, the scene looks rather unimposing—perhaps a commendation of agricultural prosperity. In reality, it was the symbolic narration of a colony's birth. Kevin Ferguson has written a short article (*The Celator,* Vol. 11, No. 12, December, 1997) describing the Roman plow—or *plough* in this case, since the author is from Canada—and its significance as a coin motif. It would be difficult for us to improve upon his succinct and enlightening observations, therefore, with his generous permission we have included it here as published.

Caesaraugusta, Spain
Caligula, AD 37-41
AE 31mm

The Roman plough: a measure of history

When it comes to the study of ancient history the Roman plough never appears to get much attention. It often is easier and more romantic to focus on the battles won and lost by the great general or the infamous emperor; rather than the plough and the poor fellow who walked behind it. There is nothing seductive about walking behind large farm animals while choking on dust, and occasionally stepping in dung; yet the Roman plough and ploughman need to be given a measure of respect for the place they hold in history. The Roman legion may have conquered the entire Mediterranean world, but it was the plough that helped to civilize it.

Much like today the Romans themselves never viewed the plough as a glamorous item. During the reign of Augustus however, when Rome was embarking upon large colonial ventures the image of the plough actually made it on to the coinage of the time. Many of Rome's colonies and provinces had developed economically to such an extent that they were given license to mint their own local bronze coinage. It is on this coinage that we encounter what the Romans were up to once the successful legions had moved on. On the reverse of the local coinage from the colony of Caesaraugusta in Spain to Parium in Mysia which is now modern day Turkey; we encounter the image of a priest or colonist walking behind a plough pulled by two oxen. It is here that we catch a glimpse of how the world was to be civilized.

The image of the ploughing colonist refers to the founding of a Roman colony, but perhaps even more significantly it represents

Rome's ability to drive back the wilderness and domesticate the land in that particular region. However, the image also presents the modern observer with something else which is much less obvious. The image is that of the man operating the plough; for he is doing much more than breaking sod. This ploughman in the typical methodical Roman fashion is in fact measuring the world.

From a treatise left behind by Vitruvius, a Roman engineer who lived during the time of Augustus, we can get a real idea as to what the ploughman was doing. According to Vitruvius, all Roman measures were derived from the human body. The smallest was the digit, then the palm; and then came that old familiar measurement known as the foot. There were 16 digits or four palms in a Roman foot. The Roman foot itself was about 296 mm, or 11-5/8 of an inch. A Roman mile was 5,000 Roman feet. Roman marching feet, and Roman farmland was measured by the feet of their ploughing oxen.

Much like modern surveying concepts the Roman mind liked to envision land in square blocks. Once the land was parcelled into blocks the Roman farmer then could make a reasonable estimate of the size of the crops he could grow; and most importantly he could get a fair idea of the potential yield for a piece of land—given the type of soil he had to work with, and of course dealing with intangibles such as weather. An ancient Roman farmer probably had a lot in common with the farmer of today.

Most, if not all, of the coin reverses depicting ploughing scenes refer to the turning of new sod. In which case the ploughman probably had the notion in his mind that he was creating an iugerum. An iugerum was begun by the precise ploughing of a furrow 120 feet in a straight line. Then another 120 foot furrow was ploughed at a right angle. This 120 by 120 foot section created an actus. Two square acti, or 120 feet by 240 feet created the unit of land measurement known to the Roman as the iugerum. It was based on a line of 120 feet because that is how far the oxen could plough before they needed a rest.

Caesarea Maritima, Samaria, AD 117-138
AE-31mm struck under Hadrian

This form of measurement was considered so practical that when the Romans founded a new city they simply incorporated the same standard on which the ploughing of land was based. A Roman surveyor would mark off the boundaries of a city using a groma and a rod. A groma was a staff with a cross that was notched in the center so it would revolve when placed on top. From the four corners of the cross, small plummets were hung with cords. It was the straight line created by two opposing cords that the surveyor used to measure a straight line. Once the line was sited an assistant laid out a ten foot rod. The end of the rod was marked, and then the groma was moved forward. Twelve markings of the ten foot rod gave the surveyor the first leg of an actus of 120 feet. Therefore every new city constructed during the time of Augustus was laid out according to the distance travelled by two oxen, one farmer, and a Roman plough.

The image of the Roman ploughman on the reverse of provincial coinage may not be glamourous, but it would appear to be timeless. Every corner of Europe that the Roman plough touched had retained and passed on at least some of the civilizing knowledge held by the man walking behind the two oxen. That knowledge has even spread to worlds then unknown to the ploughman. North America measures their land in square units regardless of the type of measurements used. The United States still measures their world in feet; something the Roman ploughman would easily understand. So when one studies the reverse of a Roman provincial coin making use of the ploughing theme; one should remember that man and his plough have had a profound effect upon world history.

Legions and the Provinces

Those colonies that were settled with legionary veterans were known as "military" colonies. The settlers typically were men who had served their commitments and distinguished themselves in the line of duty. Sulla established the first military colonies and the practice became more common in Imperial times. In some cases, an entire legion—with its officers, and men of all ranks—was settled in a new colony. On the other hand, these veterans were not exclusively deposited into unsettled border territories. The *Coloniae Romanae* had been around long before Augustus reformed the government and there were already many well established colonies in existence by the advent of the Roman Empire.

Colonial coinage often contained references to the Legions from which the settled veterans came. For example, Legionary ensigns were depicted—either alone or with the names of the Legions. Sometimes the ensigns (vexilla) were part of a founder scene, of the oxen and plow type. On a coin of the military colony Caesaraugusta, in Spain, military ensigns were depicted on the obverse and a plowing scene was selected for the reverse. At the military colony of Viminacium, a standard coin design was that of the personified province holding legionary standards.

Of course active legions also occupied the provinces, and the evidence of their presence may also be seen on coins of both the

Distribution of the remaining 25 Roman Legions following the Teutoburger Wald massacre

Spain:
IV Macedonica
VI Victrix
X Gemina

Upper Germany:
II Augusta
XIII Gemina
XIV Gemina
XVI

Lower Germany:
I Germanica
V Alaudae
XX Valeria
XXI Rapax

Pannonia:
VIII Augusta
IX Hispana
XV Apollinaris

Dalmatia:
VII
XI

Moesia:
IV Scythica
V Macedonica

Syria:
III Gallica
VI Ferrata
X Fretensis
XII Fulminata

Egypt:
III Cyrenaica
XXII Deiotariana

Africa:
III Augusta

imperial and provincial varieties. Vexilla do not by themselves assure us that the issuing city was a military colony. The reference may be to some event other than a founding, and the city might not, in fact, have been a colony at all. The garrisoning of a legion nearby was reason enough at times to place the vexilla on provincial coinage.

The Roman Legate of Syria during the probable year of Christ's birth was P. Quinctilius Varus. This was the same general who in AD 9 lost his entire army, consisting of Legions XVII, XVIII and XIX in the Teutoburger Wald massacre in Germany. Varus took his own life on the battlefield. Fifteen years earlier, at Berytos (Beirut), he issued a bronze coin with the head of Augustus on its obverse and his own name, along with legionary standards, on the reverse.

Berytos, Phoenicia, AE 21mm
P. Quinctilius Varus, 6-4 BC

A 22mm bronze issued at Heliopolis in Coele-Syria, for Philip II as Caesar, bears on its reverse the legend LEG V MACED VIII AVG COL HEL. The reverse image is a typical founder motif of two oxen pulling a plow. Behind are two legionary vexilla. Heliopolis was settled by Augustus in 16 BC, with veterans for Legion V, Macedonia and Legion VIII, Augusta. Although the active legions V and VIII were transferred from the East to Moesia during the reign of Augustus, the heritage of its founding veterans was still being acknowledged and honored some 250 years later.

Heliopolis, Coele-Syria, AE 22mm
Philip II, AD 247-249

During Gordian III's reign (AD 238-244), Viminacium in Moesia was garrisoned by legions IV and VII. A 30mm bronze coin struck during this period depicts, on its reverse, the two legions, represented by a lion and bull respectively. Between them stands the personification of Moesia holding two military standards. The abbreviation PMS in

Viminacium, Moesia Superior, AE 30mm
Gordian III, AD 238-244

the reverse legend stands for Provinciae Moesiae Superioris. The AN IIII signifies year four (AD 244) of the city's era.

As if to confuse posterity, the Romans had more than one Legion of a particular number. That is why they are referred to by their appelation and number. Legion III Parthica was not the same unit as Legion III Gallica, but they both served in the East. Coins bearing III Parthica's insignia were issued at Rhesaena in Mesopotamia, where the unit was stationed during the reign of Caracalla. The fact that Tyre, in Phoenicia, was a colony settled with Legion III-Gallica veterans is confirmed by a 29mm bronze struck under Gallienus. On this coin's reverse, the Roman eagle stands proudly before a vexillum inscribed LEG III GAL.

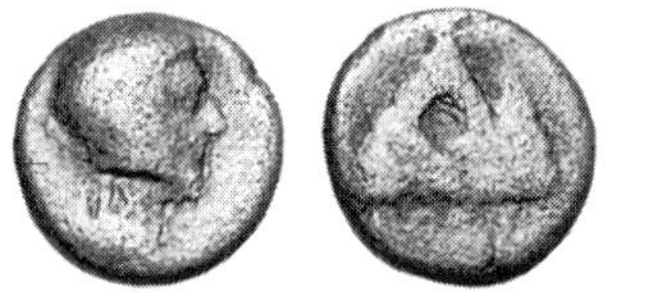

Caesarea, Cappadocia, AE 18mm
Lucius Verus, obverse c/m LXV
for Legion XV Apollonaris

Another important reference to the legions and witness of their presence is the legionary countermark on provincial coins. Countermarking was relatively common on provincial coinage in general—with some specimens bearing two, three or more impressions. For various reasons, either political or economic, the mint serving a region would recall certain coins and reissue them with a mark of certification. Often, the host coins which bear these countermarks are worn almost past the point of recognition. Being that it was recessed into the surface of the coin, a countermark withstood wear better than the natural relief. But even the countermarks are sometimes worn down. This would suggest that these coins circulated for a very long time, both prior to and after being restamped. Countermarks were applied with a punch that included an easily recognizable design. In the case of legionary countermarks, those

Sebaste, Samaria, AE 29mm
Domitian, Obv. & Rev. c/m (3)
LXF for Legion X Fretensis

Tyre, Phoenicia, AE 29mm
Gallienus, AD 253-268

punches often bore the numeric designation of the legion or legions. Troops were sometimes paid in locally circulated currency that had been countermarked for the purpose. Tracing the migration of these specially countermarked coins has revealed much new information about military campaigns and troop movements.

The movement of troops in ancient times would seem to us a complicated and arduous undertaking—without the benefit of cargo planes or convoys of troop ships. It appears, however, that units did move about quite freely. A brief excerpt from the *Notitia Dignitatum,* an official register of the late fourth century, gives us some insight into the composition of forces in Egypt at that time. Under control of the military count of Egypt were: "The fifth Macedonian legion at Memphis; the thirteenth twin legion at Babylon; the Stablesian horse at Pelusium; the Saracen Thamudene horse at Scenae Veteranorum; the third Diocletiana legion at Andropolis; The second Trajana legion at Parembole; the Theodosian squadron recently organized; The Arcadian squadron recently organized; the second squadron of Armenians in the lesser Oasis; the third squadron of Arabs at Thenenuthis; the eighth squadron of Vandals at Nee; the seventh squadron of Sarmatians at Scenae Mandrorum; the first squadron of Egyptians at Selle; the veteran squadron of Gauls at Rinocoruna; the first Herculian squadron at Scenae without Gerasa; the fifth squadron of Raetians at Scenae Veteranorum; the first Tangiers squadron at Thinunepsi; the Aprian squadron at Hipponos; the second squadron of Assyrians at Sosteos; the fifth squadron of Praelecti at Dionysias, the third cohort of Galatians at Cefro and the second cohort of Asturians at Busiris." This list was compiled perhaps a hundred years after the last provincial coins were struck, but it is not likely that the situation differed greatly in the second or third centuries as far as the organization and movement of the army is concerned.

The point is that coins moved along with people. Egypt was a bit of an exception before the reign of Diocletian, because of its closed monetary system. But aside from that, money has always tended to move with people. That is why we find coins from the mint in Carthage along with those from Alexandria or Antioch. Provincial coins did not circulate as readily, because they were not commonly used for troop payments. When they were, they were normally countermarked for the purpose. Thus, the migration of these coins is all the more significant. Upon transferring to another theater, soldiers were likely to dispose of all the local currency possible, but it is inevitable that some coins stayed in their possession.

There are, of course, many intriguing sidelights of this sort in the Roman Provincial series. For this reason, they are among the most interesting and historically relatable coins surviving from antiquity.

BIBLIOGRAPHY

Roman Provincial Expansion

Arnold, WT. *The Roman System of Provincial Administration to the Accession of Constantine the Great,* Oxford, 1914.

Barag, Dan. "The countermarks of the Legio Decima Fretensis", *Proceedings International Numismatic Congress, Jerusalem, 1963,* Tel Aviv and Jerusalem, 1967.

Brunk, Gregory G. "A Hoard from Syria Countermarked by the Roman Legions", *American Numismatic Society Museum Notes* 25, 1980, pp. 63-76.

Burnett, Andrew. "Roman Provincial Coinage of the Julio-Claudians", *Essays in Honour of Robert Carson and Kenneth Jenkins,* London, 1993.

Carson, R.A.G. "The inflation of the third century and its monetary influence in the Near East", *Proceedings, International Numismatic Congress, Jerusalem, 1963,* Tel Aviv and Jerusalem, 1967. pp. 231-250.

Crawford, Michael H. "Money and Exchange in the Roman World", *Journal of Roman Studies,* Vol. 60, 1970, pp. 40-48.

Fairley, William. *Extracts from the Notitia Dignitatum,* Translations and reprints from the Original Sources of European History, Univ. of Pennsylvania, 1899.

Ferguson, Kevin. "The Roman Plough: a measure of history", *The Celator,* Vol. 11, No. 12, December 1997.

Grant, Michael. *From Imperium to Auctoritatis, a Historical Study of the AES Coinage in the Roman Empire 49 B.C. - A.D. 14,* London, 1946.

Howgego, C.J. *Greek Imperial Countermarks,* London, 1985.

MacDowall, David W. "Countermarks of early imperial Corinth", *The Numismatic Chronicle,* 1962, pp. 113-123.

Maxfield, Valerie A. *The Military Decorations of the Roman Army,* Berkeley, 1981.

Mommsen, Theodor. *The Provinces of the Roman Empire,* original 1885, Barnes & Noble (two volumes in one) 1996.

Noot, Art. "The arms and organization of the Roman legions, *The Celator,* Vol. 7, No. 12, December 1993, pp. 6-10.

Tameanko, Marvin. "Varus, give me back my coinage" *The Celator,* Vol. 7, No. 12, December 1993, pp. 38-41.

Thomsen, Rudi. "The pay of the Roman soldier and the property qualifications of the Servian classes", *Classica et mediaevalia Francisco Blatt septua-genario dedicata,* Copenhagen, 1973.

A Tour of the Provinces

This book is not a history of provincial Rome. Theodor Mommsen's venerable work *The Provinces of the Roman Empire* is a readily accessible and a more than adequate source for that. This is a book about *provincial coins,* and the cities or provinces where they were struck. It is inevitable in the short space available here that each province is mentioned only briefly. It should be pointed out that the actual designation "province" was fluid. The list changed from time to time as new provinces were added and others were consolidated or divided. At the end of Trajan's reign there were some 45 provinces. By AD 400 there were about 120. Therefore, we have taken a rather general and simplified view in our organization of material here. The provinces listed are mostly those described by Mommsen in his pioneering work. A list of mint cities, by province, is included on pages 144-148. Of course we cannot describe every city in each province, nor is this book intended to be a catalogue of types. David Sear's *Greek Imperial Coins and their values* is a handy resource for that purpose. Our intention is to expose the reader to a broad range of material, so that one may judge the character of provincial coinage as a whole and make decisions about specific collecting interests.

Our arrangement of mints follows the plan established by Eckhel, for Greek coins, in the 18th century. This system, which starts with Spain and works its way around the Mediterranean back to North Africa, is still in use today. In *Roman Provincial Coins* (RPC) the arrangement has been modified to include North Africa along with the western provinces of Spain, Gaul and Italy. This arrangement has some merit, based on interaction between the two regions, but we have chosen here to follow the standard arrangement with a few slight deviations for logistical reasons.

The maps which are included here fall well short of the needs of the serious student and are intended only to give an impression of mint locations for the beginning collector. In Volume I of this series we included a discussion and bibliography of atlases to the ancient world. We have tried to use Latin forms of city names throughout, but due to personal familiarity with these names in their Greek form, it is easy to slip and record them in that convention. If we have missed some of the conversions, we apologize. Even so, there should be little confusion as the names are usually very similar in either language.

The Western Provinces

The western provinces issued very little "city coinage" like that found everywhere in the East. Roman expansion in this region came early, well before the advent of Empire in some cases. There were a few colonial issues and some independent issues by imperators or early emperors, but the imperial coinage of Rome quickly became the monetary instrument of Spain, Gaul, Britain, Germany, Italy and the Alpine provinces. In our survey here, the western provinces consequently occupy only a short space. This certainly does not indicate any lack of Roman presence in these provinces, nor does it suggest a lesser role for these provinces in the history of the Roman Empire. Quite the contrary, it was *because* of their importance to Rome that these provinces fell so completely under Roman administration and almost totally absorbed the Latin ways.

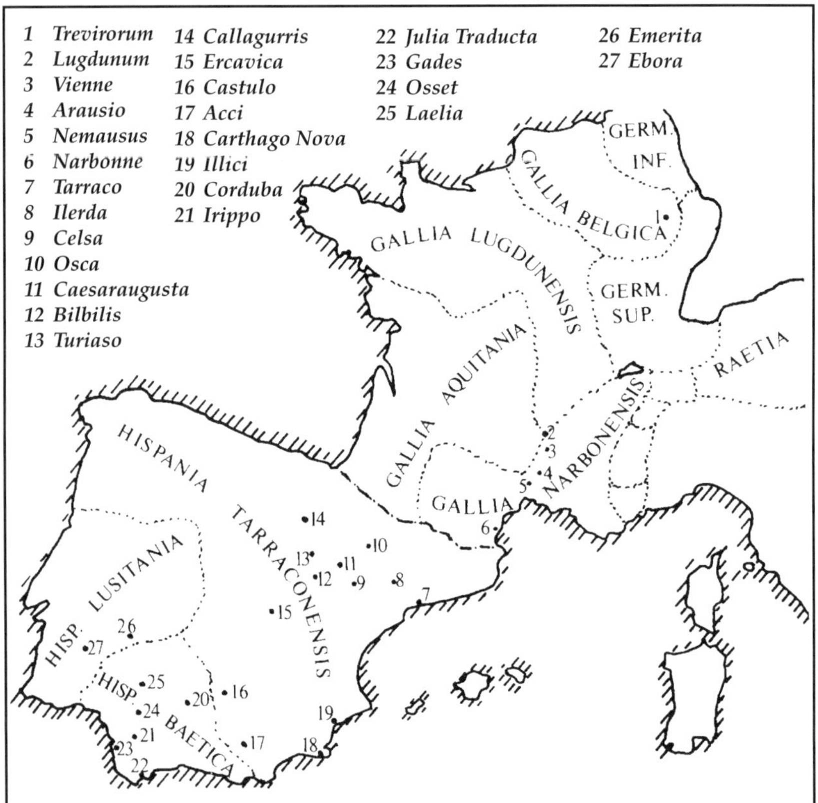

WESTERN MINTS DURING THE REIGN OF AUGUSTUS

Map by James Meyer

Romans in Spain

The Romans began striking coins in Spain (Hispania) as early as the second century BC, with denominations based on the silver denarius and the bronze as. In the first century BC, coinage became scarce, and silver issues ceased entirely, but new mints were opened by Augustus. This greatly improved the circulation of coinage and issues of both imperial and provincial style were produced during this period. The province was initially divided into two parts: Hispania Citerior ("nearer" Spain) and Hispania Ulterior ("further" Spain). That is, nearer and further on the road from Rome. Under Augustus it was further divided into three major districts: Tarraconensis, Lusitania and Baetica which included a number of mint cities (see map to left). Later in the Imperial Period, these districts were reorganized into separate provinces.

The Phoenicians were the first people to establish colonies on the Spanish coast. Consequently, the Carthaginians maintained a strong presence there until their defeat in the Punic Wars. From that time on, Spain was considered a Roman province, but the inland regions, especially in the mountains, were populated by a fierce and warlike people that were not completely subdued until the time of Augustus.

There was a flourishing of Latin culture in Spain under the Romans, and the indigenous people adopted the Roman language and ways. This led to a distinctive blend which is evidenced in Spanish literature and art of that period. Some of the famous writers to come out of the province were Lucan, Martial, Quintillian and Seneca. The country was enriched with public works, and large villas were built for the wealthy land barons who administered the province. The adornment of these villas with mosaics, sculpture and paintings was as impressive as anywhere in the Roman world. The legions in Spain were well trained and a powerful political force. During the wars between Caesar and Pompey, Spain proved to be an important battle ground. Caesar was successful at Ilerda in 49 BC and again in 45 at Munda.

Spain, uncertain city, AE as
Sextus Pompey, 45-44 BC

Carthago Nova, Spain, AE 29mm
Augustus, 27 BC - AD 14

Carthago Nova (modern Cartagena), a coastal city in the southeast, was the capital of the Carthaginians in Spain. Local silver mines produced great wealth, and

Celsa, Spain, AE 28mm
Augustus, 27 BC - AD 14

the city also prospered from trade in fish and a grass used for baskets and rope.

Celsa was a city of northern Spain in the district of Tarraconensis. It became known during the Republican period as Lepida-Celsa, and apparently achieved the status of colony under the governorship of Lepidus. The letters C V I CEL on bronzes of Augustus stand for Colonia Victrix Iulia Celsa, the colonial name adopted after the fall and exile of Lepidus. Stylistically, some of these coins are similar to those from Carthago Nova, and all of these issues share a certain coarseness of execution that is not seen on dies from the mints at Rome or Lugdunum.

Turiaso, Spain, AE 28mm
Tiberius, AD 14-37

Turiaso (Zaragoza) was a municipium in north-central Spain on the Turia river. This waterway flowed into the sea at Valentia and was the site of a famous battle between Pompey and Sertorius. Coinage was issued at Turiaso somewhat sporadically until the reign of Tiberius. His coins were the last minted there.

Colonia Romula, Spain, AE 28mm
Tiberius with Germanicus and Drusus

Colonia Romula was originally named Hispalis. It was located on the bank of the river Baetis (the modern Guadalquivir) quite a distance inland from the sea. It was settled as a military colony by Julius Caesar in 45 BC. Because of its accessibility by river to the sea, it became a center of ship building in Roman times. Today it is known as Seville.

These are only a few of the many cities in Spain which struck coins during the period of Roman domination. Although the provincial coinage ended early in this region, the political and economic importance of the province never did diminish. The legions garrisoned there played an important part in the Civil Wars of the first century AD, and the emperors Trajan (AD 98-117) and Maximus (AD 409-411) were natives of Spain.

Romans in Gaul

In the area which is analogous to modern France there were basically two regions, occupied by various tribes of Gauls, which came under Roman control. That region across the Alps was called Gallia Transalpina. That which lies in modern Italy was called Gallia Cisalpina. Although the Romans annexed a strip of land near Massalia (modern Marseilles) in 121 BC, they did not expand into the rest of Gaul until Caesar's campaigns of 58-51 BC. This area was later divided into a number of smaller provinces.

Vienna, Gaul, AE dupondius
Octavian, ca. 36 BC

The city of Vienna (Vienne) was located on the Rhone river in the region known as Gallia Narbonensis. This is of course not the same Vienna that we know today in Austria. It was under Roman control as early as 121 BC but did not achieve any prominence until the time of Augustus. A dupondius struck at Vienna for Octavian in 36 BC depicts the back-to-back heads of the future Roman emperor and his deified uncle Julius Caesar. Vienna was an active mint under the later Gallic Emperors as well.

Augusta Trevirorum
Brass quadrans, ca. 10 BC
"Germanus Indutillius"

In 16 BC, Augustus established a major settlement at Augusta Trevirorum (Trier) in Gallia Belgica—the northeast part of Gaul. From here, the administration and defense of the German frontier was managed. A brass coin, struck at or near Trier about 10 BC, features a diademed male head and the inscribed name of a local authority, Germanus Indutillius. This coin is regarded as a regional auxilliary issue, probably intended as a quadrans. It is one of the few truly provincial bronzes from Gaul.

In about 30 BC, Octavian settled a large group of legionary veterans from the Battle of Actium at Colonia Nemausus in Gaul. As a reward for their service, they were granted land and special privileges including a large mint. One of the distinctive types issued at Nemausus (modern Nimes) was a bronze coin with heads of Augustus and Agrippa back to back. On the reverse of this coin is a chained crocodile and a

Nemausus, Gaul, AE as
Augustus and Agrippa, AD 10-14

palm branch. The obvious reference is to the victory of these legionaries at Actium, by which Octavian claimed the kingdom of Cleopatra in Egypt. This type continued to be produced even after the deaths of Augustus and Agrippa. The type has been found in hoards at widely dispersed locations. This would suggest that it may have been produced specifically as payment for troops, and that it made its way throughout the empire along with the troops as they transferred from one place to another.

Heidenkopf AE radiate (enlarged)
Hybrid imitation of Tetricus II

Throughout the provinces one will find examples of local counterfeit coins. That is, coins that were struck in ancient times with the intention of passing them as legal tender. These stray pieces are merely contemporary fakes and, although interesting enough, not much more can be said of them. At times, however, severe shortages of coinage caused the massive issuing of copies of Roman coins. The workshops that produced these barbarous copies were crude, but they managed to produce a significant number of coins. When Postumus usurped authority in Britain and Gaul in AD 259 he effectively isolated the economy of those provinces. Although coins were produced in his name, the quantities were apparently insufficient to supply the entire region. From that time on, an extensive issue of barbarous radiate coins circulated about the northern provinces. One of the mints which produced copies of coinage of Tetricus I, Tetricus II and Claudius II has been excavated at a site in northwestern France called Heidenkopf. The results of this excavation reveal some startling facts (see Meyer, *RCC*). At Heidenkopf, in a substantial Roman villa, coins were made from the period of the Gallic Emperors to about AD 353—nearly a century! Even more astounding is the fact that the only types produced there were barbarous radiates and Constantinian commemoratives. It is not clear if the mint shut down between production of these two types or continued to produce the radiates the whole while. At any rate, since these are clearly local issues, they might arguably be considered provincial coinage.

Romans in Germany and Rhaetia

When Julius Caesar built a bridge across the Rhine in the summer of 55 BC, he succeeded in his objective of punishing the marauding Germanic tribes. What he also opened the door to was a 500 year long battle with these tribes. Very few Roman emperors enjoyed the luxury of peace on the Germanic frontier. Along a lightly fortified line from the Rhine to the Danube, called the Limes, Rome held together a tenuous occupation in this region.

One of the most important Roman settlements in Germany was Colonia Agrippinensis (modern Cologne or Köln). This fortified site was originally founded by Agrippa, on behalf of Octavian, with a settlement of the Ubii tribe. It was made a military colony by Claudius in AD 50 and named for his wife, Agrippina the Younger. In AD 69, under Domitian, it became the capital of the new province of Lower Germany. It was a mint city, but no provincial coins were struck there or elsewhere in Germany for that matter. Moguntiacum (Mainz) was the capital of Upper Germany and also a legionary center from which many campaigns against the Germanic tribes were launched. Another legionary garrison was established at Argentorate (Strasbourg) in what is now Alsace.

Caesar established two colonies in Rhaetia (Switzerland), one at Nyon on Lake Geneva called Colonia Julia Equestris and one near Basel called Colonia Augusta Raurica. The Romans maintained a legionary camp at Vindonissa (Windisch) during the first century. Later, as the frontier moved north, that site became a civilian settlement.

Many of the settlements in Germany and Rhaetia came under the constant threat of invasion from Germanic and later Frankish tribes. This required a vigilant and active defense as well as the personal attention of a good many emperors. Several took up residence in the region to keep a close eye on the situation. In spite of this, the provinces prospered and became thoroughly Romanized in all but the remote frontier areas.

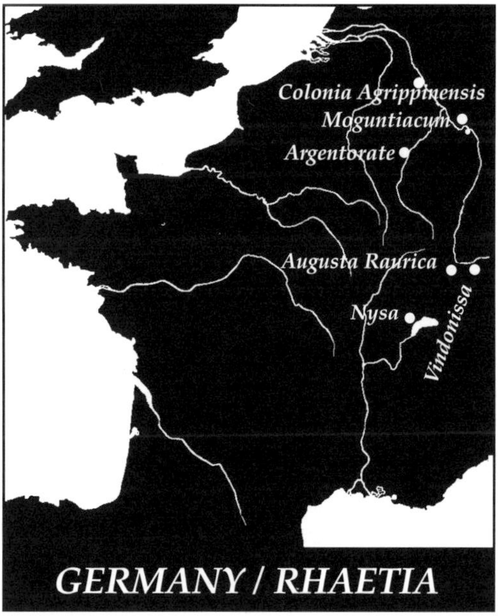

Romans in Britain

Trinovantes, AR units
Cunobeline, AD 10-43

Although Julius Caesar "conquered" Britain on a second try in 54 BC, the Romans did little to settle the province until the time of Claudius. During that 100 year period, Celtic coinage—like that of the Trinovantes illustrated here—continued to be the primary monetary instrument. Due to the classically inspired imagery on many of these coins, they were probably no more alien to a Roman soldier or merchant than a British £ or German Mark would be to an American serviceman. Some Celtic issues of this period were even modelled on circulating Roman coins. Through trade and a limited legionary presence, the imperial denarius probably infiltrated the island's economy—but there was not a firmly established Roman fiduciary system in the province.

While Claudius himself was nominally in charge of the invasion of AD 43, the workhorse Second Augusta was commanded by the future emperor Vespasian. The advancing Roman army required a secure rear guard, and with this in mind the first colonia of veterans was established at Colchester in AD 49. By 61, after suppressing the rebellion of Boudicca, the Romans had established military supremacy and were moving north with confidence. The island was occupied at that time by four legions: the Second Augusta, the Ninth Hispana, the Fourteenth Gemina and the Twentieth Valeria Victrix. Since a fully manned legion consisted of a bit more than six thousand soldiers, this probably numbered the Roman forces in Britain at about 24,000. The most successful campaigns of northern Britain were conducted under the governorship of Julius Agricola (the sub ject of a book by Tacitus) who served until AD 84. During the course of this 40 year military maneuver, six legions and several auxilliary units were deployed, although not all at the same time.

Finally, the settlements were left to the protection of three permanently assigned legions: the Second Augusta at Caerleon, the Sixth Victrix at York, and the Twentieth Valeria Victrix at Chester. These legions were the builders of Roman Britain and actually did the construction of roads, bridges, forts and even the great walls on the northern frontier. This military presence was bolstered by the employment of conscripted mercenaries from other conquered lands. Units from Spain, Syria, Asia Minor, Gaul and other provinces served at a complex network of posts throughout Britain. This further reduced the likelihood of local rebellion, since these foreign mercenaries were unlikely to side with local tribes in opposition to Roman rule.

The governor of the province was, at least until the fourth century, a military leader and much of the province's early development centered around the military presence. The difficulty of supplying a developing province with coinage, struck at Rome and transported across the whole of Europe and the Channel, must have been very great. In fact, due to the inevitable shortage, there were many locally produced copies of the Roman coins. Most of these were cast in clay molds, which have been found along with the coins in great quantities. These copies, and the early Celtic coins of the period between Caesar and Claudius, are the only real "provincial" coins of Britain—and they do not really fit into the series which we refer to as Roman Provincial Coins. After Claudius took possession of Britain in AD 43, the bronze coins from Rome became a primary instrument of commerce. The most commonly counterfeited coins were the bronzes of Claudius and Antoninus Pius—and later "barbarous radiates" imitated imperial antoniniani of several Gallic Emperors. Just who struck these coins is uncertain, and theories have ranged from official mint products to barbarian tribal issues. The excavated mint at Heidenkopf in France suggests a quasi-official mint, at least in that particular case (see p. 20).

The first Roman coins actually minted in Britain were struck during the reign of Carausius, a usurper who carved out his own empire. These followed the traditional pattern of Roman mint coinage, and even went so far as to honor the legitimate emperors Diocletian and Maximian as contemporary colleagues.

The coinage of Roman Britain is very collectable, and is in fact very popular. It is not really a part of the provincial series, in that the coins were either imperial mint issues, non-Roman issues, or unauthorized imitations of Roman issues. There are several references to coins of Roman Britain in the bibliography which follows this section.

Italy, Sicily and Sardinia

Leontini, Sicily, AE 23mm
After 210 BC (under Roman rule)

We don't generally think of Italy or the adjacent islands when we think about Roman provinces, but Rome did start out as a relatively small city. Sicily was actually the first Roman province outside of Italy. The civic coins of Roman occupation were very similar in fabric and design to the Sicilian coins which existed before the Roman conquests. This continuation of local styles in coinage was undoubtedly a purposeful act. Throughout the long history of Roman conquest and expansion we repeatedly see the gradual assimilation of Roman themes into local coinage rather than the wholesale replacement of monetary systems and numismatic images. The adoption or adaptation of foreign gods into the Roman pantheon helped to allay the fears and suspicions of indigenous populations, and coinage was a natural medium to demonstrate that Roman acceptance.

Panormus, Sicily, AE quadrans
2nd - 1st century BC

At Leontini, Panormus, Syracuse and other Sicilian cities the Greek gods continued to maintain their presence on local coinage struck under Roman rule. Gradually, however, Roman themes and systems also were introduced. A bronze from Panormus struck in the 2nd to 1st centuries BC bears the Roman denominational marks (three dots) of a quadrans. At Catana, the distinctly Roman god Janus appeared on a bronze coin of the same period. Republican bronze coins were also struck in Sicily, but these are usually catalogued as Republican issues and not "provincial". Certain issues under Augustus, and perhaps Tiberius, were also struck at Sicilian mints. The standard silver coin circulating in Sicily during this period was the denarius.

Catana, Sicily, AE 24mm
2nd - 1st century BC

The coinage of Italian provinces is relatively scarce and typically is offered in sale catalogues along with the Greek coins of pre-Roman times. Usually, the distinction between Greek and Roman Provincial must be based on the actual dating of coins and the dates of Roman annexation. The general tendency of numismatic cataloguers has been to treat Roman occupation coins as something other than provincial. This makes little sense, however. The problem is one of definition and acceptance—much like the distinction between imperial and provincial. As provincial coins gain in popularity, which is clearly happening in our generation, these divisions will become more clear, or at least by concensus more definable.

ITALIAN PROVINCES

Venetia et Histria
Aemilia
Liguria
Flaminia et Picenum Annoarium
Tuscia et Umbria
Picenum Suburbicarium
Campania
Apulia et Calabria
Lucania et Brutii
Samnium
Valeria
Alpes Cottiae

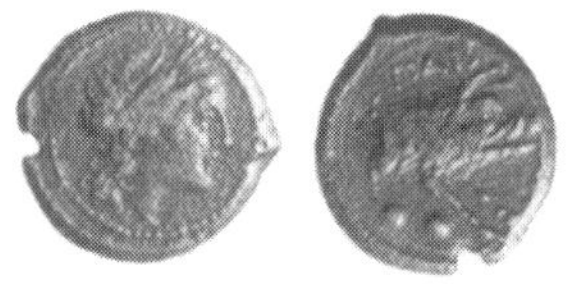

Paestum, Italy, AE sextans before 89 BC

Paestum, like the other Italian cities, became a municipium in 90/89 BC. It struck coinage in a sort of quasi-autonomous status, perhaps even to the time of Augustus. For a discussion of the provincial coinage of Italy, and a bibliography of the most current articles relating to this confusing area, see *Roman Provincial Coinage*, pages 157-161. RPC does not, however, address the earlier issues by former Greek cities in Italy.

The island of Sardinia produced several interesting coin types, one of which was formerly ascribed to Carthage. A bronze struck during the time of Augustus with the inscription KAR VENERIS in retrograde has been reattributed to Sardinia because the type is often found there and has never been found in hoards from Carthage or elsewhere in Africa.

Caralis, Sardinia, AE 30mm Time of Augustus and Tiberius

BIBLIOGRAPHY

The Western Provinces

Askew, G. *The Coinage of Roman Britain,* London (reprint) 1980.
Bédoyère, Guy de la. *The Finds of Roman Britain,* London, 1989.
Brickstock, R.J. *Copies of the Fel Temp Reparatio Coinage in Britain* (British Archaeological Reports, No. 176), Oxford, 1987.
Burns, Thomas S. and Bernhard H. Overbeck. *Rome and the Germans as seen in coinage,* (Emory University) Atlanta, 1987.
Casey, P.J. *Roman Coinage in Britain,* Aylesbury, 1984.
De la Tour, H. *Atlas de Monnaies Gauloises,* Paris , 1892.
Goodwin, Tony. "Barbarous copies of the 3rd and 4th centuries". *The Celator,* Vol. 7, No. 4, April, 1993, pp. 38-41.
Grant, Michael. *Aspects of the Principate of Tiberius,* ANS Numismatic Notes and Monographs 116, New York, 1950.
Heiss, A. *Description Générale des Monnaies Antiques de l'Espagne,* Paris, 1870.
Hill, G.F. *Notes on the Ancient Coinage of Hispania Citerior,* ANS Numismatic Notes and Monograms 50, New York, 1931.
Hill, Philip V. "Barbarous Radiates, Imitations of Third-Century Roman Coins", *ANS Numismatic Notes and Monographs* 112, New York, 1949.
Hilt, Michael. "The History of Legio XXI Rapax", *The Celator,* September, 1995, pp. 10-24.
Hunter-Blair, Peter. *Roman Britain and Early England, 55 B.C. - A.D. 871,* New York and London, 1966.
Kollgaard, R. "The history and coinage of Iberia Part 2: The Roman conquest of Spain", *The Celator,* Vol 7, No. 7, July 1993. pp. 18-23. also, "The history and coinage of Iberia Part 3: Spain in the late Republic and early Empire", *The Celator,* Vol 7, No. 8, August 1993. pp. 10-15.
Laing, Lloyd R. *Coins and Archaeology,* (mostly Britain) London, 1969.
Mack, R.P. *The Coinage of Ancient Britain,* London, 1975.
MacKendrick, Paul. *Romans on the Rhine.* New York, 1970.
Meyer, James. "Visit to a Gallic Mint", *Roman Coins and Culture,* Vol. 2, No. 4, 1986.
Reece, Richard. *Coinage in Roman Britain,* London, 1987.
Tameanko, Marvin. "The broken coins of Colonia Augusta Nemausus" *The Celator,* Vol. 10, No. 9, September 1996, pp. 6-11.
Thompson, P.R. "Roman Britain and its coinage", *The Celator,* Vol. 9, No. 12, December, 1995, pp. 32-41.
Webster, Graham. *The Roman Imperial Army,* 3rd. Ed., London, 1985.

The Balkans and Greece

The provinces of Noricum, Pannonia and Dacia were incorporated into the Roman sphere over a period of some two hundred years. The motivation for expansion into these regions was partly to secure raw materials—a gold rush initially took the Romans to Noricum—and partly to secure the northern frontiers to allow stable development of the Mediterranean rim countries. As a result, these provinces were military oriented, and a nearly constant drain on the treasury of Rome. Unlike the cities farther south, they did not issue any civic coinage of their own.

Moesia is a different story. Provincial coins were struck at Tomis from the time of Caligula on. By the reign of Commodus, at least five mints were in operation in Moesia Inferior. The mint of Viminacium, in Moesia Superior, was opened during the reign of Gordian III. These mints produced a tremendous quantity and variety of coinage. The extent of this coinage is unknown, but a huge hoard of bronze coins from mints in this region has brought to light a great many types that were previously unknown. An added bonus is that the soil conditions in this region are favorable for patination of bronze. The coins from Moesia and parts of Thrace often possess a beautiful green, brown or black patina. Unfortunately, the material currently on the market is so plentiful and diverse that no one has adequately catalogued it.

The coinage of Thrace and Macedonia is better recorded, but many new types from Thrace have also come to light in recent years, making the current catalogs rather outdated. For the beginning collector, the entire Balkan region offers extraordinary opportunity for useful research, and acquisition of rare and unappreciated types—often at extraordinarily low prices.

Noricum, Pannonia and Dacia

Noricum was a state and subsequently a Roman province on the south side of the Danube between Rhaetia and Pannonia. It occupied what is modern Austria and part of southeastern Germany. Latin legends appear on coinage of the region as early as the second century BC due to Roman gold mining activities there. Noricum did not fall under Roman control however until about 35 BC. It became a full province under the reign of Claudius. Although a legion was garrisoned there in the second century AD, no provincial mints are known. It was eventually combined with Pannonia.

Pannonia

Dacia

AR antoninianii

Trajan Decius, AD 249-251

The region which became the province of Pannonia had been contested by Romans and local tribes from 119 through the entire first century BC. It was finally subdued by Tiberius in AD 9, after a serious three-year war, and made a province. Pannonia was split under Trajan into two provinces—Upper and Lower. In the fourth century, a major imperial mint was active at Siscia, one of the capitals of a divided province. Here too there is an absence of civic coinage. Issues beginning under Philip I (Sear *Greek Imperial*, 3873) bear the inscription PROVINCIA DACIA, but these were probably struck in Moesia. During the reign of Trajan Decius, a series of imperial coins honored the provinces of Pannonia and Dacia, or more probably the legions of these provinces.

Dobrudja, in modern Romania, was incorporated into the Roman territories in 29/8 BC following a crushing defeat of the local populations. Local resistance continued, however, and a tribal leader named Decabalus became King of Dacia in AD 87. He won several victories against the Romans, but was finally defeated by Trajan in AD 105. This campaign and victory was commemorated in great detail on the monument known as "Trajan's Column" which still stands in the center of Rome. From that time, Dacia became a Roman Province. Due to its indefensibility, Aurelian withdrew the Roman army and administration from Dacia in AD 274. Local settlers stayed behind and were assimilated into a stock which became the "Romanian" people. Like Noricum and Pannonia, Dacia did not produce any provincial coinage.

Moesia

Moesia was conquered by the army of Octavian in 30 BC, but did not become a full province of Rome until the reign of Tiberius. In AD 86, Domitian divided the province into Moesia Superior (upper) and Moesia Inferior (lower). Tomis became the capital of lower Moesia and Viminacium later became the capital of Moesia Superior. The province was an important source of enlistees for the Roman army, and several emperors came from Moesia.

Viminacium (modern Kostolac) became a Roman camp in the first century AD, and served as the headquarters for Trajan during the Dacian Wars. It was not established as a military colony, however, until the time of Gordian III (AD 239), and dated its era in Latin numerals from that year.

One of the prevalent motifs on the city's coins was a standing personification of the province, Moesia, accompanied by a bull (Legion VII) and lion (Legion IV) representing the legions permanently stationed there. This coinage circulated widely throughout the province and indicates the importance of the city. Viminacium was overrun by Attila in AD 441 and finally destroyed completely by the Avars in 582.

Viminacium, Moesia Superior
Gordian III, AE 30mm, AD 243

Viminacium, Moesia Superior
Philip I, AE 27mm, AD 247

Viminacium, Moesia Superior
Mariniana, AE 27mm, AD 254-55

Many of the coins struck at mints in Moesia Inferior during the third century utilized the convention of facing busts. Some included two members of the imperial family, others linked an imperial personage with a deity, often Serapis. These double portraits are very popular among collectors of provincial coinage. The reverses of issues from mints in this province are very interesting as well. Many have depictions of Dionysus, Athena, Aesculapius, Hercules and other popular figures. They also include scarcer figures such as Nemesis, Triptolemos and Demeter. Some of the bronzes feature radiate busts, while others feature laureate busts. This may have some relationship to the value of the coin, but there is not any clear distinction other than the crown.

Markianopolis, Moesia Inferior AE 28mm, Gordian III , AD 238-244

Tomis, Moesia Inferior, AE 26mm Philip II (as Caesar), AD 244-46

Nicopolis ad Istrum, Moesia Inferior AE 28mm, Elagabalus, AD 218-222

Tomis, on the Romanian coast of the Black Sea, was the capital of lower Moesia until the second century. Coins were struck at that city from early in the imperial era. Tomis was the city to which Augustus banished the poet Ovid. It could not, therefore, have been a cultural center of note. It was, nevertheless, an important trading center and grain storage facility with close ties to the cities on the northern coast of Asia Minor.

Marcianopolis (Rekna Devnia in northeastern Bulgaria) was founded by Trajan and named after his sister Marciana. It replaced Tomis as the capital of Moesia Inferior and issued provincial coins from the time of Commodus to the middle of the third century. Coins of Marcianopolis often bore interesting architectural motifs on the reverse.

Among the other cities issuing provincial coins in Moesia Inferior were Callatis, Dionysopolis, Istrus, and Nicopolis ad Istrum.

Thrace

The actual boundaries of Thrace and Moesia Inferior changed from time to time, and the historical record is not precise. It is therefore likely that the collector will find coins of certain cities listed variously under Moesia or Thrace. For example, Grant places Odessos in Moesia while Sear places it in Thrace. The Romans annexed Thrace after the defeat of the Macedonian Kingdom in 168 BC. The local Odrysian king Cotys II became a client king of Rome and Thrace was ruled by a succession of puppet kings until AD 46 when Rhoemetalces III was murdered and Thrace became a Roman province. The provincial capital was established at Perinthus. Under the Flavians, colonies were established at Deultum (Colonia Flavia Pacensis Deultum) and Flaviopolis. A provincial Koinon was established at Philippopolis under Antoninus Pius or earlier.

Perinthos, Thrace, AE 28 mm
Geta, AD 209-212

Perinthus, later named Heraclea, is the modern Eregli in Turkey. The city is located on the Sea of Marmara, south of Istanbul. It was an active mint, and grew in importance under the Tetrarchy. Being on an important crossroad, it was the site of several skirmishes and power struggles during the Imperial Period.

Deultum, Thrace, AE 25 mm
Julia Mamaea, AD 222-235

Odessus is the modern Varna in Bulgaria—on the west coast of the Black Sea. It was associated with the Pontic cities of Asia Minor and belonged to the Koinon of Pontic cities. It fell to the Romans in 72 BC and was affiliated with cities of Moesia, but also seems to have been at times a part of Thrace.

Odessus, Thrace, AE 29 mm
Gordian III, AD 238-244

Macedonia

Macedonia was located in the central part of the Balkans, north of Greece and west of Thrace. The Romans fought two wars with the Kings of Macedonia. Philip V was defeated in a major battle at Cynoscephalae in 197 BC, but continued to rule under an agreement with Rome. In 176 his son Perseus was defeated in battle at Pydna and the dynasty was eliminated. In its place was established four autonomous republics. During this period, autonomous coins with the names of Roman officials were issued. Macedonia became a province in 146 BC with its capital at Thessalonica.

The tetradrachms issued under Roman rule, with the loosely styled head of Alexander, were struck in great numbers and are relatively common. The first issue of this series, which is rare, bears the initials of the praetor, one L. Julius Caesar (not the dictator) along with the name of the quaestor Aesillas. On the reverse of these coins is a quaestorial moneychest or *cista,* the club of Herakles (related to Macedonian foundation myths) and the quaestorial *sella* or chair, all within an olive wreath.

Macedon, Roman rule, AE 24mm
L. Fulcinnius (Quaestor)
ca. 166-165 BC

Macedon, Roman rule, AR tetradrachm
Aesillas (Quaestor), ca. 90-60 BC

Philippi, in eastern Macedonia, was a Roman city from about 130 BC, but achieved fame as the site of a famous battle in 42. At this place, Antony and Octavian met Brutus and Cassius, the assassins of Julius Caesar, and ended Republican hopes forever. After the battle, Antony established Philippi as a military colony with veterans from the engagement. Following the Battle of Actium, Augustus refounded Philippi as Augusta Julia with a praetorian cohort.

Philippi, Macedon, AE 27mm
Augustus, 27 BC - AD 14

Epirus

Epirus was located in the region that is now northwestern Greece and southern Albania. It is a mountainous country, famous for the quality of its horses and cattle. The Epirotes supported King Perseus of Macedon in his war against the Romans, and as a result the country was devastated by the Roman army in 167 BC. Ancient sources report that 150,000 captives were sold into slavery. This was not the first experience of the Romans with Epirus. They had earlier come into open conflict with the Epirote King Pyrrhus during his Italian expeditions. When Macedon was made a province in 146, Epirus was attached to it. Coins struck in Epirus under Roman rule honor Zeus Dodonus, a local cult figure.

Octavian further depopulated the country after the Battle of Actium, but it recovered slowly to become a separate province in the second century. Following the Battle of Philippi, a colony of veterans was settled at Dyrrhacium (Colonia Julia Veneria). The main city of Epirus during the Imperial Period was Nicopolis, which was founded on the site of Octavian's victory at Actium.

Epirus, AE 20mm
Under Roman rule, after 146 BC

Corcyra, the modern island of Corfu, is the northernmost of the Ionian islands. It lies just off the coast of ancient Epirus. Because it lies at the narrowest point of the Adriatic Sea it was used as a commercial port for trade with Italy. The Romans took control of Corcyra in 229 BC and later attached it, along with the rest of Epirus, to the province of Macedon.

Corcyra, Epirus, AE 26mm
Plautilla, AD 197-217

Coins of the Imperial Period reflect maritime themes and also the historic connection to Corinth (Pegasus) which had established an early colony on the island.

Corcyra, Epirus, AE 26mm
Plautilla, AD 197-217

Achaea

The Roman province of Achaea, established by Augustus in 27 BC, was the closest thing approximating modern day Greece. It consisted of Thessaly, central Greece and the Pelopponesus. The two main cities of Greece, Athens and Corinth, continued to produce coins during the Roman period. Athens was a free city, but Corinth was established as a Roman colony by Julius Caesar in 44 BC. Both cities struck provincial coins into the third century AD. Other coin issuing cities of Achaea included Tanagra, Thebes, Chalcis and Carystus.

Excepting Corinth, the coins of the Peloponnesus are few and rare. Sparta and Argos were the only cities with any notable activity, although coins were also issued from Sicyon, Patrae, and Dyme. A few rare issues of "Fleet Coinage" were issued from uncertain mints. Crete was administratively attached to Cyrenaica in Africa, and issued a fair number of types with imperial portraits under the Julio-Claudians. Also issued on the island were coins in the name of a Koinon. A few islands in the Aegean and Ionian Seas issued coins sporadically during the Roman era. We have mentioned the island of Cyprus in this section, even though, like Crete, it did not fall under administrative control of the Province of Achaea.

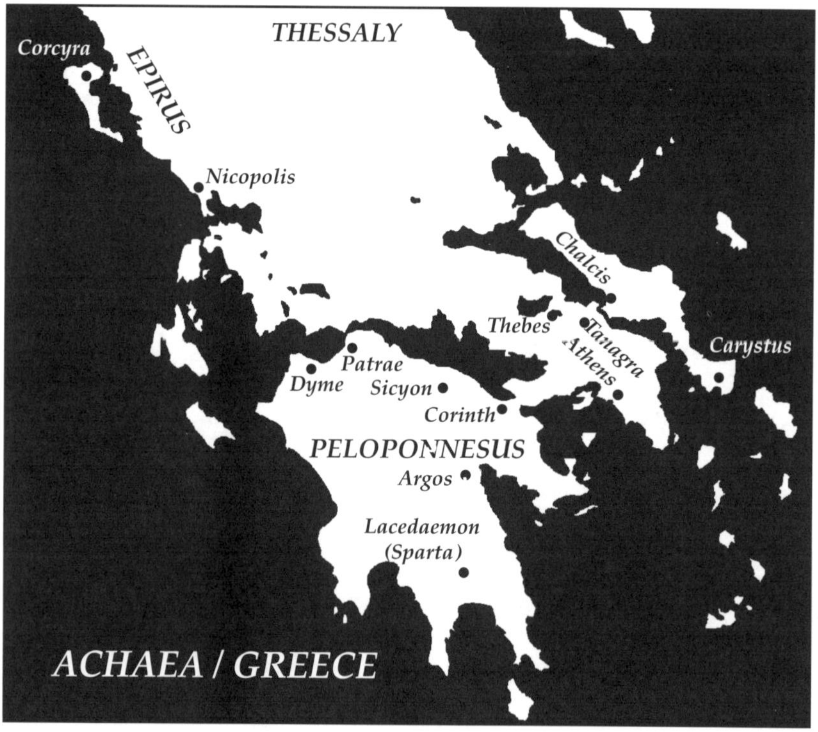

The league of Thessalian cities that had cooperated effectively in Hellenistic times continued to maintain close ties under the Romans. The chief city of this federation was Larissa, and the city had a long history of mint activity. Thessaly was incorporated into the province of Achaea by Augustus, but later it was transferred back to the province of Macedonia. Under Diocletian, it became a separate province, but league coins were no longer issued by that time. Athena Alkidemos, a familiar motif from the Hellenistic silver coins which were struck early in the Roman period, appears much later on a bronze struck during the reign of Marcus Aurelius. The endurance of these images is remarkable, and it is not unusual to see local motifs survive hundreds of years and several political changes.

Thessaly under the Romans
AR double victoriatus
ca. 1st century BC

Thessaly was known for its lush pastures and the excellent horses raised there. Throughout the history of the region its coinage featured this characteristic with horses portrayed in a multitude of poses. A bronze of the Koinon, struck under Caracalla, depicts Victory in a quadriga—of Thessalian horses no doubt.

KOINON ΘΕCCΑΛωΝ
The Thessalian League, AE 24mm
Marcus Aurelius, AD 161-180

The provincial issues from cities in central Greece are scarce, and few of them produced coinage over any length of time. Most of the coinage that was struck in the first century BC continued the styles and themes of the pre-Roman era. This coinage is usually found listed in catalogues as "Greek" coinage, in spite of the fact that it was struck under Roman occupation, and even following annexation.

KOINON ΘΕCCΑΛΩΝ
The Thessalian League, AE 23mm
Caracalla, AD 197-217

The City of Athens

By the time of the Roman occupation, Athens had declined commercially to the status of a provincial city. Its venerable history was still an inspiration to the Romans, however, and the city was allowed many privileges and was bestowed with many honors. The Julio-Claudians undertook large scale restoration projects and the emperor Hadrian was a great benefactor of the city. In fact, Athens was like a University town, where scholars and artists of all kinds gathered. The Romans had a penchant for Greek literature and art, and imported all kinds of masterpieces, as well as the artists who produced them. Hadrian built a large library there in addition to the other public works he sponsored.

One of the privileges allowed Athens was the right to strike "pseudo-autonomous" coinage. As a result, we find during the Imperial Period some very interesting bronze coins with allusions to the city's illustrious past. These are very popular today among collectors and due to their relative scarcity, are rather difficult to obtain. None of the coins from Athens bear imperial portraits.

One series of bronze coins features a group of scenes related to the city's founding. For example, a 25mm bronze depicts the mythological contest between Athena and Poseidon for the possession of the city. Others depict the city's famous Acropolis and buildings (see the section of *Masterpieces* later in this volume).

Athens, AE 20, 21 & 25mm
Time of the Antonines
(city foundation scenes)

The "New-Style" silver tetradrachms of Athens with the head of Athena Parthenos obverse, and an owl standing on an amphora reverse, continued to be struck at the city until the Imperial Period. Aside from the magistrate's marks and symbols, these are still Hellenistic coins in every respect. One of these issues bears the mark of Sulla, who had moved east with his army in response to the threat of Mithridates the Great, king of Pontus.

The Peloponnesos

Corinth was the most prominent city of the Peloponnesus in the Hellenistic Period, but was destroyed in 146 BC when the Romans conquered Greece. The city was basically uninhabited for the century preceding its refounding by Julius Caesar in 44 BC. After the repopulation, Corinth prospered again. It was built on a strategic location, and was an important maritime center. The full name of the colony at Corinth was COLONIA LAVS IVLIA CORINTHVS. This is normally abbreviated CLI COR on the provincial coins of that city. The city was governed by two magistrates (Duovirs) who served jointly. Their names are inscribed on a long series of bronze coins. Many of the provincial issues bear scenes relating to the mythology of the city's founding, similar to the series struck at Athens.

Corinth, AE 26mm
Lucius Verus, AD 161-169

Another Peloponnesian city, famous in Hellenistic times, was Lacedaemon or Sparta. The city was ruled by local dynasts who served sporadically at the pleasure of the Roman emperor up until the reign of Claudius when it became a free city. A portrait of the ruling magistrate appears on an issue struck prior to the Battle of Actium.

Sparta, AE 20mm, 43-31 BC
Magistrate Atratinos

Patrae was a convenient harbor outside the western mouth of the Gulf of Corinth. It served as a staging point for Mark Antony, and coins were struck here with the portrait of Cleopatra as Isis. A colony of legionary veterans was established at the city by Augustus in 14 BC with the new name Colonia Aroe Augusta Patrensis. The legionary reference is seen on subsequent issues, including one under Claudius which is illustrated here.

Patrae, AE 26mm
Claudius, AD 41-54

Crete, Cyprus and the Islands

Crete, AR drachm
Caligula, AD 37-41

The main mints on the Island of Crete were at Gortyn and Cnossus. From these mints, a fair number of Julio-Claudian portrait coins were issued in both silver and bronze. One example, illustrated here, bears well executed portraits of Caligula and the deified Augustus. Another portrays Nero and his wife Octavia as Sol and Luna. Coinage in the name of the Koinon of Crete was issued up to the time of Antoninus Pius when the local mints closed.

KOINON ΚΥΠΡΙΩΝ
Cyprus, AE 33mm
Caracalla, AD 197-217
Temple of Aphrodite at Paphos

Salamis was the principal city and capital of the island of Cyprus. It is not the most famous of Cypriot sites however. Paphos was, according to Greek mythology, the birthplace of Aphrodite. It was a famous place in ancient times and its important temple to the goddess was a major attraction. The portrayal of this site on rare issues of the "Koinon Kyprion" is one of the most popular of architectural coin types.

Cnossus, Crete, AE 27mm
Nero and Octavia, AD 54-68

Not very many of the Greek islands struck coinage during the Roman period, but among those that did were Lemnos, Lesbos, Amorgos, Ios, Melos, Naxos, Astypalaea, Cos, Rhodes, Samos, Samo–thrace, Tenedos, Thasos and Zakynthos. Cult images were popular motifs on these issues—often set within distyle (2 column) or tetrastyle (4 column) temples. See illustration to the left.

Samos, Islands off Ionia, AE 30mm
Gordian III, AD 238-244

BIBLIOGRAPHY

The Balkans and Greece

Amandry, M. *Le Monnayage des Duovirs Corinthiens,* Paris, 1988.

Bompois, H.F. *Examen Chronologique des Monnaies frappées par la Communauté des Macédoniens avant, pendant et après la Conquete Romaine,* Paris, 1876 (Chicago, 1980 reprint).

Carson, R.A.G. "Coinage and history in Pannonia in the third century A.D.", *Arheoloski vestnik* (Lubljana, 1972), vol. 23, pp. 27-34.

Elmer, Georg. "Die Münzpragung von Viminacium und die Zeitrechnung der Provinz Ober-Moesien", *Numismatische Zeitschrift,* Vol. 68 (1935), pp. 35-43.

Fisher, Roger S. "Two Notes on the Aesillas Tetradrachms: Mint Attribution and a Die Control System", *ANS Museum Notes* 30, New York, 1985.

Gaebler, H. *Die Antiken Münzen Nord-Griechenlands: Vol III, Makedonia und Paionia,* Berlin, 1935 (often referred to as AMNG).

Hoddinott, R.F. *Bulgaria in Antiquity,* New York, 1975.

Lengyel, A. and G.T.B. Radan. ed. *The Archaeology of Roman Pannonia,* University Press of Kentucky, Lexington, 1980.

MacKendrick, Paul. *The Dacian Stones Speak,* University of North Carolina Press, 1975.

MacKenzie, Andrew. *Archaeology in Romania,* London, 1986.

Oeconomides, M. *E nomismatokopia tes Nikopoleos,* Athens, 1975 (reviewed by Colin M. Kraay, "The coinage of Nicopolis", *Numismatic Chronicle,* 1976, pp. 235-247

Pick, B. *Die Antiken Münzen Nord-Griechenlands: Vol I, Pt. 1, Dacien und Moesien,* Berlin, 1898.

Pick, B. and K. Regling. *Die Antiken Münzen Nord-Griechenlands: Vol I, Pt. 2, Dacien und Moesien,* Berlin, 1910.

Rosecrans, J.J. Jr. "The Province of Dacia and its effects on Roman imperial coinage", *North American journal of numismatics* (1967), Vol. 6, no. 8, pp. 251-255.

Strack, M.L. *Die Antiken Münzen Nord-Griechenlands: Vol II. Thrakien,* Berlin, 1912.

Svoronos, J.N. *Numismatique de la Crète Ancienne,* Macon, 1890.

Touratsoglou, Y. *Coin Circulation in Ancient Macedonia (c. 200 B.C. - 268-286 AD),* Athens, 1993.

Touratsoglu, I. *Die Münzstätte von Thessaloniki in der römischen Kaiserzeit (32/31 v. Chr. bis 268 n. Chr.)* Vol. 13 of the series Antike Münzen und Geschnittene Steine, 1988.

Asia Minor and Mesopotamia

The settlement of Asia Minor (modern day Turkey) and the region known as Mesopotamia was a lengthy process, and one that required many accommodations. Initially, the entire region was considered part of a large ambiguous province—loosely referred to as Asia. Over time, it became a fully developed region with many smaller provinces and a variety of governmental structures.

The Romans were active militarily in Asia during the early years of the first century BC. A long series of wars with the Pontic king, Mithridates, had caused the Romans to establish a military presence and the consequential support system that entails. While Mithridates was occupying Roman attentions in the northern and western regions, Piracy was flourishing in Cilicia. Unable to tolerate the increasing interference with maritime commerce, Rome sent Pompey into Cilicia to subdue the marauders. This was a successful venture in the short term, but it led to ever increasing demands on Rome to keep political stability in the region.

When Mark Antony assumed ownership of the East, he consolidated power in Asia Minor and forged a provincial system that lasted for centuries. The authorization for individual cities to strike their own coinage, whether in the name of the ruler or in their own names autonomously, was an important aspect psychologically as well as economically. For us, as collectors, it was a wonderful occurrence because it fostered a mammoth production of diverse types and extraordinary historical vignettes. It is through these city coins that we have learned much of what is known today about the region. There is much more to discover, and the coins of Asia Minor and Mesopotamia are laden with opportunity for the scholar as well as the amateur.

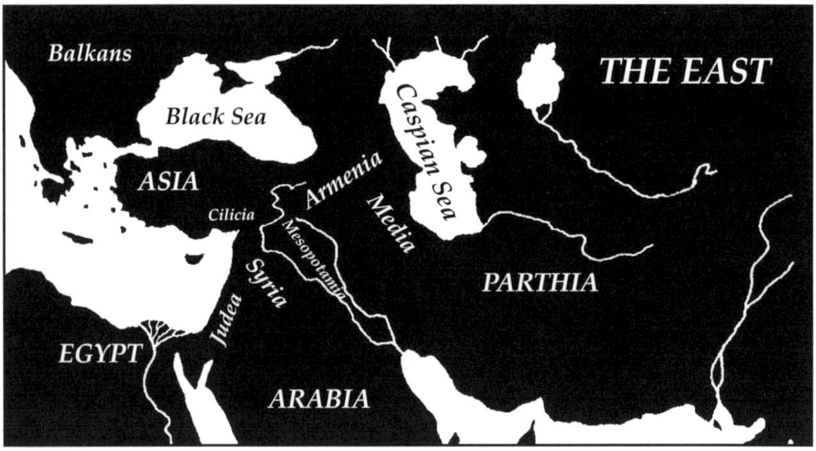

The Province of Asia

The province of "Asia" consisted of the old kingdom of the Attalids in western Asia Minor. The Roman people, in the early first century BC, actually inherited this rich kingdom in a bequest from the last of the Hellenistic rulers. It therefore became a senatorial province. Asia ranged from Bithynia in the north to Lycia in the south and from the Aegean Sea east to Galatia. In other words, it was a large tract of land. Augustus settled military colonies at the cities of Alexandria Troas, and Parium, but the 500 or so previously established communities remained virtually intact and basically unhindered by Roman government.

One of the interesting features of civic coinage in this region is the appearance of "Alliance" coins between cities of importance. Also appealing to the collector is a wonderful diversity of religious types. Many of these cities were famous for their temples and shrines, which had attracted worshippers and the curious for centuries.

Because the region was already civilized and prosperous, Roman occupation had much less effect on daily life here than it did in some other provinces where the entire infrastructure changed. In Asia, only a few improvements were needed.

Stratoniceia, Caria
AE 36mm, AD 193-211
Septimius Severus

Aphrodisias, Caria, AE 28mm
Senate, ca. AD 200-300

Commune Asia, AE 34mm, struck at Pergamum?
Augustus, 27 BC-AD 14

The pattern of legionary reference in the iconography of coins struck at military colonies is fairly consistent. Therefore, it should not be a surprise that an "autonomous" bronze coin of Alexandria Troas still bears the legion's vexillum more than two hundred years after its founding. The turreted city goddess, Tyche, has by this time become a standard obverse type on minor bronzes of the non-imperial portrait variety. There can be little doubt that this coin is "Roman" and the term "autonomous" is really a misnomer. By the third century, the power of the emperor had reached a point that no city could claim to be autonomous, not even Rome.

Alexandria Troas, AE 20mm
ca. 3rd c. AD, Tyche/Eagle
Legionary vexillum on obverse

Ilium was the Troy of Homeric fame. It was, because of its history and the story of Aeneas, a popular place with educated Romans. Many emperors contributed to the city's beautification and prestige. A small bronze coin from Ilium, struck during the Imperial Period, reflects the legends of Rome and Troy. On its obverse is depicted the She-Wolf and Twins alluding to the foundation of Rome. On the reverse is Hector, striding left in battle dress, which is a reference to the Trojan War.

Ilium, Troas, AE 19mm
ca. AD 117-192

Cyzicus, Mysia, AE 20mm
Kore Soteira, ca. 1st-2nd c. AD

The province of Asia included many wealthy cities, and the iconography of its coins is rich as well. Literally thousands of types beckon the curious and treat the inquisitive. It is unfortunate that we can show only a few here, but the others will be waiting for you!

Erythrae, Ionia, AE 32mm
Otacilia Severa (wife of Philip I), AD 244-9

Alliance Coins

The fascinating alliance coins of cities in the Roman province of Asia have long been a subject of discussion and debate among numismatists. The idea that these cities could form independent alliances while under the dominion of Rome is difficult to fathom. Clearly, these alliances were not military in nature. What then did they represent? It does not seem that economic pacts were the occasion for these issues.

A recent monograph by Dr. Ursula Kampmann (see bibliography) sees this series as an attempt by Asian cities to "practice foreign policy under Roman rule". The arguments for various theories are extremely complex and the final word has yet to be written on this issue. Fortunately, the precise motivation for this impressive series (which may not be a "series" in the strictest sense) is not relevant to every collector. It is possible to collect coinage of a particular period, or iconographic similarity, without fully understanding the details of its origin.

The very nature of these coins, and the fact that they are enigmatic, makes them collectable. We find the cities, represented by their patron deities, on coins of very large and relatively consistent module. Also, the inscriptions are reflective of the union and clearly as important to the composition as the figural elements.

It should be said that the beginning collector of Roman Provincial coins is not likely to stumble across one of these alliance coins in a junk box—at least not in anything approaching a collectable grade. They do appear with some regularity, however, in public auctions and occasionally on fixed price lists.

Apollo and Artemis as Miletus and Ephesus in Alliance, AE 36mm Marcus Aurelius, AD 161-80

Smyrna and Nicomedia in Alliance, AE 36mm Marcus Aurelius, AD 161-80

Asklepios and Artemis as Pergamum and Ephesus in Alliance, AE 36mm Gallienus, AD 253-60

Cistophoric Tetradrachms

The *cistophori* derived their name from the cista or basket which was part of a particular cult worship in Asia. It means literally "One who carries the cista", meaning of course that the basket is carried on the coin. The design on early issues of this coin type included a Dionysiac cista out of which emerged a serpent. It was called a Cista Mystica.

The denomination, a silver tetradrachm, originated under the Attalid kings of Pergamum and was retained by the Romans when they inherited that kingdom in 133 BC. During the Imperial Period, the cistophori were different in the respect that they bore imperial iconography and Latin legends, but they apparently circulated along with earlier Hellenistic coins of the same denomination. The Roman cistophori were once thought to have been struck at only a few mints, but that view has changed and there is now a long list of mints where they are believed to have been struck (see facing page). In addition to the number of mints, the denomination was struck over a fairly long period of time.

The Roman cistophori are quite popular among collectors because on the one hand they are made of silver, and on the other they are large coins. This allows for rather striking portraits that do not appear in any other silver issue of the Romans at that time. One of the more popular cistophori is an issue by Mark Antony which depicts the imperator along with his wife Octavia. The coin comes in two varieties, one with their conjoined heads on the obverse (illustrated here) and another with the head of Antony (much enlarged) on the obverse and a smaller head of Octavia, above a cista, on the reverse.

Ephesus, Ionia, AR cistophorus
Antony & Octavia, 39 BC

Several varieties of the cistophorus were issued under Augustus. One reverse depicts a garlanded altar with two stags, another the Capricorn—which was the natal sign of Augustus. One type struck at Ephesus (illustrated here) depicts a group of six wheat stalks tied together. This is a common motif that occurs on many provincial coins.

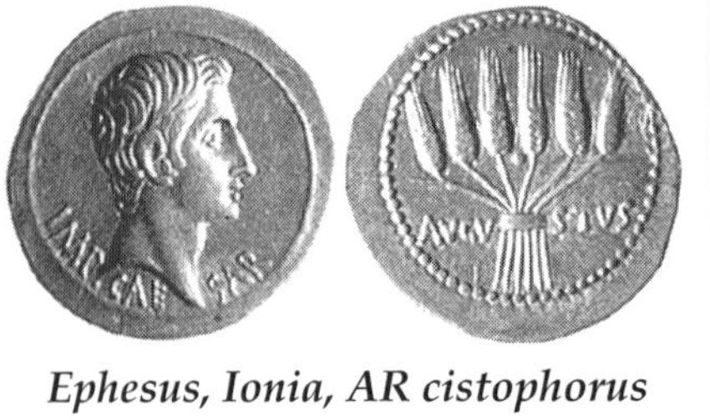

Ephesus, Ionia, AR cistophorus
Augustus, 27 BC - AD 14

Among the more outstanding portrait cistophori is one struck at Ephesus with the conjoined portraits of Claudius and his wife Agrippina the Younger. Not only is the portrait exceptional, the reverse of this coin presents a rare depiction of the cult statue Diana Ephesia. This is the Greek Artemis of Ephesus whose temple was one of the seven wonders of the ancient world.

Another type struck at Ephesus, under Domitian, depicts three military standards with an eagle above. From this, and the types mentioned previously, it is clear that the imagery on cistophori was not always provincial in nature—even if the circulation was relatively limited.

Like most imperial denominations, cistophori are often datable by the titulature or rank mentioned in the inscriptions. Although they were struck in the province of Asia for local use, and are in reality no different than the colonial issues with Latin legends, the cistophori are often catalogued as imperial issues in sale catalogues. In fact, they are included in *Roman Imperial Coins,* which would be reason enough for most cataloguers to include them with the imperial coins.

One cannot escape, however, the reason and place of issue. Regardless of the inscriptions and the general character, these coins are as provincial as any "autonomous" bronze struck in the highlands of Anatolia.

Cities issuing cistophori

Adramyteum	*Mysia?*
Aezani	*Phrygia*
Apameia	*Phrygia*
Aphrodisias	*Caria*
Apollonis	*Lydia?*
Bithynia	*(Commune)*
Ephesus	*Ionia*
Eumeneia	*Phrygia*
Laodiceia	*Phrygia*
Miletus	*Ionia*
Mylasa	*Caria*
Pergamum	*Mysia*
Sardis	*Lydia*
Smyrna	*Ionia*
Stratoniceia	*Lydia?*
Synnada	*Phrygia*
Thyateira	*Lydia*
Tralles	*Lydia*

? = uncertain. There are also various unidentified mints.

Ephesus, Ionia, AR cistophorus

Nicomedia, Bithynia, AR cistophorus
Hadrian, AD 136

Bithynia and Pontus

Bithynia was a region in northwestern Asia Minor which extended from the Sea of Marmara to the Black Sea. Like the province of Asia, Bithynia was bequeathed to Rome by a deceased client king. With the death of Nicomedes IV in 74 BC, the line of Bithynian Kings ended and Rome became administrator of a vast territory in northern Asia Minor. Bithynia was united with Pontus and annexed as a Roman province in 63 BC. In 29 BC, Nicomedia became the seat of the Bithynian Koinon.

Tium, AE 15mm, AD 138-161
Marcus Aurelius as Caesar

Nicaea, AE 24mm
Caracalla, AD 197-217

Bithynium, AE 25mm
Gallienus, AD 253-268

The number of coin issuing cities in the province reached 29 by the second century AD. At that time, the emperor Trajan sent Pliny the Younger to Bithynia to check the extravagance of local administrators. It was from here that he sent Trajan a famous letter about Christians and their practices.

Hadrian was especially partial to Bithynia, being that it was the home of Antinoüs, his "favorite". He established a Legate at

Koinon Bithynia, AE 34mm, Hadrian, AD 117-138

Nicomedia (modern Izmit), the provincial capital.

Apameia, AE 17mm
Mark Antony?, ca. 42-40 BC

Nicaea (modern Iznik) contended bitterly with Nicomedia for leadership of the province. The city was prone to elaborate displays of titulature on its coinage and hosted many games and festivals as a show of importance. Architectural types are common. In the time of Constantine the Great, Nicaea was selected as the site of an important ecumenical council. From that time, it finally equalled Nicomedia in importance, although the latter became an imperial mint.

Sebastopolis, originally named Dioscurias, was a city on the eastern coast of the Black Sea in the region known as Colchis. The city was known for its export of salt, timber, linen and hemp. It was also an important link to trading with the tribes of the Caucauses. The name Sebastopolis was acquired during the reign of Augustus (Sebastos in Greek). It apparently diminished in importance during the first century.

Sebastopolis, Pontus, AE 32mm
Geta, Year 208 (AD 205/6)
Stoa of Herakles

Zela was an inland city in Pontus and a cult center of Anaitis (Anahiti). It was the site of a Roman disaster, where some 7,000 troops were lost in a battle against Mithridates VI. Seventeen years later, Julius Caesar avenged the defeat at this same city by prevailing over the forces of Pharnaces II of Pontus. His subsequent Triumph at Rome was the occasion in which he raised the sign with the famous words Veni, Vidi, Vici. The coins issued at Zela under Septimius Severus (illustrated here) depict the Temple of Anaitis with an unusual triple pediment.

Zela, Pontus, AE 30mm
Septimius Severus, Year 143 (AD 206/7)

Phrygia / Galatia

Sebaste, Phrygia, AE 18mm
Augustus, 27 BC - AD 14

Amorion, Phrygia, AE 21mm
Augustus, 27 BC - AD 14

Philomelium, AE 30mm
Philip I, AD 244-249

Phrygia and Galatia were interior regions of Asia Minor on the western side of the great central plateau. They lay to the south of Bithynia and north of Lycia and Pisidia. To the west they bordered on the province of Asia and on the east Cappadocia. It was a region with many cities, over fifty of them striking coins. Among the more important not illustrated here were Acmoneia, Aezanis, Apamaea, Cibyra, Cotiaeum, Hierapolis, Laodiceia ad Lycum, Pessinus and Tavium.

Ancyra (modern Ankara) became the capital of the Roman province of Galatia, and center of a koinon, following the death of the Roman Client King Amyntas in 25 BC. A famous monument to Augustus at Ancyra preserves on the temple walls the text of the *Res Gestae Divi Augsti* outlining the official version of the political life of Augustus. The coinage of Phrygia sometimes includes the names of local magistrates and priests. For example, a coin from Eumenia (illustrated below) bears the name of Ioulios Kleon who served as Archierus Asias or Chief Priest of Asia during the reign of Nero. The coins of Phrygia and Galatia are numerous and often difficult to attribute. As a result, they are often neglected and offer fertile ground for the collector who wishes to build an important collection on a limited budget.

Eumenia, Phrygia, AE 19mm
Nero, AD 54-68

Ancyra, Galatia, AE 23mm
Bust of Senate, ca. 2-3rd c. AD

Lycia

Lycia was a mountainous region, located in the southwest corner of Asia Minor. It was a very independent region, administered by a federation of cities, and the Romans tended to leave it alone. Augustus confirmed Lycia's freedom in 29 BC. Nonetheless, the federation struck coins in the name of Augustus, Tiberius and Caligula. It was united with Pamphylia as one province in AD 43 by Claudius. The Lycian league coinage was continued under the empire, and silver drachms were produced in the style of earlier Hellenistic Period issues. They carried the portrait of the reigning emperor rather than a head of Apollo. These were issued through the reign of Trajan and circulated widely.

Masicytes, AR drachm
Augustus, 27 BC - AD 14

The most prolific coinage of Lycia during the Imperial Period occurred during the reign of Gordian III. A bold issue from Cyane was struck in the name of his wife Tranquillina, and a series of coins in the name of Gordian was struck at Myra. Saint Nicholas, the famous bishop of Myra from whom the legend of Santa Claus originated, would undoubtedly have seen these coins in circulation during his lifetime. Ironically, they depict on the reverse a cult statue of Artemis within a distyle temple.

Cyane, AE 31mm
Tranquillina, AD 241-244

Myra, AE 31mm, Gordian III, AD 238-244

Pamphylia

Pamphylia was the region on the southern coast of Asia Minor to the east of Lycia. The most notable feature, aside from its rugged Taurus mountains, is a strip of coastal area known today as the Turkish Riviera. This fertile alluvial plain was the home to several important cities in Roman times. In 36 BC King Amyntas of Galatia gave Pamphylia to Mark Antony and it was transferred several times between the provinces of Lycia and Galatia during the Imperial Period. It eventually became a province of its own. Throughout the period, a Koinon of confederated cities continued to operate.

Aspendus was an important harbor on the Eurymedon river, about eight miles inland. It was a prosperous city, and minted coins well into the third century AD. The remains of Aspendus include the best preserved theater in Asia Minor—built to seat an audience of 7,500. It was constructed about AD 160 and dedicated to Antoninus Pius. Aqueducts served the coastal cities of Pamphylia, and remains of the impressive structure at Aspendus are still visible. The coin from Aspendus illustrated here portrays Hephaistos, the blacksmith of the gods, working a shield with his hammer. Provincial coins of Aspendus sometimes feature the two wrestlers which are commonly seen on silver staters of the Hellenistic Period.

Aspendus, AE 31
Maximinus I, AD 235-238

Not too far from Aspendus was the city of Perga. It too was prosperous during the Roman period and its coinage is rich in local religious iconography—especially in Asian cult figures.

Perga, AE 21 mm
Septimius Severus, AD 193-211

The third major city on the western edge of the "Riviera" was Side. This seaport was important enough to the Romans to be given the accolade *Navarchis.* Like many other cities of Asia Minor, Side continued to use Hellenistic motifs on its provincial coinage. The bronze of Domitian illustrated here depicts Athena and a pomegranate—traditional types from the city's past.

Side, AE 21 mm
Domitian, as Caesar, AD 69-79

Pisidia / Lycaonia

Pisidia was an inland district north of Pamphylia and Cilicia. It overlapped at times with the provinces of Lycaonia, Phrygia and Galatia which together made up the general interior of Asia Minor west of Cappadocia. There were some 30 cities in Pisidia which struck provincial coins. The most important of the Pisidian cities was Antiochia (modern Yalvaç) which is usually referred to simply as Antioch or Antioch in Pisidia. This is not to be confused with the Syrian city of much greater importance.

Etenna, Pisidia, AE 18mm
Orbiana, ca. AD 225
wife of Severus Alexander

Antioch was declared a free city by the Romans in 188 BC following their victory over Antiochus III. It was re-founded as a Roman colony shortly after 25 BC. Provincial coinage continued at Antioch until the time of Claudius Gothicus, which is relatively late. The large sestertius-sized issues of Septimius Severus, and later rulers, bear the letters SR which apparently stand for *Senatus Romanus.*

Antioch, Pisidia, AE 33mm
Gordian III, AD 238-244

Many of the coins struck at obscure central plateau cities, like that of Etenna illustrated here, bear portraits of imperial family members which are difficult and expensive to obtain in the imperial series. Surprisingly, these can often be found in junk boxes of mixed Greek bronzes.

Cremna, modern Girme, was made a Roman Colony (Colonia Iulia Augusta Felix Cremnensium) in 25 BC following the death of Amyntas. The status of *ius italicum* gave Cremna the same rights as an Italian city. In other words, they were exempted from land taxes and were given the right of municipal self government. The motif chosen for the coin illustrated here honors Cybele, the great mother or Magna Mater—a distinctly Eastern goddess who became very popular with the Romans.

Cremna, Pisidia, AE 37mm
Julia Domna, ca. AD 193-217

Termessus Major, Pisidia,
AE 22mm, 3rd c. AD
The mythic hero Solymos

Termessus was a fiercely independent inland city of Pisidia which held the distinction of being the only city to have survived a siege by Alexander the Great. Due to population pressure, the city established a colony of the same name in Lycia, about 50 miles west of the mother city. It too struck coins and therefore we have issues from Termessus Major and Termessus Minor. Termessus became an autonomous state under the Romans in 71 BC. Even after it had been incorporated into the Roman province of Galatia, during the reign of Augustus, the city continued to issue coin types without imperial portraits. Many of these issues bear the image of a local hero, Solymos. Two very recent and excellent articles deal with this series (see bibliography for Kosmetatou and Tameanko).

Isauria was sandwiched in between Pisidia and Lycaonia, bordering Pamphylia on its south. It never was a province in any real sense of the word and its cities were mostly fragmented pirate hideouts. The largest mint was at Isaura, which produced some lovely issues under the Severans.

Lycaonia was an ill defined region in the central highlands which bordered on and overlapped Pisidia, Galatia, Cappadocia and Isauria. Lycaonia was under the reign of Amyntas until his death in 25 BC and then for a while under the Cappadocian kingdom. Finally, until AD 72 it was ruled by the Roman Client King, Antiochus IV of Commagene. The main resources of Lycaonia were the great salt lake (modern Tuz Gölü) and mining of copper and lead. The main city was Iconium (Konya), which much later became the capital of the Seljuq Turks. The execution of dies in these remote areas was not always as refined as one might see in Asia or Syria, nor even in Cilicia. The "SR" of Pisidian Antioch appears at Iconium as well.

Isaura, Isauria, AE 25mm
Caracalla, AD 197-217

Iconium, Lycaonia, AE 29mm
Gallienus, AD 253-268

Cilicia

Cilicia was strategically important to the Romans as it provided a toe-hold in southeastern Asia Minor and a springboard for campaigns to the east. It was an excellent marshalling point for supplies, and its ports served as gateways to the Levant and Egypt. It was also a breeding ground for Pirates which ravaged the entire Mediterranean.

In 67 BC, Pompey the Great led an expedition which partially stabilized the region and brought much of it under Roman influence. The interior, however, was left under the authority of Tarcondimotus, who ruled from Heiropolis as Toparch, and eventually as Client King of Cilicia. He was succeeded by his son Philopator who died during the reign of Tiberius. Cilicia was divided into two regions, rough or "Tracheia" in the west and smooth or "Pedias" in the east. This was due to the mountainous character of the former and the flat plains of the latter. There were several important cities in Cilicia, the two most prolific in their coinage were Tarsus and Anazarbus. The coinage of these cities is discussed on the following pages. Some, including Tarsus, Seleuceia, Elaiussa, Aegeae and probably others, produced silver coinage during the Roman period.

Philadelphia, AE 22mm
Trajan, AD 98-117

Flaviopolis, as one may surmise from its name, was founded as a Roman city under the Flavian dynasty. Frequent depictions of the Dioscouri on coinage of this city indicates a cult worship of the twins. The example illustrated here, in addition to the Dioscouri reverse, depicts the Caesars Herennius Etruscus and Hostilian in a composition that may have been intended to portray them allegorically as the Dioscouri.

Hieropolis-Castabala, AE 22mm
Monogram of Tarcondimotus?

There were many small cities in Cilicia, like Philadelphia, Augusta, Mopsus, etc. which struck abundant coinage. The coins of

Flaviopolis, Cilicia, AE 26mm
Herennius Etruscus and Hostilian
as Caesars, Year 177 (AD 249/50)

Cilicia are very well catalogued in the SNG catalogue of the collection of Eduardo Levante (SNG Switzerland - Levante). There are also a great many specialized works on provincial coins, by city, which we unfortunately cannot expand on in this survey due to space.

Anemurium was located on the western edge of coastal Cilicia. It became an important commercial center during the third century with a prolific coinage with a diversity of types. The specimen illustrated here presents the hero Perseus holding a short sword in his right hand and the severed head of Medusa in his left. The single letter "A" before the ethnic is actually a date, i.e. regnal year 1 (AD 235/6) of the reign of Maximinus Thrax.

Anemurium, AE 35mm
Maximinus I, AD 235/6

Seleukeia ad Calycadnum, modern Silifke, was presumably founded by or in the name of Seleucus I Nicator. The city was built on the banks of the Calycadnus river and due to its harbor, was the most important city of western Cilicia. The coins struck at Seleukeia, particularly during the third century are quite impressive, and reflect the prosperity that the city must have enjoyed. The figure of Nike advancing was a common theme on Hellenistic Period coins from Seleukeia and may also be seen centuries later on the coinage of Roman emperors including Gallienus as illustrated here.

Seleukeia ad Calycadnum, Cilicia
AE 30mm, Gallienus, AD 253-268

Syedra issued a number of large bronze coins with interesting reverses, including the one shown here which honors Salonina, the wife of Gallienus.

Syedra, Cilicia, AE 30mm
Salonina (wife of Gallienus), AD 253-268

Tarsus

Tarsus, Cilicia, AE 29mm
Elagabalus, AD 218-222

Tarsus was a major metropolis in Roman times. It was the place where Cleopatra and Mark Antony met, and the home of Saul. In a continuing battle between Tarsus and Anazarbus for pre-eminence among cities of Cilicia, Tarsus was honored (at least under the reign of Elagabalus) to host the *Ciliciarch*—the leader of the Cilician assembly or koinon. This official was the high priest of the imperial cult and organizer of the games honoring the divine emperors. On the reverse of a coin struck at Tarsus, during this period, these divinities are represented by small heads (imperial busts) adorning the Ciliciarch's crown. Alongside is the crown of the demiurgos, or highest official of the city. The abbreviation AMK in the exergue stands for "first" "greatest" and "most beautiful" (see table of inscriptions). This was a phrase used extensively by both Tarsus and Anazarbus. Also found in the composition (among the heads) are the numbers ΓB (3/2) which stand for "superior of the three eparchates" and "keeper of two imperial temples". This too was a claim frequently advanced by Anazarbus on its coinage. Another fascinating coin type depicts the Tyche of Tarsus seated, with Lycaonia (personification of the province) crowning from behind, while personifications of Cilicia and Isauria approach with crowns. The river god Kydnos is shown swimming at Tyche's feet, as in the famous statue from Antioch.

Tarsus, Cilicia, AR tetradrachm
Domitian, AD 81-96

Tarsus, Cilicia, AE 35mm,
Septimius Severus, AD 193-211

Anazarbus

Anazarbus, in the central part of the large Cilician plain, was refounded as Caesarea ad Anazarbum by Augustus—apparently during a visit to Cilicia in 19 BC. It was formerly under the rule of the Tarcondimotid dynasty. The first Roman portrait coins were struck during the reign of Claudius and from that time until the capture of Valerian by Shapur the Great, the city issued literally hundreds of diverse and sometimes spectacular types. The corpus of coins from this city, published by Ruprecht Ziegler, lists over 800 different dies. The city itself was built on a flat plain beneath a 600 foot escarpment and acropolis. It hosted three neocorate temples and a great many games, which are recorded on the city's coins. Several emperors visited the city, and in AD 221, Elagabalus accepted the title *demiurgos* (the highest official) of the city. As if to rub salt in the wound, Anazarbus struck a coin type with the bust of Elagabalus on its obverse and on the reverse a motif historically employed by Tarsus—the lion attacking a bull. This prompted Tarsus to elicit a similar acceptance of the position at their city by Severus Alexander. The rivalry was clearly intense.

Anazarbus, AE 34mm
Severus Alexander, AD 229/30

Anazarbus, AE 25mm
Elagabalus, AD 218-222

Anazarbus, AE 30mm
Diadumenian, AD 217-218

A Triumphal arch, built at Anazarbus during the reign of Septimius Severus, is featured on an impressive bronze of the period. Other architectural types include a number of the city's temples, shrines, the fortified acropolis and the impressive aqueduct which crossed a wide expanse of the Cilician plain.

Antiochus IV in Cilicia

Antiochus IV, Epiphanes, was descended from a long line of Kings of Commagene. His homeland had become a Roman province in AD 17, but Caligula restored the kingdom to his friend in AD 38. Along with the lands of his patrimony, he was given control of parts of Lycaonia and most of Cilicia. He served the Romans during the reign of Nero in their wars against the Parthians and again under Vespasian in the war against the Jews.

Epiphanes & Callinicus
AE 22mm, AD 72
struck at Selinus in Cilicia

Antiochus reigned until AD 72, when he was accused of conspiring with the Parthians and was deprived of his kingdom. He lived out his life in Rome either as a private citizen or in confinement.

Antiochus IV, AE 20mm, , AD 38-72
struck at Elaeussa-Sebaste in Cilicia

In Cilicia, he issued a series of bronze coins bearing his portrait and those of his wife Iotape and their sons Epiphanes and Callinicus. During this time, the major cities of Cilicia were producing civic coins, both with imperial portraits and non portrait iconography. The exact relationship between Antiochus IV and the various city councils is a perplexing question. It can be assumed that the authority he possessed in this region was not unlike that of the toparchs who ruled before him and served at times as magistrates of the cities nominally under their rule. The result was a very loose kingship by our modern way of thinking.

Iotape, AE 21mm, , AD 38-72
struck at Anemurium in Cilicia

Antiochus IV, AE 26mm, , AD 38-72
struck at Anemurium in Cilicia

Cappadocia

Cappadocia, in the eastern highlands, was a rough and mountainous region known for its fine horses. It was ruled by the Roman Client King Archelaus from 36 BC to AD 17 when he died at Rome. The territory at that time was extensive and even included some cities on the Cilician coast. Under Tiberius, it was made a Roman province and became the site of many imperial estates. Timber and stone were the main exports.

Caesarea ad Argaeum, the capital of Cappadocia, was given that name during the reign of Augustus. Before that it was known as Mazaca. According to Josephus, the city was originally founded by the Biblical Mesech, son of Japhet. Caesarea was located at the foot of Mount Argaeus, a sacred mountain, which is depicted on many of the city's coins from the Roman period. The mountain is typically depicted with a cult figure standing in a grotto or at the top. On some coins, like the bronze of Septimius Severus illustrated below, the mountain is depicted as a model atop an altar.

Caesarea, Cappadocia
AR Didrachm, Nerva, AD 98

Caesarea, AR didrachm
Hadrian, AD 117-38

The mint at Caesarea was extremely productive, especially in silver issues. Much of the silver coinage circulating in Asia Minor was struck there in the denominations of didrachm, drachm and hemidrachm. The city fell to Shapur the Great after the capture of Valerian. Although it was recovered, it never achieved the same importance after that time. The dates on Roman coins of Caesarea are regnal dates.

Caesarea, AE 30mm
Septimius Severus, Year 13 (AD 205/6)

Although provincial silver coins were only produced in a few provinces, the output from those mints was very great. Consequently provincial silver in today's market is much less expensive, on average, than equivalent imperial coins.

Commagene

Commagene was located in the extreme north of Syria or what is now southeastern Turkey. The capital, Samosata, was originally a royal seat of the Commagenian kings. These kings, from the time of Pompey, served Rome as client rulers. When Antiochus III died in AD 17, Tiberius made Commagene a Roman province and struck coins there bearing his portrait and Latin legends (see page 1 of this volume). The kingdom was restored, however, in AD 38 when Caligula appointed his boyhood friend Antiochus IV to the throne of his lineage. The kingdom was actually expanded beyond its original boundaries (see page 57) and Antiochus ruled successfully, if somewhat harshly, until AD 72. He had two sons, Epiphanes and Callinicus, who were groomed to inherit the throne. Unfortunately, a reported intrigue with the Parthians led to the king's deposition and the end of any dynastic dreams. Coins from Commagene sometimes reflect the astrological signs of the royal family, Scorpio and Capricorn, and other local symbology like the Armenian tiara.

After the fall of Antiochus, Commagene was incorporated into the province of Syria, with a koinon or federal council. Later coins struck for Roman emperors often bear the familiar Tyche of Antioch seated on a rock with a river god swimming at her feet.

Samosata, AE 18-19mm,
Epiphanes & Callinicus, AD 72

Samosata, AE 28mm
Antiochus IV, AD 38-72

Samosata, AE 24mm
Philip I, AD 244-249

Mesopotamia

Mesopotamia means literally "the land between the rivers". It refers specifically to the land between the Tigris and Euphrates, which is one of the world's oldest centers of civilization. The customs and traditions of this region are deeply rooted and it has for all of recorded history been a hotbed of political activity and military conflict. The Romans had long dreamed of conquering the East, like Alexander, but they were thwarted first by the Parthians and then by the Sasanians. They were not, however, above trying. Repeated excursions into and beyond Mesopotamia resulted in a long string of Roman disasters. Only the Emperor Trajan was able to establish a stable military presence, and that was short lived. Edessa (modern Urfa) was a city in northwestern Mesopotamia on a tributary of the Euphrates. It was ruled in imperial times by a succession of Oshrene kings who served as clients of Rome (see facing page). Edessa was an early Christian center and one of the kings named Abgar supposedly wrote a personal letter to Jesus Christ receiving not only a written reply but a disciple named Addai. Oshrene was made a Roman province in AD 195 and Edessa became a colony under Caracalla in AD 215.

Edessa, Billon tetradrachm

Nisibis, Mesopotamia, AE 26mm

Hatra, AE 23mm, 2nd-3rd c. AD

The city of Nisibis was right at the point of conflict, and Roman outposts were established there with some regularity. They were overrun with equal regularity.

Hatra was an oasis in what is modern Iraq, about 50 miles south of Mosul. It was under Roman control for only a short time, but bronzes were issued there with a peculiar upside down or backwards SC. The obverse of these interesting coins depicts the sun god Shamash accompanied by an Aramaic legend.

Kings of Edessa

Edessa, the capital of the kingdom of Osrhoene, was founded by Seleukos I. Its name comes from the Macedonian city which was the burial place of kings. After the Roman elimination of Seleukid power in the region, Edessa became a free city and tended to support the Parthian kings. It was captured several times by the Romans but never could be held for very long.

In AD 167, Lucius Verus defeated the Parthians in Mesopotamia and reinstalled Ma'nu VIII, Philoromaios, on the throne as a client king. He had been deposed by the Arsacids in 163. Ma'nu ruled until his death in 179 and was succeeded by his son Abgar VIII (The Great). Edessa was an early and important center of the Syrian church, and during this time one of the members of Abgar's court, a man named Bardesanes, was converted to Christianity. It has been suggested that a cross on the tiara of Abgar VIII may have Christian meaning. Following a reign of 35 years, Abgar VIII was succeeded by his son, Abgar IX, Severus. The unfortunate son ruled for only a year and a half before being deposed by Caracalla in AD 215/6. Caracalla was murdered two years later at Edessa and the city fell back under Arsacid control.

The Kings of Edessa did not regain power until the time of Gordian III when Abgar X was installed on the throne. This appointment is depicted on bronze coins of the reign of Gordian as illustrated below. It is not known whether Abgar X was a son or grandson of Abgar IX. At any rate, he ruled only two years as King of Edessa.

There are more than 25 varieties of coinage struck by the kings of Edessa, in spite of their limited tenure. In virtually every case, the ruler is depicted wearing the distinctive tiara of the Osrhoene kings.

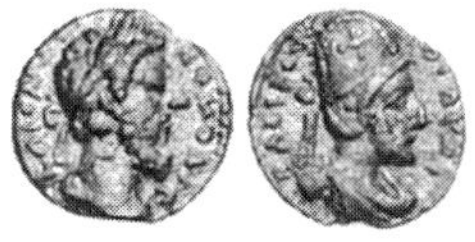

Commodus / Abgar VIII
Edessa, AE 15mm, AD 180-192

Septimius Severus / Abgar VIII
Edessa, AE 23mm, AD 193-211

Gordian III / Abgar X
Edessa, AE 30mm

Armenia

Armenia was a mountainous country in northeast Asia Minor, lying to the east of the Euphrates river. There are very few coins from the Roman period which can be considered provincial issues and they are exceedingly rare. Most coins with Armenian references were struck by the mint at Rome and include claims of conquest and subjugation by Roman expeditions. Surprisingly, the only reference that deals specifically with Armenian reference coins struck under the Romans is a small book in Armenian by Paul Z. Bedoukian (see bibliography). The two coins illustrated here are extracted from that reference. The satrap Artaxias was established in Armenia, with Roman support, following the defeat of Antiochus III in 190 BC. The kings of that dynasty are therefore known as Artaxiads. They ruled with varying degrees of freedom, but the greatest king of the dynasty was Tigranes II, who expanded the kingdom south into Syria and west into Asia Minor. Tigranes was restrained by Lucullus (69 BC) and became at least nominally a partner, if not subject, of Rome. Three decades later, Mark Antony attempted to consolidate Roman power in Armenia, but suffered great losses against the Parthians and was eventually forced to withdraw.

Following the Battle of Actium, Augustus (Octavian) inherited all of Asia Minor including Armenia. Tigranes III, who had been appointed by Augustus, died in 6 BC and the Armenians apparently installed his successor, Tigranes IV, without Roman approval. A period of negotiation finally brought confirmation about AD 1 and prompted the issue of a bronze coin bearing the heads of Tigranes IV and Augustus.

Tigranes IV, AE 25mm with Augustus, ca. AD 1 (Bedoukian 1)

Artavasdas, AR drachm with Augustus, AD 2-4 (Bedoukian 2)

Armenia was coveted by the Parthians, and constant threats against the country required the attention of Nero, Vespasian, Trajan, Hadrian and the Antonines. A treaty in the time of Nero placed the Arsacid king Tiridates on the throne of Armenia as a client king of Rome. Later, the Sasanians placed their own vassals on the throne and the conflict persisted for centuries.

The Provinces and Selected Cities of Asia Minor

BIBLIOGRAPHY

Asia Minor and Mesopotamia

Akurgal, E. *Ancient Civilizations and Ruins of Turkey,* Istanbul, 1983.

Bean, G.E. *Aegean Turkey,* London, 1966.

_____. *Turkey's Southern Shore,* London, 1968.

_____. *Turkey beyond the Maeander,* London, 1971.

_____. *Lycian Turkey,* London, 1978.

Bedoukian, Paul Z. *Roman Coins and Medals Relating to Armenia,* (1971 edition in Armenian. Translated by L.A. Saryan and serialized in *The Celator,* 1998).

Kampmann, Ursula. *Die Homonoia-Verbindungen der Stadt Pergamon, oder Der Versuch einer kleinasiatischen Stadt, unter römischer Herrschaft eigenständige Politik zu betreiben,* Saarbrücken, 1996.

Kleiner, F.S. and S.P. Noe. *The Early Cistophoric Coinage,* ANS Numismatic Studies No. 14, New York, 1977.

Kosmetatou, Elizabeth. "The Hero Solymos on the Coinage of Termessos Major", *Swiss Numismatic Review,* No. 76, 1997, pp. 41-56.

MacDonald, David J. *The Coinage of Aphrodisias,* RNS, London, 1976.

Metcalf, W. *The Cistophori of Hadrian,* ANS Numismatic Studies No. 15, New York, 1980.

Ramsay, W.M. "Studies on the Roman Province Galatia", *Journal of Roman Studies,* VII, 1917.

_____. "Colonia Caesaris (Pisidian Antioch) in the Augustan Age", *Journal of Roman Studies,* VI, 1916.

Slocum, John J, "Another Look at the Coins of Hatra" *ANS Museum Notes* 22, 1977.

Stark, Freya. *Rome on the Euphrates,* New York, 1966.

Sydenham, E. *The Coinage of Caesarea in Cappadocia,* London, 1933.

Tameanko, Marvin. "The coinage of Termessos: a mountain fortress city", *The Celator,* Vol. 12, No, 2, 1998.

Waddington, W.H. *Recueil Général des Monnaies Grecques d'Asie Mineure,* Paris, 1904-12.

Williams, G. *Eastern Turkey: A Guide and History,* London, 1972.

Wruck, W. *Die Syrische Provinzialprägung von Augustus bis Traian,* Stuttgart, 1931.

Ziegler, Ruprecht. "Münzen Kilikens als Zeugnis kaiserlicher Getreidespenden", *Jahrbuch für Numismatik und Geldgeschichte,* Vol. 27, 1977, pp. 29-67.

_____. *Untersuchungen zur Münzprägung von Anazarbos,* Vienna, 1993.

The Levant

The countries bordering the Eastern Mediterranean are often referred to as the Levant. Although this definition is a bit vague, and the region extends inland for some distance, numismatists generally consider coins of the Levant, at least during the Roman Provincial period, as those struck in the provinces of Syria and Judea. Even this distinction is rather vague, as the Roman "city coins" of Judea typically include the Transjordan issues—which are certainly not on the Mediterranean. There are, according to David Hendin, thirty-eight cities which fall into this broadly defined category. There are also issues from adjacent Roman provinces of the Middle East which could be considered a part of this general grouping. For our very limited purposes, and for the sake of convenience, let us simply include within the Levant all of those Roman coin issuing cities between modern day Turkey and Sinai, excepting Mesopotamia, which has already been discussed.

Syria was divided into several districts which included Seleucis, Pieria, Cyrrhestice, Chalybonitis, Coele-Syria, Trachonitis and the Decapolis. Seleucis was the most fertile region, in the northwest between the Amanus mountains and the sea. Pieria was a contiguous region named after the mountain of the same name. The two districts are usually mentioned together as Seleucis-Pieria. Cyrrhestice occupied that land between Commagene and Antioch and Chalybonitis was also located in the northeast of Syria. Coele-Syria was a valley district which bordered on Phoenicia to the south, while Trachonitis lay further east. The Decapolis (literally "ten cities") extended into northeastern Palestine. The boundaries of "Syria" changed greatly, and at times even included Commagene and the coastal cities of Phoenicia.

Judea was also, at times, considered part of Syria. At other times it was designated as a separate province. The city coinage of Judea is well covered in Hendin's readily accessible *Guide to Biblical Coins,* and we will not attempt to elaborate on that coinage here. It will suffice to illustrate a few of the more popular types and touch on some of the most important cities. Samaria and Phoenicia are sometimes treated as separate provinces as well. The principality of Palmyra issued a few rare types during the provincial period and, for a short time, extended their influence over virtually all of this region.

We cannot begin to present a comprehensive view of this massive coinage, and will be able only to touch briefly on the nature of the coins struck here. Our focus, understandably, will be on those cities whose coins are generally of greatest interest or accessibility to collectors or students of the ancient world.

Antioch on the Orontes

The city of Antioch, modern Antakya, was founded by Seleucus I Nicator, a general of Alexander the Great, in 300 BC. The site is strategically located at a point where the Orontes river cuts through the mountains from Syria to the sea. Thus, it has from very early times been a crossroad for trade as well as a political, cultural and religious center. It was a very early center of Christianity and played an important role in the forging of doctrine which led to the great schisms of the fourth and fifth centuries. Its population has been estimated at up to a half million inhabitants during the Roman period, and the resulting demand for coinage, both for domestic use and external trade, was substantial. The provincial coins of Antioch are admittedly not as rich or diverse in iconography as many of the coins struck farther to the north in Asia Minor, but they conservatively reflect important historical events over a very long period of time. The city enjoyed access to two major seaports, its own harbor at Seleuceia and the nearby port of Laodicea ad Mare.

Tyche of Antioch

Although the coinage of Antioch is extensive, there has not been a comprehensive study of the city's coinage. Rather, the periods have been treated in isolation. One of the most artistically distinctive coin types from Antioch and its ports, depicted a local cult statue of widespread fame. There are few primary sources which discuss ancient works of art, and we are fortunate to have the words of both Pliny the Elder and Pausanias on this subject. Both have commented on the work of a certain Eutychides of Sikyon, who was commissioned to create a statue in bronze for the city of Antioch. Pliny the Elder (1st century AD) reported that "Eutychides represented the river Eurotas [Orontes]. Of this figure it has often been said that art has made it more liquid than the river itself." Pausanias (2nd century AD) said "Eutychides of Sikyon, a pupil of Lysippos, made a statue of Fortune for the Syreans who live on the Orontes, at whose hand it receives great honor." An additional comment by the chronicler John Malalas (reign of Justinian) indicates that the statue was, at that time, still housed in a shrine above the river Orontes. Pliny placed the date of this work at 296 BC, which is only shortly after the city's founding as a Seleucid city.

Tyche was the deified personification of Chance or Fortune—which became increasingly important during the Hellenistic period. Every city had a Tyche, crowned by turrets, to symbolize the role of guardian. This particular representation, as the personification of Antioch, depicted Tyche seated on a rock with one foot resting on the shoulder of a youth swimming beneath her. Tyche's hand holds a wheat stalk, symbolizing abundance. The youth is a personification of the river Orontes.

The fame of Eutychides' original sculpture is attested to not only by the survival of later copies, both as statues and statuettes, but also by the appearance of this personification on innumerable coins and other media over an extended period. Its influence became so strong that the noted historian W.W. Tarn credits this sculpture with ultimately making a city's Fortune the city goddess. Considering that all subsequent renderings seem to stem from this original work, and that by Imperial times the image became essentially religious, the argument seems reasonable.

The full sculpture first appears on coinage during the reign of Tigranes II of Armenia, who ruled in Antioch from 83-69 BC. This adoption of a venerable Antiochene motif for the reverse type may have been an attempt on the part of Tigranes to ingratiate himself with the local population.

During the Imperial period, the Tyche of Eutychides appears at Antioch on coins of Augustus, Septimius Severus, Elagabalus, Severus Alexander, Julia Mamaea, Trajan Decius, Herrenius Etruscus, Hostilian, Trebonianus Gallus, Volusian, Valerian, and perhaps others. Coins with the Tyche motif were struck at both of Antioch's port cities, and was adopted by a number of other cities—especially those located on rivers, as a generic representation of their local deity.

With the capture of Valerian and most of Roman Asia by the Sasanian king Shapur I in AD 253,

Laodicea ad Mare, AR tetradrachm
Septimius Severus, AD 193-211
Tyche of Antioch, anchor at feet

Antioch, AE 30mm, Trebonianus Gallus
Cult statue of Tyche in tetrastyle shrine
river god Orontes swimming below

Antioch, AR tetradrachm (x1.5)
Trajan, AD 98-117
Tyche & the river Orontes

the motif temporarily disappears. It reappears on a small bronze coin of Antioch which formerly was thought to be struck under the reign of Julian II, but is now recognized to be part of a series issued by Maximinus II (AD 309-313).

The final appearance of this motif at Antioch falls in the Romaion (Byzantine) series. Although typically crude in its draftsmanship, the reverse design of the pentanummia struck at Antioch under the reign of Justin I (Wroth 75-82) bears the familiar Tyche of Eutychides. Depictions of works of art, or for that matter any narrative subject, are extremely rare in the Byzantine series. The fact that this statue honored a pagan deity makes its selection as a motif on one of the State's most conservative instruments all the more remarkable. The sculpture must have inspired immense public sentiment even at this late date. The reverse type of Tyche is repeated on the reverse of bronze coins struck at Antioch jointly by Justin and his nephew Justinian (Sear, *Byzantine* 133).

The fate of this magnificent sculpture is uncertain, but it probably met with the same demise that most of the famous bronze sculptures of antiquity suffered—the metal being melted down for coinage or weapons by some conquering army. It is not clear how long the sculpture actually survived; perhaps it perished during the sack of Antioch by the Sasanians in AD 540, shortly after the pentanummia were issued.

The "SC" Coins of Antioch

Antioch was made capital of the Roman province of Syria by Pompey in 64 BC. Then, Julius Caesar granted the city autonomous status in 49/48 BC, from which date the city era is calculated. The people of Antioch enjoyed a special relationship with Rome—perhaps to the chagrin of many Romans. A large immigration of Syrians to Rome in the first century caused open indignation. A series of bronze coins from Antioch maintained a simple motif for much of the Roman period, bearing on their reverse a simple "SC" within a wreath. This abbreviation is probably for the same *Senatus Consulto* that is a common feature on Roman Imperial coins and signifies that the Roman Senate had given its approval for the issue. Syria was, however, an imperial rather than senatorial province. The SC device is not often seen on provincial coinage. It has been suggested that its use was a purposeful attempt to disassociate the coinage from its place of issue. In other words, the coinage was issued for imperial purposes rather than local trade. This suggestion is sensible and would seem to be supported by the fact that the SC bronze coins circulated widely in the Levant. They were often counterstamped by local legions. It is doubtful, however, that they were issued solely for troop payments or any other singular purpose. The coins of this series are quite readily obtainable in the market and form a coherent collecting specialty that is not over-studied or overly popularized.

Antioch, AE 30mm

Antioch, AE 27mm
Vespasian, AD 69-79

Antioch, AE 18mm

Antioch, AE 18mm
Diadumenian, AD 217-218

“Syrian” Tetradrachms

Antioch, Syria, AR tetradrachm
Nero, AD 62/3 (AIP=yr. 111)

Antioch, Syria, AR tetradrachm
Pescennius Niger, AD 193-194

Laodicea ad Mare, Syria
AR tetradrachm
Geta as Caesar, AD 198-209

Ake-Ptolemais, Phoenicia
AR tetradrachm
Caracalla, AD 215-217

The "Syrian" tetradrachms form a very interesting and collectible series—which receives much less attention than one would expect. Actually, the term "Syrian" is a bit of a misnomer since some of the coins included in this series were struck at mints outside of Syria proper. Of course the boundaries of Syria were so vague, and changing, that one could hardly quibble about the distinction. They are, however, a series distinctly separate from the cistophoric tetradrachms of Asia.

These issues are styled after the coins of Antioch, and clearly belong to the same group. The predominant motif is the eagle standing on a thunderbolt, but this is not exclusive. A few varieties have mint names in the exergue, but most are distinguishable only by mint symbols which have been deciphered through persistent scholarly research. Although originally based on the late Hellenistic tetradrachms, the actual amount of silver in these issues varied greatly. Many of the later issues are actually considered billon, rather than silver, because of the great debasement in precious metal content.

The Syrian tetradrachms are commonly found in rather large hoards, suggesting that they were used for financial exchanges on a larger scale than simple daily commerce.

Byblus, Phoenicia
Billon tetradrachm
Diadumenian, AD 217-18

Antioch, Syria, AD 244
Billon tetradrachm
Otacilia Severa

Antioch, Syria, AD 244
Billon tetradrachm
Philip II as Caesar

Berytos, Phoenicia
Billon tetradrachm
Caracalla, AD 215-217

Caesarea Maritima, Samaria
Billon tetradrachm
Diadumenian, AD 217-18

Antioch, Syria, Billon tetradrachm
Philip I, AD 246

Antioch, Syria, Billon tetradrachm
Trajan Decius, AD 249-251

Emisa

Emisa, AR tetradrachm
Julia Domna, AD 215-17

Emisa, Syria, AE 30mm
Caracalla, AD 216/7
The Black Stone

Emisa, also sometimes spelled Emesa, was a Syrian city on the east bank of the Orontes river—south of Apamea. It was the native city of Julia Domna, the powerful matriarch of the Severan Dynasty. Her grandnephews, the future emperors Elagabalus and Severus Alexander, were also raised there. The family was descended on Domna's side from a high-priest of the local cult of sun worshippers. The god of this Semitic cult, known as Elagabal, was worshipped in the form of a conical black stone. It is thought that this stone was probably a meteorite. The first depiction of the stone on a coin seems to be that on a tetradrachm of Caracalla. When Elagabalus, who took this name as high-priest at Emisa, came to power he had the stone transported to Rome—where he had an elaborate temple built for it. Coins were struck depicting this journey to Rome, with the stone being carried in an elaborate carriage. His cousin and successor, Severus Alexander, accepted the more traditional Roman gods and beliefs—at least in public—and the stone's worship was discontinued at Rome. It must, however, have been returned to Syria undefiled. On a bronze coin of Uranius Antoninus, a later usurper from Emisa, the Black Stone was depicted back at its home within a hexastyle temple. In comparing the details of this coin with an earlier bronze struck at Emisa under Caracalla, it is clear that the temple was one and the same as that which originally housed the sacred stone.

Emisa, Syria, AE 32mm
Uranius Antoninus, AD 253-254

Chalcis

Chalcis was located at the foot of Mount Anti-Lebanus in Coele-Syria otherwise called Chalkidice. It is now known as Mejdel Anjar. Chalcis was a principality of fluctuating importance, ruled by a succession of Roman Tetrarchs—a rank somewhat less prestigious than king. At its zenith, it extended as far as the sanctuary of Baalbek, and included parts of Massyas and Abilene. The tetrarchs who issued coins from this principality included Ptolemy, his son Lysanius and Zenodorus who was probably related. Cleopatra acquired the land from Mark Antony, and issued coins from there shortly before the Battle of Actium. It was inherited by Octavian after Actium, and Zenodorus was confirmed as tetrarch (see *Client Kings*). However, he was eventually removed in 20 BC for gross mismanagement of the government.

The region fell under the kingdom of Herod the Great of Judea until 4 BC, and then in 41AD after a period of Roman rule was entrusted to Herod's grandson of the same name—referred to as Herod of Chalcis. A great grandson of Herod called Aristobulus of Chalcis ruled from AD 53 to 92. He is depicted on a bronze coin of Chalcis along with his wife Salome of the "Dance of the Seven Veils" fame. The principality ceased striking coins late in the first century AD. Many of the coins issued at Chalcis were subsequently countermarked.

Chalcis, AE 20mm
Ptolemy (Tetrarch), 85-40 BC

Chalcis, AE 18mm
Ptolemy (Tetrarch), 85-40 BC

Chalcis, AE 23mm
Ptolemy (Tetrarch), 85-40 BC

Chalcis, AE 23mm
Cleopatra and Antony, 32-31 BC

The Decapolis

The Decapolis was, as its name suggests, a league of ten cities. It was established by Pompey the Great following his campaigns in the Levant about 65 BC. Today, although the cities are essentially Syrian, their issues are often catalogued along with the Judean city coins.

Damascus, Syria, AE 24mm
Cleopatra, 37/6 BC

Damascus was located in southern Syria, at an important crossroad between Palmyra, Phoenicia and Judaea. It was first occupied by the Romans in 65 BC and shortly thereafter made a member of the Decapolis. Antony granted the city to Cleopatra as a gift, but it fell into the hands of Octavian after the Battle of Actium. Caligula ceded the city to the Nabataean king Aretas IV in AD 37, but it was brought back into the Roman province of Syria in AD 62. Damascus was raised to the status of a colony by Severus Alexander.

Among the more interesting provincial coins from Damascus is an anepigraphic portrait coin of Cleopatra VII. This is probably not a Roman coin in the strictest sense of the word, but the relationship between Mark Antony and Cleopatra brought Egypt and its possessions into the Roman sphere as a practical matter if not as a diplomatic technicality.

Gadara, Decapolis, AE 26mm
Gordian III, AD 240/1

Gadara, a city east of the River Jordan, was brought under Roman influence by Pompey the Great in 63 BC. It was attached by Augustus to the kingdom of Herod the Great but became part of the Province of Syria on his death in 4 BC. The city was destroyed in AD 66 during the Jewish revolt. The historic founding of Gadara was commemorated on a bronze coin issued during the reign of Gordian III which depicts the flagship of Pompey and bears the inscription ΠΟΜΠ ΓΑΔΑΡΕΩΝ. Some have argued that the ships on these inland city coins represent sham naval battles staged at local games. The precise allusion is uncertain, but the reference to Pompey is clear.

Abila was a city of the Decapolis in Coele-Syria, about which little is known. Under the name Claudiopolis, it was the capital of the tetrarchy of Abilene. A series of coins was struck in AD 166/7 for Marcus Aurelius, Lucius Verus and Commodus. The 24mm bronze of Lucius Verus illustrated here is dated LC (year 230 of the Pompeian era) in the exergue.

Abila, Decapolis, AE 24mm
Lucius Verus, AD 166/7

Originally known as Susita, the Roman Hippos was another city of relative obscurity. It had been destroyed by Alexander Jannaeus and was rebuilt by Pompey, after which it belonged to the Decapolis. The coin struck in the name of Lucius Verus was undoubtedly tied to his successful campaign against the Parthians and concurrent tour of the Levant. Its reverse depicts Tyche holding a horse in her hand. An earlier coin struck under Antoninus Pius had on its reverse a scene of Tyche standing and holding a horse by the bridle. Hippos, which means horse, is the Greek translation of the Hebrew word for horse—*Sus* (from Susita).

Hippos, Decapolis, AE 23mm
Lucius Verus, AD 160-169

Practically nothing is written about the Decapolis member Capitolias. It is known that the city was located at the modern Beit er-Ras and that it was one of the cities liberated by Pompey. Its era is dated to 98 AD, during the reign of Trajan, therefore it would seem that the city was refounded. Inscriptions on some of the coins from this city would seem to indicate that it was a sanctuary. Coins of Marcus Aurelius and Lucius Verus have temple reverses, and at least one bears an abbreviated inscription meaning "sacred, inviolate and autonomous." The variety illustrated here bears a head on the reverse that has tentatively been identified as Alexander the Great.

Capitolias, AE 25mm
Commodus, AD 189/90

Phoenicia

Ancient Phoenicia corresponded approximately to modern day Lebanon. It had a very long and rich history of colonization and maritime trade, which continues to surface in the iconography of its coins into the Roman period. One of Phoenicia's most famous products was purple dye obtained from the murex shell. This was the dye used for the imperial toga. The murex is often seen as a subsidiary element in the field of Phoenician coins.

Berytus, modern Beirut, was a harbor city and a jewel of the trading world. It was especially famous for its wine and silk. Augustus established a military colony there in 14 BC and the familiar COL BER appeared on coins of that city for centuries. A coin struck in the reign of Claudius depicts the standards of legions V Macedonica and VIII Augusta Gallica which were stationed in Berytus at the time. Grant refers to the city as "a Latin island in a Semitic ocean". The plowing founder scenes and legionary standards are the city's most common types.

Berytus, Phoenicia, AE 22mm
Claudius, AD 41-54

Berytus, Phoenicia, AE 19mm
Gordian III, AD 238-244

Sidon, Phoenicia, AE 21mm
Augustus, 10/9 BC

Sidon was made a Roman colony by the emperor Elagabalus, who gave it the name Colonia Aurelia Pia Metropolis Sidon. It too was a coastal city, and possessed two commercial harbors. The city reckoned its era from 111 BC and was recognized as an autonomous city by Pompey and Augustus. The specimen from Sidon illustrated here, with a portrait of Augustus, has on its reverse the mythological scene of Europa being abducted by Zeus, in the guise of a bull. This is a popular local myth which appeared on coins of Phoenicia with regularity in the Hellenistic as well as the Roman periods.

Tyre was actually built on a rocky island a couple hundred yards off the coast. It was connected to the mainland by an artificial jetty which thus formed two protected harbors. It became the headquarters of Rome's eastern navy during the Principate. A bronze coin struck at Tyre during the reign of Elagabalus is described in the British Museum Catalogue as bearing a serpent entwined around an ovoid baetyl. In this particular case, could it be that the baetyl is, at least symbolically, the conical Black Stone of Emisa? This meteorite was so much a part of the emperor's personal heritage and beliefs that it was transported from Syria to Rome and made a part of the Roman religious pantheon(see *Emisa* on page 72). The entwined serpent normally is an invocation to the gods of fertility either for a dynastic heir or for the fertility of life in general. Elagabalus certainly went through enough wives in the search for genetic immortality.

Tyre, Phoenicia, AE 27mm
Elagabalus, AD 218-222

Byblus, the Biblical Gebal, claimed to be the world's oldest city. It supported an active cult worship to Adonis, the lover of Aphrodite. An impressive sanctuary to Astarte-Aphrodite is depicted on bronze coins of Macrinus and Diadumenian struck at Byblus. The specimen here bears a youthful portrayal that is probably one of the more accurate portraits of the young prince.

Byblus, Phoenicia, AE 24mm
Diadumenian, AD 217

Dora was also a coastal city, in the north of Phoenicia, which sometimes was included as part of Judea. Like many other cities in the region, it was liberated by Pompey in 63 BC. Dora dates its era to that year. Provincial coins were struck there until the reign of Caracalla. Types include Tyche, galleys and the mythical founder, Doros. On some, the title *Navarchis* was claimed. On the specimen illustrated here, Doros is depicted on the obverse. The reverse presents Tyche holding a standard. Dora has been inhabited continuously since the second millennium BC.

Dora, Phoenicia, AE 21mm
Reign of Nero, AD 66/7

Judea

The Roman Provincial coinage of Judea is extremely popular among collectors and requires careful study. The average condition of specimens found in this region is low due to very poor preservation. Those pieces that are well preserved, with good surfaces and nice patinas command exceptional multiples in price. The cities of Palestine, Syria, Samaria, Phoenicia, and the Decapolis changed hands so many times that it is impossible to assign some of them to a single region. If the reader finds a coin attributed to the same city in different provinces or districts, it should not be too surprising nor too distressing. It is simply a circumstance of the confusing history.

Ascalon was a coastal city in the southwestern corner of Israel along the Gaza strip. Its history is complicated by political turmoil among its neighbors. The city has eras starting in 104/3 BC and 58 BC. It was a cultural center and oddly enough was famous for its onions. Ascalon retained its status as a "free city" through the Roman period.

Ascalon, AE 19mm
Vespasian, AD 69-79

The city of Jerusalem was almost totally destroyed, and the Temple was razed, during the First Jewish Revolt (AD 70). A permanent legion was stationed there to control the area. In about AD 130, the emperor Hadrian refounded the city as Aelia Capitolina and made it a colony. After that, Jews were forbidden to enter the city. Provincial coins were issued through the reign of Valerian.

Aelia Capitolina, AE 22mm
Antoninus Pius, AD 138-161

Ake-Ptolemais is known today as Acre and is another of the cities that has been continuously occupied since the second millennium BC. It was a residence of Roman military governors and staging point for legionary operations.

Ake-Ptolemais, Judea, AE 24mm
Year 5, Caesarean Era, 44/3 BC
Eagle countermark

Agrippa II ruled in Judea for nearly 50 years and issued an extensive coinage. He was a Client King of Rome and supported Rome in the Jewish War. By AD 66/7 he was awarded the title King of Judea. The small bronze illustrated here is one of a series thought to recognize that accession. It bears double accession dates which have given rise to much debate. Agrippa II struck coins under Claudius, Nero and the Flavians almost exclusively with their portraits.

Paneas?, AE 13mm
Agrippa II, AD 66/7

Sepphoris was known by a multitude of names: Autocratoris, Neronias, Irenopolis and Diocaesarea, just in the Roman period. After Pompey's conquest of Judea it became a district capital. The city was taken by a rebel named Judas on the death of Herod the Great and subsequently reoccupied by the Roman Legate P. Quinctilius Varus—the same general who lost three legions in Germany. Varus burned Sepphoris to the ground. It rebounded to become the largest city in Galilee by the time of the First Jewish War.

Sepphoris, Judea, AE 23mm (x1.5)
Trajan, AD 98-117

The city of Anthedon was only two miles from Gaza on the Mediterranean coast. It was made part of the kingdom of Herod the Great after Actium. Provincial coins were struck here by the Severans.

Anthedon, AE 21mm
Severus Alexander, AD 222-235

Gaza was a trading center at the edge of the desert where caravans brought goods from Arabia. The city has a long history of provincial coinage from the first century BC to the time of Gordian III. The mintmark of the city is in Phoenician script.

Gaza, Judea, AE 28mm
Antoninus Pius, AD 213

Samaria

Samaria was a district extending along the coast of Palestine from Caesarea in the south to Joppa in the north. Coins from the cities in this district are often catalogued as Judean coins.

The most well known of the Samarian cities today is Caesarea Maritima. Not because of its historical record, but because of the extensive archaeological excavations that have been in progress at the site. A massive harbor and many important buildings have been uncovered, bringing to light a city of great importance. The city was called Stratonis Turris in Hellenistic times, meaning "Strato's Tower". The name was taken from a large tower built by an early king of that name. Pompey added the city to the Roman province of Syria, but it was gifted to Herod by Augustus in 30 BC. Herod built a great harbor on the site of the earlier Hellenistic port and adorned the city with temples, a theater, hippodrome, aqueducts and granaries. Vespasian was proclaimed emperor at Caesarea in AD 69 and made the city a colony. Caesarea was the birthplace of the historian Eusebius.

Caesarea Maritima, AE 23mm
Severus Alexander AD 222-235

Neapolis, AE 25mm
Julia Domna, AD 193-217

Sebaste, AE 23mm
Julia Soaemias died AD 222

Neapolis in Samaria, modern Nablus, was founded by Vespasian in AD 72. It is from that date that the city era is calculated. Provincial coins were struck there from the time of Domitian to Volusian. Neapolis supported Niger in the war with Severus. According to Hendin, as a punishment no coins were allowed to be struck there during the reign of Severus. The specimen illustrated here of Julia Domna may well have been issued by her son Caracalla.

The city of Sebaste was once known as Samaria and was renamed by Herod in honor of Augustus. Sebaste became a Roman colony under Septimius Severus.

Arabia Petraea

The Nabataean kingdom was annexed by Rome during the reign of Trajan, making Arabia a Roman province. Prior to this, the Nabataeans had produced a long series of drachms bearing the portraits of their kings. Farther east, the Himyarites struck silver coins bearing the portrait of Augustus. The latter seem to have been inspired for purposes of trade, rather than by any political concession, and do not fit practically into the provincial series.

The expansion of the empire was commemorated on a series of imperial coins as well as on provincial issues. The capital of the province was Bostra, an oasis city in the desert south of Damascus. The coinage of this province has not been adequately studied, and only recently have several issues which formerly were attributed to Caesarea in Cappadocia been reassigned to Arabia.

Bostra, AR drachm
Trajan, AD 112-117

Not too surprisingly, the types previously been thought to be an issue of Caesarea, and now are being reconsidered as issues from Arabia, bear references to the desert. The camel on a silver drachm (illustrated here) has been seen by numismatists in the past as a reference to the subjugation of Arabia. More likely, it is merely the adoption of a familiar local image as was the practice throughout provincial mints. The local city goddesses had, by the Roman period, evolved as personifications of Tyche (see Antioch) and the turreted figure is so identified on a coin of Elagabalus from Bostra (left) inscribed TYXH.

Bostra, AE 24mm
Elagabalus, AE 218-222

Bostra, Billon tetradrachm, AD 247-9 (Philip II)

BIBLIOGRAPHY

The Levant

Bellinger, A.R. *The Syrian Tetradrachms of Caracalla and Macrinus,* ANS Numismatic Studies No. 3, New York, 1940.

Bland, R. "Six hoards of Syrian tetradrachms of the third century AD", *The Numismatic Chronicle,* 1991, p. 1-33.

Delbrück, R. "Uranius of Emesa", *Numismatic Chronicle,* 1948.

Dohrn, T. *Die Tyche von Antiochia,* Berlin, 1960.

Gait, Robert I., Malcolm E. Black and Brian E. Joyce. "Syrian and Phoenician tetradrachms A.D. 202-254, Part I: *The Celator,* Vol 10, No. 5, May, 1996, pp. 6-19; Part II, June, 1996, pp. 32-38.

Hendin, David. *Guide to Biblical Coins,* third edition, Nyack, NY, 1996.

Kadman, L. *Corpus Nummorum Palaestinensium.* Vol. I, *Coins of Aelia Capitolina;* Vol. II, *Coins of Caesarea Maritima;* Vol IV, *Coins of Akko Ptolemais,* Jerusalem, 1956-61.

Kindler, A. and A. Stein. *A Bibliography of the City Coinage of Palestine From the 2nd Century B.C. to the 3rd Century A.D.,* 1987.

McAlee, Richard G. "Vespasian's Syrian Provincial Coinage", *American Journal of Numismatics,* 7-8, 1995-96, pp. 113-143.

_____. "The Severan Tetradrachms of Laodicea", *American Numismatic Society Museum Notes* , 29, 1984, pp. 43-59.

Meshorer, Y. *Jewish Coins of the Second Temple Period,* Tel Aviv, 1967.

_____. *The Coinage of Aelia Capitalina,* Jerusalem, 1989.

Prieur, M. *Syro-Phoenician tetradrachms - A Corpus by Types from 57 B.C. to AD 253,* Paris, forthcoming.

Rosenberger, M. *City-Coins of Palestine,* 3 Vols., Jerusalem, 1972-77.

_____. *The Coinage of Eastern Palestine,* Jerusalem, 1978.

Sayles, Wayne G. "Antioch's statue of Fortune became the model for city goddesses", *The Celator,* Vol. 8, No. 7, July, 1994, pp. 18-20.

Sear, David R. "The stone of Emisa on a tetradrachm of Caracalla", *Numismatic Fine Arts Journal* #32, 1986, Beverly Hills, California.

Seyrig, H. *Notes on Syrian Coins,* ANS NNM 119, New York, 1950.

Spijkerman, A. *The Coins of the Decapolis and Provincia Arabia,* Jerusalem, 1978.

Sydenham, E.A. *The Coinage of Caesarea in Cappadocia,* London, 1933.

Wruck, W. *Die Syrische Provinzialprägung von Augustus bis Traian,* Stuttgart, 1931.

Zimmermann, Linda. "Meteorites: Sacred stones of ancient Rome", *The Celator,* Vol. 9, No. 1, 1995, pp. 12-13.

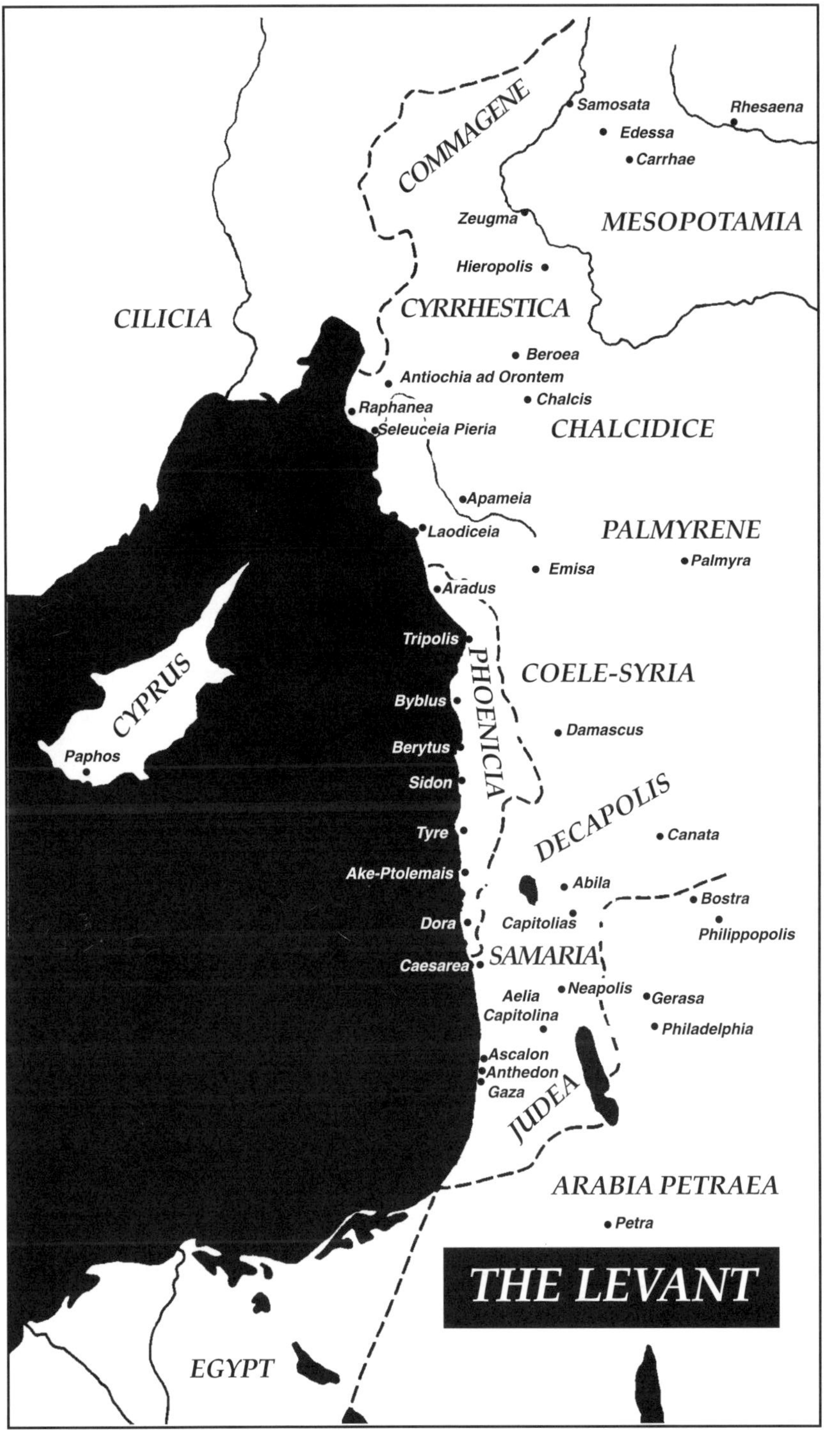
COMMAGENE
Samosata
Rhesaena
Edessa
Carrhae
Zeugma
MESOPOTAMIA
Hieropolis
CILICIA
CYRRHESTICA
Beroea
Antiochia ad Orontem
Chalcis
Raphanea
Seleuceia Pieria
CHALCIDICE
Apameia
Laodiceia
PALMYRENE
Emisa
Palmyra
Aradus
Tripolis
PHOENICIA
COELE-SYRIA
CYPRUS
Byblus
Damascus
Berytus
Paphos
Sidon
DECAPOLIS
Tyre
Canata
Ake-Ptolemais
Abila
Bostra
Dora
Capitolias
Philippopolis
Caesarea
SAMARIA
Aelia Capitolina
Neapolis
Gerasa
Philadelphia
Ascalon
Anthedon
Gaza
JUDEA
ARABIA PETRAEA
Petra
THE LEVANT
EGYPT

Of Sphinxes, Crocodiles & Heroes: Collecting the Coinage of Roman Egypt

by Kerry K. Wetterstrom

Personification of the Nile
AE drachm of Hadrian
year 18 (AD 133/4)

Ancient Egypt conjures up immediate images of the Great Pyramids and Sphinx at Giza, the tomb of the boy Pharaoh Tutankhamun and its discovery by archaeologist Howard Carter, and the various Egyptian deities such as Horus, Isis and the Apis bull. Unfortunately, the great pharaohs of ancient Egypt did not issue any coinage, with the rare exception of one of the last native pharaohs, Nektanebo II, who issued a gold stater around 350 BC.

Coinage was not to become a regular part of Egyptian life until Alexander the Great conquered Egypt in 332 BC, about a thousand years after King Tut's death. It was one of Alexander's generals, Ptolemy, that finally started striking coinage in Egypt on a regular basis. He first struck in the name of Alexander, and then later under his own name as king or pharaoh of Egypt and with his own portrait on his coins—an honor usually reserved for the gods.

Several hundred years later, Ptolemy's descendants were still striking coins with his portrait on them, but this was to end when Cleopatra VII lost Egypt in 30 BC to Octavian (later known as Augustus), the future emperor of Rome. Augustus isolated both Egypt and its economy from the rest of the Roman Empire. He realized that it was too important to be left as a semi-independent state, for the food supply of Rome depended on its harvests. And, he forbade any Roman senator to set foot on its soil without his permission lest they should have designs on Egypt's wealth for their own purposes.

One consequence of Augustus' actions was the development of a coinage that combined facets of the Greek, Roman and Egyptian cultures. The coinage of Roman Egypt, or Alexandrian coinage (in reference to the mint city of Alexandria) as it is most often called by its aficionados, developed rapidly after the 1st century AD. The mint officials and die-engravers at Alexandria were given great latitude in their choice of reverse designs and motifs and thus emerged a coinage of unparalleled interest to today's collector!

As with most all Roman Provincial coinage, the obverse design of Alexandrian coinage portrayed the current ruling emperor (or a member of his family, a secondary ruler, or a favored associate such as Antinoüs under Hadrian). The legends were in Greek. The choice of reverse designs, for the most part, constitutes a unique selection of types not seen elsewhere. The reverse types are what attract most collectors to the Alexandrian series. Among these types are:

(1) The gods of Egypt, Greece and Rome (and combinations thereof).

(2) Personifications of various virtues such as Nike (Victory), Dikaiosyne (Equity), Eirene (Peace) and Elpis (Hope), to mention just a few, as well as the personifications of the cities of Alexandria and Rome.

(3) Commemorative issues for the Egyptian nomes (an administrative province of Egypt).

(4) Mythological types such as the Twelve Labors of Hercules, Apollo's triumph over the satyr Marsyas, the Judgment of Paris and astrological types such as the twelve signs of the Zodiac .

(5) General allegorical or commemorative reverse types borrowed from Greek or Roman coinage, or in some cases unique.

Another facet of Alexandrian coinage that enhances its popularity is that it can be collected by year. Each coin is dated, usually on the reverse, with the ruling emperor's regnal year and using the Egyptian calendar rather than the Roman or Julian calendar. The Egyptian new year began on August 29th, hence an emperor that came to power on July 1st and ceased to rule the Empire on October 1st of the same year actually had two regnal years in Egypt. On the coinage we encounter two different representations for "year". The Greek word "ETOYC" for year, in the genitive case, is used infrequently whereas the symbol "L" is most often used to

Marcus Aurelius, AD 169/70
Billon tetradrachm, year 10 decennial

Aurelian, Billon tet., year 5, AD 273/4

Hadrian, Year 19, AD 134/5
AE drachm
date spelled out
L ENNEAKΔ

represent "year". The symbol "L" is possibly a "development of a conventional sign, taken from the demotic script, where it means 'year'; or, perhaps less likely, it is a reduced form of the first letter of ETOYC." Another theory is that "L" is a modification of an ancient Egyptian hieroglyph for year.

The actual year itself is either spelled out in Greek (i.e. such as TETAPTOY for 4 — see table below) or the corresponding letter from the Greek alphabet is used to designate the year (i.e., Δ for 4). Usually, just the Greek number is used in conjunction with the symbol "L". This means that a collector, such as myself, with a "pennyboard" mentality can collect Alexandrian coins by year for each issuing Emperor. The only caveat being that not every emperor struck coins for every one of his regnal years as the Alexandrian mint produced coins only when they were needed.

Table of dates on Alexandrian coinage

Year	Greek Equivalent	
1	A	
2	B	ΔΕΥΤΕΡΟΥ (*)
3	Γ	ΤΡΙΤΟΥ
4	Δ	ΤΕΤΑΡΤΟΥ
5	Ε	ΠΕΜΠΤΟΥ
6	ς or S	
7	Ζ	ΕΒΔΟΜΟΥ (*)
8	Η	ΟΓΔΟΟΥ (*)
9	ΗΑ(*)	ΕΝΑΤΟΥ
10	Ι	ΔΕΚΑΤΟΥ
11	ΙΑ	ΕΝΔΕΚΑΤΟΥ
12	ΙΒ	ΔΩΔΕΚΑΤΟΥ
13	ΙΓ	ΤΡΙΣΚΑΙΔΕΚΑ
14	ΙΔ	
15	ΙΕ	
16	Ις or IS	
17	ΙΖ	
18	ΙΗ	
19	ΙΘ	ΕΝΝΕΑΚΔ
20	Κ	and so on (ΚΑ, ΚΒ, etc.)
30	Λ	and so on (ΛΑ, ΛΒ, ΛΓ, etc.)
40	Μ	Dates past year 42 are not seen in the Alexandrian series
(*)	seldom encountered	

The spelled-out version of the date (i.e. ΕΝΔΕΚΑΤΟΥ) can be encountered on the coins in a multitude of abbreviated forms (i.e. ΕΝΔΕΚΑΤ or ΕΝΔΕΚ).

The Alexandrian denominational system is derived from the Ptolemaic system, with direct influences from Roman coinage. After his defeat of Antony and Cleopatra, Augustus continued the Ptolemaic system for a time and bronze coins dated before his assumption of the title Augustus are of the same size and weight as the issues of Cleopatra (and likewise bear the marks of value of Π and M—for 80 and 40 drachms respectively). Until AD 20, the Romans retained the Ptolemaic silver coinage as legal tender and chose not to issue any silver at Alexandria. Due to the closed economy of Egypt, neither imperial nor other provincial issues were permitted to circulate within its borders. The Ptolemaic silver drachm was valued at six obols, but apparently commanded a premium when exchanged for bronze.

Augustus, AE 80 drachms (Π on reverse)

Tiberius introduced the billon tetradrachm with a silver content approximately that of the Roman denarius, and it was equated in value with the former Ptolemaic silver tetradrachm (which was, indeed, nothing more than billon itself by the time of Cleopatra and continued to circulate into the reign of Nero) and with the Roman denarius.

Officially, this new billon tetradrachm was valued at 6 obols but private commerce used anywhere from a 6 to 7.25 obol standard as papyrus records indicate. Silver drachms of Roman Egypt are known only under Claudius, who issued both drachms and didrachms in billon. Both are extremely rare today.

After the assumption of his new title, Augustus issued bronze coins on the old Attic standard, with a bronze drachm of six obols (although no drachms were actually issued during his reign). The new bronze issues continued, with slight modifications in size and weight, until the reign of Nero. Then, two new denominations were introduced—the drachm and hemidrachm. Since Nero's drachm was approximately the same size and weight as the Roman sestertius, they have traditionally been equated. Whether this is valid, since the Alexandrian system of coinage was totally fiduciary, remains debatable and the exact identification of the various Alexandrian bronze issues is still uncertain.

Three denominations in bronze were struck for Claudius (diobol, obol, and dichalkon); five for the emperors Nero through Domitian (drachm and hemidrachm added); six for Trajan through Marcus Aurelius (chalkon added); and three for Commodus, Septimius Severus, Caracalla, Macrinus and Diadumenian (drachms, hemidrachms and

Table of Alexandrian Coin Denominations

Billon tetradrachm

AE drachm

AE hemidrachm

AE diobol

AE dichalkon

AE obol

AE chalkon

Note: All coins illustrated are of the emperor Hadrian (AD 117-138) diobols). Sporadic, isolated issues of bronze are known for later rulers—the most important of which were drachms. These, mostly commemorative in nature, were issued by Severus Alexander and his family, Philip I and family, and Gallienus and family.

On the whole, the coinage of Roman Egypt was crudely manufactured at all stages—including die-engraving, flan manufacture and preparation, and the actual striking of the coins. Still, it manages to maintain a charming quality about it. Once a collector is hooked, it usually is for good! There were some excellent examples of the coiner's art struck at Alexandria, with the zenith of coinage from Roman Egypt occurring during the reigns of Hadrian and Antoninus Pius. Overall, their coins were far superior to anything else that ever came out of the Alexandrian mint.

Septimius Severus and Julia Domna Billon tetradr., year 8 (AD 199/200)

Alexandrian coinage, especially the bronze issues, was heavily circulated well into the Byzantine period—accounting for the lack of high grade examples known today. Coins were only minted when needed, and not always on a regular basis. Hence, there are periods when certain denominations were not minted. Sometimes, for economic reasons, an emperor such as Septimius Severus (whose imperial coinage is quite common) minted very few coins at Alexandria.

Since the average condition of surviving Alexandrian bronzes is probably 'Fine', coins in higher grades usually command a premium in the market. Flan cracks are very common, especially on the larger diameter pieces, as the planchets were cast, reheated and then struck. Bronzes without flan cracks, corrosion, porosity and encrustation also command a premium, but the collector should not downgrade a coin too severely for these faults as they occur frequently even on high grade specimens.

Tetradrachms are more readily available in high grade, due to the fact that they were often hoarded. It seems strange to hoard a coinage that did not have much, if any, intrinsic value and was fiduciary in nature, but the people who buried these coins must have had some sort of faith in their currency and government. Tetradrachms, from about the reign of Commodus onward, are rare when "silvered" (i.e., bearing a noticeably higher concentration of silver on the surface) and as such usually command a premium.

The percentage of silver in the billon tetradrachms ranged from around 50% or higher for some issues of Tiberius to about 4% during the reign of Marcus Aurelius and then 16% during Commodus' reign.

After Commodus, the tetradrachms are not considered "billon" any longer, rather they are at this point called "potin", and their silver content ranges from about 10% during Severus Alexander's tenure to less than 1% for issues of Diocletian. It was during the reign of Diocletian that the Alexandrian coinage of Roman Egypt was to end.

Domitius Domitianus
Potin octadrachm, Year 2 (AD 297/8)

An usurper, known as Domitius Domitianus, revolted in Alexandria for at least part of the years 297 and 298 AD. During his rebellion, Domitius reformed the Alexandrian coinage by introducing two new denominations—the octadrachm (or hexadrachm?) and didrachm. He kept the tetradrachm already in use. His exact reasons for this are unknown, and he also minted Roman-style folles at Alexandria for external trade in the Empire. All of his coins are extremely rare today, and mark the end of the Alexandrian series of coinage as well as that of Roman provincial coinage as a whole. After Diocletian regained control of Egypt, he converted its currency system over to that of the rest of the Roman Empire.

An important aspect of collecting Alexandrian coinage, or any other series of coins for that matter, is having a few good reference books. Fortunately, the Alexandrian series has been well published over the past century. Many of these books are still available at reasonable prices as they have been continuously reprinted. A beginning collector can get by with just one or two books, depending on whether they decide to collect the billon tetradrachms or the bronze series or both.

A few recommendations would be: *The Tetradrachms of Roman Egypt* by Col. James W. Curtis (a former vice-president of the American Numismatic Association); *Catalogue of Alexandrian Coins,* by J.G. Milne; and *Monete Imperiali Greche, Numi Augg. Alexandrini* by G. Dattari. A call to your favorite numismatic bookseller should result in you acquiring any of these three volumes at a modest cost!

Hopefully, at this point, you now have a good grasp of some of the many ways one can collect the coins of Roman Egypt. The next four sections of this chapter will examine some sub-series of Alexandrian coinage: The "Labors of Hercules" and "Sothic Cycle" drachms of Antoninus Pius, Mythological themes and the Nome series.

The "Labors of Hercules"

A series of bronze drachms portraying the labors and / or adventures of Herakles (also known by the latinized version of his name—Hercules) were struck in Alexandria in seven different years of the reign of Antoninus Pius. These range from Year 4 (140 / 141 AD) to Year 24 (160 / 161 AD), with Year 10 being the most prolific in terms of specimens extant today.

The Twelve Labors of Hercules are most often attributed by classical scholars to have been penance and atonement for Hercules' madness by which he killed six of his own children, and two of his brother's, mistaking them for his enemies. When Hercules recovered his sanity, he went to the Oracle of Delphi to be purified and was told to serve King Eurystheus for twelve years—performing whatever "Labors" might be determined for him. His reward for this was to be immortality (by today's standards of morality, it seems contradictory to give Hercules a reward for performing penance!). He was hindered at all times by Hera (the wife of Zeus) while trying to complete these labors, but was aided by others in the Greek pantheon. Interestingly, the Greek name Herakles means "Hera's Glory". Since Hercules was fathered by Zeus and Alcmene, this was a direct affront to Hera and part of the reason for her hatred of Hercules.

Antoninus Pius, AE drachm Year 10, (AD 146/7) Hercules strangling the Nemean Lion

The First Labor: The Nemean Lion. The first labor imposed on Hercules by Eurystheus was the conquest of the Nemean lion. This invulnerable, ravaging beast had a pelt impervious to iron, bronze or stone. After trying various weapons on the lion, to no avail, Hercules was able to choke it to death as seen on the Alexandrian coin type. He then managed to skin the lion with its own claws. Thereafter, the lion's skin became his standard raiment.

The Second Labor: The Lernaean Hydra. The Alexandrian reverse type is often thought to portray the giantess Echidna raising her son Hydra against Hercules in defense. This theory is proposed by Col. James Curtis and others. The mythical variations are so many for this labor that it is difficult to give an effective summary. One variation is that an enormous crab came to the aid of the Hydra by nipping Hercules' foot, and in reward for the crab's service, Hera set its image among the twelve signs of the Zodiac. This is an obvious attempt by ancient writers to tie in the labors of Hercules to the Zodiac.

Curtis believed that the coin type referred to the earliest form of the Labor (before later writers had embellished Hydra with a multitude of heads, each of which could be replaced by two when cut off). This is probably close to the truth. Echidna is depicted as half woman, half serpent.

Dr. Hans Voegtli in *Bilder Der Heldenepen In Der Kaiserzeitlichen Griechischen Münzprägung* (Basel, 1977) proposed that this is actually Hydra in his giantess form or Hydra with a female's upper body, ("Hydra mit weiblichem Oberkorper"), not Echidna. Therefore, the Alexandrian reverse type would be portraying Hercules directly in conflict with Hydra. This type is not unique to Alexandria, as it also occurs in Perinthos on coins of Septimius Severus.

Antoninus Pius, AE drachm Year 10, (AD 146/7) Hercules killing the Lernaean Hydra

The Third Labor: The Cerynean Stag. Hercules was required to capture the stag, with its brazen hooves and golden horns, alive and bring it from Oenoe to Mycenae. He chased the stag for one full year before it finally tired and he captured it—as shown on the coin type.

Antoninus Pius, AE drachm Year 10, (AD 146/7) Hercules capturing the Cerynean Stag

The Fourth Labor: The Erymanthian Boar. In this adventure, Hercules is given the task of capturing alive the fierce boar which ravaged the slopes of Mt. Erymanthius. He frightens it from its lair, chases it into deep snow, and there captures it and binds it with chains. The coin type shows Hercules approaching Eurystheus, who cowered in terror in a bronze jar, when he saw Hercules with the struggling beast about his shoulders.

Antoninus Pius, AE drachm Year 10, (AD 146/7) Hercules capturing the Erymanthian Boar

The Fifth Labor: The Augean Stables. Hercules' fifth task was to clean the vast stables of King Augeas, in which the accumulated filth of many years lay undisturbed. Hercules diverted the waters of a nearby river through the stables, effectively cleaning them in a single day. The coin type symbolically portrays Hercules advancing toward a pile of rocks, from which a lion-head spout pours water into a shallow vase. A rake leans against the rocks. This pictorial representation of the labor was a direct copy from a master image that was used in other artistic media, such as mosaics, which have also survived. The same is true for most of the representations of Hercules' labors chosen by the Alexandrian die-engravers for this series.

Antoninus Pius, AE drachm
Year 10, (AD 146/7)
Hercules cleaning
the Augean Stables

The Sixth Labor: The Stymphalian Birds. A thickly wooded marsh in Stymphalos in Arkadia provided a natural refuge for these birds, who became so numerous that Hercules was given the task of eliminating them. Some accounts state that the birds had razor-edged feathers, or that they were man-eaters, or that they were women, daughters of Stymphalus and Ornis, whom Hercules killed because they refused him hospitality. In any event, Hercules secured a bronze rattle made by the god Hephaistos, with which he frightened the birds out into the open. He then quickly shot them with arrows. The coin type depicts Hercules, with the lion skin over his head and shoulders, drawing his bow for a shot. Two birds tumble down before him.

Antoninus Pius, AE drachm
Year 6, (AD 142/3)
Hercules shooting
the Stymphalian Birds

The Seventh Labor: The Cretan Bull. Hercules was here given the task of capturing alive the bull on which Europa arrived in Crete—or by other accounts, the bull that King Minos withheld from sacrifice to Poseidon and which sired the Minotaur. Hercules captured the bull, after some minor adventures, showed the bull to Eurystheus, and released it. The coin motif depicts the actual capture, as the hero grasps the bull by the head.

Antoninus Pius, AE drachm
Year 6, (AD 142/3)
Hercules capturing
the Cretan Bull

The Eighth Labor: The Mares of Diomedes. In this rather gruesome saga, Hercules is required to secure the four flesh-eating horses of Diomedes, son of the war-god Ares. He does so, after a terrible battle, by killing Diomedes and feeding his body to his own horses. This act tamed the Mares and enabled them to be brought safely to Mycenae, where Eurystheus dedicated them to Hera and set them free on Mt. Olympus. The coin motif depicts Hercules about to smite one of the mares with his club. Diomedes is seen lying prostrate before Hercules.

Antoninus Pius, AE drachm
Year 5, (AD 141/2)
Hercules taming
the Mares of Diomedes

The Ninth Labor: Hippolyte's Girdle. In this labor, Hercules is charged with obtaining the magic golden girdle of Ares worn by Hippolyte, queen of the Amazons. Although there are numerous variations of how Hercules actually obtained the girdle, the prevalent version is that after defeating the Amazonian army, Hercules removed the girdle from the fallen body of the queen. The coin type shows Hercules in the act of seizing the girdle from Hippolyte, depicted prostrate on her fallen horse.

Antoninus Pius, AE drachm
Year 10, (AD 146/7)
Hercules removing
Hippolyte's Girdle

The Tenth Labor: The Cattle of Geryon. In this labor, Hercules was unable to journey to the "Farthest West," the land of the monster-man Geryon (brother of Echidna); without first forcing Helios to yield the "Golden Cup of the Sun" for the journey. After reaching the "Farthest West," he had to contend with the two-headed watchdog Orthus and with the herdsman Eurytion, son of Ares, both of whom he killed before finally confronting Geryon. Hercules killed Geryon and then loaded the slain monster's vast herd of cattle on board the "Golden Cup" and returned. The

Antoninus Pius, AE drachm
Year 4, (AD 140/1)
Hercules stealing the
Cattle of Geryon

coin type depicts Hercules holding two charging bulls of Geryon whose dead body lies below.

The Eleventh Labor: The Apples of the Hesperides. The Hesperides were Atlas' daughters, to whom Hera had entrusted the tree that grew golden apples. After they were caught pilfering the apples, Hera sent the ever-watchful serpent Ladon to coil around the tree as its guardian (as depicted on the coin type). Hercules was sent by Eurystheus to secure the holy golden apples of the Hesperides. After difficulties in locating the garden, Hercules could not pick the apples himself. He got Atlas to do this for him by holding the sky on his own shoulders. Atlas, however, had to be tricked by Hercules into resuming his heavy burden. Varying from the myth, the coin type shows Hercules reaching for an apple while the serpent Ladon, with an arrow through his neck, hangs dead from the branches of the tree —correctly part of the original myth.

Antoninus Pius, AE drachm
Year 10, (AD 146/7)
Hercules picking the Apples of the Hesperides

Antoninus Pius, AE drachm
Year 4, (AD 140/1)
Hercules capturing Cerberus

The Twelfth Labor: The Capture of Cerberus. This, the most terrible and difficult of the labors, required Hercules to invade Hades itself. He was to bring back the three-headed watchdog of Hell, Cerberus (another of Echidna's delightful offspring). After several adventures and hardships, and with the help of Athena and Hermes, the task was accomplished. The coin type depicts Hercules emerging from the portal of Hades, dragging by a rope the reluctant Cerberus.

While the inspiration for selecting these types may be a bit of a mystery, the coins themselves tell us that engravers from at least two schools were employed to create the dies. They may have belonged to the group of traveling die-engravers that cut other Roman provincial coin dies, or perhaps they were local artists trained in different media.

It is very well known that the "Labors of Hercules" and the other mythological drachm series motifs appeared in other forms of art, including mosaics, during the same period. A large contemporary mosaic found in Spain depicts the "Labors of Hercules" in almost exactly the same manner as they appear on the Alexandrian drachms of Antoninus Pius.

In discussing this mosaic, M. Tarradell *(Arte Romano En Espana)* observed: "We know that there were travelling workshops of mosaic workers who worked according to models or 'cartoons' which they repeated in the most diverse places. Mosaic, therefore, is to a very great extent an art without any provincial frontiers, and it is possible to find in places very far removed from one another the same motifs treated in identical fashion. Frequently a mosaic discovered in Spain presents characteristics very close to those of others from the region of the Danube or from the African provinces."

There is strong evidence that these images were shared by artists working in different media and that a more or less standard iconography had emerged by the period under consideration. That some of them are better suited to a rectangular rather than circular aspect is obvious. Nevertheless, the standard iconography was adapted to a presentation in the round often enough on coins and circular relief sculpture.

The reason why these coins just discussed were struck in Alexandria, and why during the reign of Antoninus Pius, is often debated. One theory, first proposed by Joseph Grafton Milne, is that Alexandria might have been following Rome's lead in "an attempt to revive the interest of the Romans in their archaeology and antiquities by representations of historical or mythological scenes or objects of art." Therefore, those in charge at the Alexandrian mint arguably produced these "series" of coins to follow this line of thinking. By so doing, they issued a grouping of coins completely foreign to the native Egyptians, but of obvious importance to those with Greek influence in their backgrounds.

Another theory is that during this time period of Pius' reign there was a governor from Greece, or that general area, appointed over Egypt. It was this governor, therefore, that commissioned these mythological coins to be minted for his own reasons and purposes—perhaps even as gifts for visiting dignitaries. He supposedly governed approximately ten years and then was replaced. Some of the odd year issues such as during years 10 and 24 are explained as having been minted to complete or add to someone's "sets" — so to speak. A third argument is that these coins were commemorative issues related to the observance of the Sothic cycle (see following section).

As a final thought, it is possible that the Roman love for astrology and mythology, Egyptian interest in the Sothic cycle, and the general tendency of both to celebrate religious and historical events, might simply have escalated from a modest commemorative proposal into a much more elaborate project. In any case, what has survived is a fascinating series of coins that are beautiful, evocative and similar in design and purpose. The result is a highly collectible sub-series which has the merit of defined limits and yet substantial challenge to the collector.

The Sothic Cycle and Zodiac coins

It has been thought for some time that the Zodiac or Astrological series minted in Alexandria in Pius' regnal year 8 (AD 144/5) was inspired by or related to the commencement of a new "Sothic Cycle" which occurred in AD 139. Unlike most civilizations in antiquity, the Egyptians used the solar not the lunar calendar. The moon played an unusually minor role in their mythology. The Egyptian year consisted of three seasons of four months each—Inundation, Germination and the Warm Season. One of the first astronomers at Memphis (or Heliopolis) must have noticed early one morning, before dawn on the first day of Inundation, that the bright star Sothis (or Sirius, the Dog Star) appeared on the eastern horizon on this day at the same moment as the sun. Impressed with this "heliacal rising of Sothis" it was decided to make it a subordinate point of departure for the Egyptian year. This conjunction of the three events of the rising of the sun, rising of Sothis, and the start of Inundation occurred only once every 1461 Egyptian years. This period constituted a Sothic Cycle.

Modern research has established that a Sothic cycle would have commenced in approximately 1322 BC, during the 19th Dynasty of Pharaonic Egypt. This is confirmed by ancient scribal records. Therefore, the cycle would have reappeared during the second year of Antoninus Pius' reign. It seems plausible that the Zodiac, and perhaps the Hercules, series of drachms were commemorative issues honoring this rare and important event in Egyptian culture. Alternatively, in his persuasive article "Sirius Rising: Commemorating the Anniversary of the Sothic Cycle" (*SAN*, Vol. XIX, No. 1, 1995, pp. 15-18), Dr. Michael Molnar argued that: "the drachmas depicting the zodiacal signs may have been inspired by the Sothic anniversary through the astrological metaphor of the *Thema Mundi*; however, there is no firm evidence connecting these coins to the event. It seems more plausible that the drachmas were struck because astrology

Antoninus Pius, AE drachm
Year 8, (AD 144/5)
Zodiac Wheel

Antoninus Pius, AE drachm
Year 8, (AD 144/5)
The Sun in Leo

Antoninus Pius, AE drachm
Year 8, (AD 144/5)
The Moon in Cancer

was important to the people of Alexandria who had in their midst at this time a great astrologer and astronomer, Claudius Ptolemy."

There can be little doubt that the influence of Claudius Ptolemy was widely felt in Alexandria. Whether the coins in this series came into being as a commemoration of the Sothic Cycle, or simply as the reflection of a broader interest in Astrology, the series is quite remarkable.

The first coin type of the series features a Zodiac Wheel which portrays the Moon and Sun, and the five known planets: Mercury, Venus, Mars, Jupiter and Saturn. Each is coupled with their domiciliary constellations. The rest of the series "represents the various constellations of the Zodiac with the planet which was in conjunction with each during the year of the start of the new Sothic Cycle."

We have presented here only a selection of the types, but there are 12 in all. Both the day houses and the night houses of each planet are represented. The Sun has no night house, and the Moon has no day house.

Antoninus Pius, AE drachm
Year 8, (AD 144/5)
Venus in Libra

Antoninus Pius, AE drachm
Year 8, (AD 144/5)
Jupiter in Pisces

Antoninus Pius, AE drachm
Year 8, (AD 144/5)
Mars in Scorpio

Antoninus Pius, AE drachm
Year 8, (AD 144/5)
Saturn in Capricorn

Antoninus Pius, AE drachm
Year 8, (AD 144/5)
Saturn in Aquarius

Astrology was a subject of interest to Near-Eastern civilizations as early as the third millennium BC. In fact, many of the symbols seen in Sumerian and Babylonian astrological motifs are repeated in later Greek art. The representation of celestial figures as personifications was a well established convention on Greek painted vases by the 5th century BC. Like much of Roman art, the imagery of astrological personifications in this coin series stems from earlier Greek prototypes. The styles of representation may vary, as discussed in the following section, but the general iconography is one of evolution and consistency. Not too surprisingly, for the Romans were a conservative lot.

Domicilia of The Planets

Planet:	Day House:	Night House:
Sun	Leo	none
Moon	none	Cancer
Mercury	Gemini	Virgo
Venus	Libra	Taurus
Mars	Aries	Scorpio
Jupiter	Sagittarius	Pisces
Saturn	Aquarius	Capricorn

Mythological Themes in Roman Egypt

Antoninus Pius, AE drachm
Year 5, (AD 141/2)
The Judgement of Paris

Surely, the fascinating mythological scenes on drachms of this period also fit into a grander iconographic program for the entire series. The narrative depictions of such popular myths as "The Rape of Persephone", "The Flaying of Marsyas", "Perseus and Andromeda", "The Judgement of Paris", and several isolated adventures of Hercules, are thematically similar to the motifs of the "Hercules Labors" and "Astrological" coins. However, in contrast to the latter, these coin motifs were almost exclusively derived from the parallel arts of painting and mosaic with little or no modification for presentation in the round. This is clear from the standard theater-like positioning of the subjects. The method by which the artist approached perspective in the Marsyas narrative, for example, is certainly not that of a sculptor or traditional coin die engraver. Throughout this mythological series, figures are typically portrayed in a "panoramic" style.

The Judgement of Paris, which was ultimately the cause of the Trojan War, began when a gathering of the gods at the wedding of Peleus and Thetis was interrupted by Eris ("Strife"), who threw on the banquet table a golden apple inscribed "to the fairest." Hera, Athena and Aphrodite all immediately laid claim to this apple. Zeus politically referred the decision to Paris, the lost mortal son of Priam—King of Troy. Hermes led the goddesses to Mount Ida where Paris was a herdsman.

Paris' chief amusement was setting his bulls to fight one another and then crowning the victor with flowers and the loser with straw. He then pitted his best against the champions of his neighbors' herds—all of which were defeated. When he offered to set a golden crown upon the horns of any bull that could defeat his own, Ares turned himself into a bull, and won the prize. Paris' unhesitating award of the golden crown to Ares surprised and pleased the gods which is why Zeus chose him to arbitrate the three goddesses' dispute over the golden apple. All three goddesses tried to influence Paris' decision by bribery, but Aphrodite triumphed by guaranteeing Paris the world's most beautiful mortal woman as a wife—Helen of Sparta.

The Alexandrian coin presents Athena, Hera and Aphrodite on a raised platform to the right of Hermes and Paris. Hermes is shown pointing toward Aphrodite while looking back at Paris; Hera is looking back at Athena—a presage of things yet to happen.

The Flaying of Marsyas: The satyr Marsyas acquired the discarded flutes of Athena who threw them away in disgust for she did not like how they disfigured her mouth when she played. Marsyas gradually became so proficient in their use that he challenged Apollo himself to a music contest. Apollo accepted with the condition that the victor could do as he pleased with the other. Having then vanquished the conceited Marsyas, Apollo chose to have him flayed alive as his punishment for having the audacity to challenge a god. The coin type depicting this flaying scene is known from Year 8 at Alexandria.

Antoninus Pius, AE drachm
Year 8, (AD 144/5)
Flaying of Marsyas

Hercules and Prometheus: For giving mankind the gift of fire—previously known only to the gods on Mt. Olympus—Prometheus was sentenced by Zeus to being chained naked to a pillar in the Caucasian mountains. Every day, year in and year out, a greedy vulture-eagle tore at Prometheus' liver. There was no end to the pain, because every night his liver grew whole again. Hercules, coming upon Prometheus during his travels, felt compassion for him and asked Zeus for his release. Zeus agreed only when the centaur Chiron said he would take Prometheus' place in order to escape the incurable wound inflicted upon him by Hercules. Chiron was also immortal, but gave this up to escape his pain. On this coin (possibly a hemidrachm), Hercules is shown aiming his bow and arrow at the vulture-eagle that tormented Prometheus—who is chained to the pillar on the right. The coin illustrated, formerly part of the John Work Garrett collection and then the K.K. Wetterstrom collection, is the only surviving example known at this time. It currently, and probably permanently, resides in the collection of Köln University.

Antoninus Pius, AE drachm
Year 24, (AD 160/1)
Hercules freeing Prometheus

Hercules and the Centaur Pholos: Hercules, on his way to capture the Erymanthian boar, was entertained by the Centaur Pholos, whom one of the ash-nymphs bore to Silenus. The other centaurs grew angry when they smelled the strong wine from their communal wine jar and knew Pholos had offered it to Hercules. They attacked Hercules while Pholos hid in terror. In his attempt to defeat the centaurs, an arrow

Antoninus Pius, AE drachm
Year 6, (AD 142/3)
Hercules conversing with Pholos

Antoninus Pius, AE drachm
Year 24, (AD 160/1)
Perseus and Andromeda

Antoninus Pius, AE drachm
Year 5, (AD 141/2)
Hercules wrestling with Antaeus

inadvertently struck the centaur Chiron, who was an old friend of Hercules and his mentor. This is the wound discussed in the Prometheus myth above. Hercules tried to help Chiron, but to no avail as we know. The coin type portrays Hercules, holding a lyre, clasping the arm of Pholos as the two apparently converse. To the right, an attendant is drawing wine.

Perseus and Andromeda: Perseus, the slayer of Medusa, was returning from this deed when he caught sight of the naked Andromeda chained to a sea-cliff, and instantly fell in love with her. Cassiopeia had boasted that both she and her daughter Andromeda were more beautiful than the Nereids. They complained of this insult to their protector, Poseidon, who sent a flood and a female sea-monster to devastate Philistia, where Cassiopeia and Andromeda lived. When the King consulted an oracle, he was told that his only hope was to sacrifice Andromeda to the sea monster. This was Andromeda's predicament when Perseus saw her. Perseus killed the sea monster and took Andromeda as his wife. The coin type portrays Perseus on the left helping Andromeda down from the sea cliff.

Hercules and the Giant Antaeus: Antaeus, the son of Poseidon and Mother Earth (or Gaia), was in the habit of forcing strangers to wrestle with him until they were exhausted, whereupon he killed them. Not only was he a strong and skillful athlete, but whenever he touched his mother, the earth, his strength revived. Hercules was determined to end this barbarous practice. He wrestled Antaeus and, realizing that the Giant was a son of Mother Earth, lifted him in the air until he crushed him to death. This is the scene portrayed on the coin type.

Nome Coinage

The so-called "Nome" coinage of Alexandria, which has recently been studied and researched with new perspectives and vigor, is another fascinating sub-series to collect (see Jennifer A. Sheridan, "The Nome Coins of Alexandria, Another Look", *ANSMN* 33, 1988, pp. 107-110; and Keith Emmett, "Egyptian and Roman Cults Mix in Nome Coinage", *The Celator,* January 1988, pp. 13-14). The primary difference between the regular issue Roman-Egyptian coinage and the sub-series Nome coinage is the epigraphical use of the nome's ethnic or an abbreviation thereof on the reverse of the coin.

Trajan, AE drachm
Year 12, (AD 108/9)
Saïte Nome

The ethnic serves to identify the nome in conjunction with the design motif or type also employed on the reverse. The reverse type was supposed to be indicative of the local cult of the Egyptian religion worshipped in each particular nome, city or administrative entity (not all of the ethnics in question actually represented a nome but the designation as a class has served to satisfy the titular instincts of numismatists).

Under the Roman emperor Domitian the first nome coins, of the hemidrachm denomination, were issued in his 11th Alexandrian regnal year (91/92 AD). Nome coins of the drachm denomination were issued under Trajan during his Alexandrian regnal years 12-15 and 20 and under Hadrian from regnal years 6-8 (these coins are extremely rare). This Nome drachm series was continued by Antoninus Pius and Marcus Aurelius Caesar during Pius' regnal year 8.

A new denominational series of Nome coins was issued by Hadrian during his 11th Alexandrian regnal year (126/127 AD). This remarkable series consisted of the two smallest denominations—obol and dichalkon. The reverse type of the dichalkon is always the nome symbol held by a standing figure/deity on the obol reverse type.

It should be noted, at this point, that most of the names, if not all, used to designate the nomes on the Alexandrian coinage, such as Herakleopolites or Hermopolites, were the Greek interpretations devised by the Ptolemaic dynasty. They assimilated the local cult god with its nearest equivalent in the Greek pantheon to arrive at an appropriate

Hadrian, AE obol
Year 11, (AD 126/7)
Panopolite Nome

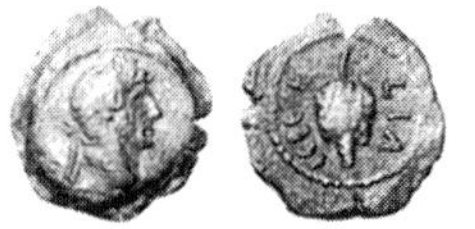

Hadrian, AE dichalkon
Year 11, (AD 126/7)
Lower Sebennyte Nome

name for the nome. The Romans continued this assimilation process by further merging the reverse types with attributes of the Horus/ Isis cult which was extremely popular during Roman times. Thus a study of Roman-Egyptian nome coinage is only indicative of the nomes, cities, etc. as they probably existed during the second century AD with their Greco-Roman attributes and not as they existed under the Pharaonic dynasties.

The word "nome" itself is the anglicized Greek word nomos. This word in Greece proper usually is "found in the sense of 'law.'" In Magna Graecia, however, "it was used in a sense derived from its basic meaning of 'apportionment, division' as a name for the standard unit of silver coinage, the equivalent of a stater in Greece and Asia Minor." It was from this sense that it was applied to the "divisions" of Egypt.

Joseph Grafton Milne was probably the first to correctly surmise that the nome coinage was struck in Alexandria itself and not in the nomes as tradition maintained. Milne based his conclusion on the similarities in style and fabric and the fact that Alexandria was the administration center for most of Egypt (see J.G. Milne, "The Nome Coins of Egypt", *Ancient Egypt,* 1932, pp. 73-78). This argument was supported when Carl W.A. Carlson noted in a 1973 article in the journal of the Society of Ancient Numismatics *(SAN)* that an obverse die link existed between a drachm of Antoninus Pius with a "Mercury in Gemini" zodiac reverse (Dattari 2962) and a drachm of the Mareote nome (Dattari 6293). Recently, Milne's conclusion has been further corroborated by the discovery of a reverse die intended for a dichalkon of the Phthemphutite nome that was recut from a die accidentally engraved with the ethnic for the Phtheneotite Nome (Sheridan, "Nome Coins"). In addition, an obverse die link between a standard Alexandrian obol of Hadrian and an obol of the Arsinoite nome was illustrated by Sheridan. These die analyses provide conclusive evidence that Alexandria was the mint-city for the nome coinage.

With Alexandria firmly established as the mint-city for the nome coinage, the other question that has been a major dilemma for numismatists is the raison d'etre for this remarkable series of coins. Evidence is inconclusive for the suggestion that these coins were intended to circulate in the nomes themselves. The rarity of these coins would tend to argue against any large scale circulation in the *chora* (the area of Roman-Egypt outside of the capital city of Alexandria), especially when compared to the extremely large numbers of surviving Alexandrian coinage.

The Nome coinage may have been issued for commemorative reasons such as "gifts" for nome administrators or religious officials (Wetterstrom, *Historical Coin Review*, Vol. XIII, No. 2, 1988, pg. 20). Another possibility for two issues in the Nome series would be as Decennial commemoratives for Domitian and Hadrian. Pius' issues of his regnal year 8 could be explained as commemorative issues, of the Great Sothic Cycle, coupled with the Zodiac issues of the same year. The importance of the Great Sothic Cycle to the Egyptians cannot be overestimated, and it is possible that the Alexandrian mint officials held nothing back in their commemoration of this event. The rarity and sporadic issue of the nome coinage in general would specifically eliminate the theory that they were only additions to the regular stock types of the Alexandria mint. Unfortunately a definitive answer eludes us. Hopefully, continuing study will further illuminate the Nome series and enhance our understanding of this enigmatic, but fun to collect, series.

BIBLIOGRAPHY

Roman Egypt

Blum, Gustave. "Numismatique D'Antinoos", Extract from *Journal International D'Archéologie Numismatique*, Athens, 1914, pp. 33-70, 5 plates.

Christiansen, Erik. *Coins of Alexandria and the Nomes, A Supplement to the British Museum Catalogue*, London, British Museum Occasional Paper No. 77, 1991. Corrections (about 300) to the original catalog by Poole and 992 new entries for coins acquired by the BM since the original publication of Poole's work.

_____. *Sylloge Nummorum Graecorum. The Royal Collection of Coins and Medals. Danish National Museum. Vol. 41. Alexandria-Cyrenaica*, Copenhagen, 1974.

_____."The Roman Coins of Alexandria (30 B.C. to A.D. 296): An inventory of hoards", *Coin Hoards*, Volume VII, The Royal Numismatic Society, London, 1985, pp. 77-140.

_____. *The Roman Coins of Alexandria.* Two Volumes, Aarhus, Denmark; 1988.

Curtis, Col. James W. "The Coinage of Roman Egypt: A Survey", Reprinted from *The Numismatist*, January-August, 1956.

_____. *Tetradrachms of Roman Egypt*, New York, 1990 reprint.

Dattari, Giovanni. *Monete Imperiali Greche — Numi Augg. Alexandrini. Catalogo della collezione G. Dattari*, Volume I (Text), Volume II (Plates), Cairo (originally published in 1901 but still available as a reprint, one of the largest collections ever published with over 6,000 coins listed, in Italian but not too difficult to use for the non-Italian reader).

De Rouge, J. and F. Feuardent. *The Coinages of the Nomes and Prefectures of Roman Egypt,* Chicago (reprint) 1979.

Feuardent, Felix. *Collections Giovanni di Demetrio, Numismatique, Égypte Ancienne, Deuxième Partie — Domination Romaine*, Paris, 1873.

Förschner, Gisela. *Die Münzen Der Römischen Kaiser In Alexandrien, Historisches Museum Frankfurt am Main*, Frankfurt, 1988.

Geissen, Angelo & Wolfram Weiser *Katalog Alexandrinischer Kaisermünzen der Sammlung des Instituts für Altertumskunde der Universität zu Köln*, Five Volumes, Köln, 1972-1984.

Haatvedt, Rolfe A. & Enoch E. Peterson. *Coins from Karanis — The University of Michigan Excavations, 1924-1935*, Ann Arbor, 1964. Over 30,000 coins were uncovered at Karanis of which 24,257 are Alexandrian. The catalogue individually describes 1396 Alexandrian coins.

Kapossy, Balázs. "Alexandrinische Münzen im Bernischen Historischen Museum," *Schweizerische Numismatische Rundschau (Swiss Numismatic Review)*, Vol. XLV, 1966, pp. 51-115, pl. I-VII.

König, Ingemar. *Alexandrinische Münzen in der Original und Abgußsammlung der Universität Trier — Einführung und Katalog*, Trier, 1988.

Langlois, Victor. *Numismatique Des Nomes D'Égypte Sous L'Administration Romaine*, Paris, 1852.

MacDonald, George. *Catalogue of Greek Coins in the Hunterian Collection, University of Glasgow. Volume III: Further Asia, Northern Africa, Western Europe*, Glasgow, 1905. Catalogues 1193 Alexandrian coins in the Hunterian collection.

Milne, Joseph Grafton. *Catalogue of Alexandrian Coins. University of Oxford, Ashmolean Museum*, Oxford, 1933 with a Supplement by C.M. Kraay, London, 1971.

Mionnet, Théodore-Edme. *Description de Médailles Antiques, Grecques et Romaines*, Volume 6, Paris, 1813 and Supplément, Volume 9, Paris, 1837. Catalogues 3992 Alexandrian coins in Volume 6 and 758 additional coins in Volume 9 of the supplement. Still important as many of the coins are not published elsewhere.

Poole, Reginald Stuart. *Catalogue of the Greek Coins in the British Museum, Alexandria and the Nomes*, London, 1892.

Rémy, Bernard (with the collaboration of Michel Amandry). *Chambéry Musée Savoisien — Catalogue des monnaies romaines d'Alexandrie (Egypte)*, Milan, 1994.

Rougé, J. de & Felix Feuardent. *The Coinages of the Nomes and Prefectures of Roman Egypt*, Text in French, Chicago, 1979. Reprint from *Revue Numismatique* (Nouvelle Série, Tome XIV, 1869-1870) and of Feuardent's work from the Demetrio collection.

Skowronek, Stefan. *On The Problems Of The Alexandrian Mint*, Warsaw, 1967. Subtitle is "Allusion to the Divinity of the Sovereign Appearing on the Coins of Egyptian Alexandria in the Period of the Early Roman Empire: 1st and 2nd Centuries A.D."

Tameanko, Marvin. "The Pharos of Alexandria on ancient coinage", *The Celator*, Vol. 7, No. 7, July, 1993, pp. 6-12.

_____. "The fertility snake on Roman coinage struck at Alexandria", *The Celator*, Vol. 8, No. 7, July, 1994. pp. 6-12.

Tôchon d'Annecy, Joseph François. *Recherches Historiques Et Géographiques Sur Les Médailles Des Nomes Ou Préfectures De L'Égypte*, Paris, 1822.

Voegtli, Hans. *Bilder Der Heldenepen In Der Kaiserzeitlichen Griechischen Münzprägung*, Basel, 1977. Covers the "Labors of Hercules" series from Alexandria.

Vogt, Joseph. *Die Alexandrinischen Münzen. Grundlegung Einer Alexandrinischen Kaisergeschichte*, Two Volumes (text and tables), Stuttgart, 1924.

West, Louis C. & Allan C. Johnson. *Currency in Roman and Byzantine Egypt*, Princeton, 1944.

The Romans in Africa

The first Roman presence in Africa came as a result of the conflict with Carthage in Sicily. This led to the Second Punic War and eventually to the Roman victory of Scipio Africanus over Hannibal at Zama, Numidia in 202 BC. From that time on, the Romans settled and developed Tunisia and built many great estates and cities. Africa eventually became so Romanized that it produced several great leaders. We normally think of the third century in terms of great African leaders, like Septimius Severus, or the Gordians, but the province was fully developed long before that. The wife of Vespasian, Flavia Domitilla, was for example from Sabratha—and Mauretania was ruled by a boyhood friend of Octavian. The governors of Numidia in the Imperial Period were frequently elevated to Consul upon completion of their term. It is clear that Africa was not thought of as a backwater.

The geography of Africa divides it into two sections. In the east were Egypt and Cyrenaica, and in the west Syrtica (Tripolitana), Numidia and Mauretania. Like Asia Minor and the Levant, the boundaries between districts, and even their names, changed over time and can tend to confuse a collector who is not steeped in the history of the region. The Romans themselves often referred to the province of "Africa" in non-specific terms, much as we do today. The provincial coinage of Africa, excepting Egypt, is not extensive. Whether this is because of limited production or simply that it has not yet been brought to light by "unofficial finds" is not certain. In any event, collectors specializing in the provincial coinage of Roman Africa will find that the offerings in a typical sale catalogue will be limited to only a few choices. Much research has yet to be done in this field.

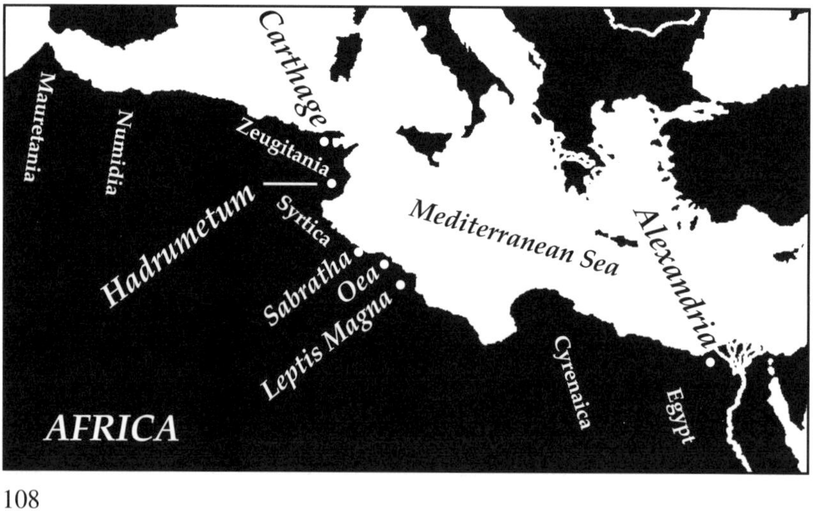

Cyrenaica

Cyrenaica was in what we know today as eastern Libya. It extended from the gulf of Syrtes Major east to Egypt. It was isolated from Egypt by deserts, and consequently had more ties by sea to the Greek world. The medicinal plant Silphium, from which the port of Cyrene became famous, was still the major export of Cyrenaica in the first century BC. The Romans were quick to exact a tax on it once they gained control. Cyrenaica became a province in 74 BC, but was later given by Antony to Cleopatra Selene, the infant daughter of Cleopatra of Egypt, and later wife of Juba II of Mauretania. It was combined with Crete, and restored as a province, after Antony and Cleopatra were defeated at Actium. That status was again lost as the result of a Jewish rebellion during the reign of Trajan (AD 115).

Coinage struck at Cyrene, the capital, bears the expected mix of Greek and Latin influence. On both of the examples illustrated here, the obverse depict the horned Zeus Ammon. The reverse of a 26mm bronze struck by the Quaestor Aulus Pupius Rufus depicts a *sella castrensis,* or camp chair. This was undoubtedly a mobile furnishing which symbolized authority. Another bronze, struck about five years earlier by Quaestor L. Lollius, depicts the sella Curulis. This was the term for the chair of office belonging to a curule magistrate. This chair of state was used only by the emperor (or equivalent), consuls, praetors, censors and curule aediles. Its use indicates that the offices held in this province were considered to be very important. Occasionally, we find the portrait as well as the name of a provincial official on the coinage of Africa under the Principate.

Province of Cyrenaica, AE 26 mm
Quaestor Aulus Pupius Rufus, 30-27 BC

Province of Cyrenaica, AE 31 mm
Quaestor L. Lollius, ca. 35 BC

Syrtica

The name Tripolis comes from the African federation of "Three Cities" Leptis, Oea and Sabratha (Abrotonum). A glance at the map of Africa shows that these cities were in close proximity on the Syrtican coast. One should be careful not to confuse this region with the Tripolis in Phoenicia.

Leptis Magna was the easternmost of the three coastal cities. It was under Roman rule during the reign of Augustus, and issued coinage in his name, but not with the rights of citizenship. The city received colonial status under Trajan. Leptis was a trading center for ivory, which was brought across the Sahara from central Africa. The "African Emperor", Septimius Severus, was born at Leptis and did much to honor the city once he came to power.

Leptis Magna, AE 23mm
ca. 1st Century BC

Oea (Tripoli) was situated in a coastal oasis, with a small but pleasant harbor. It was added to the Roman province of Africa in 146 BC. Like Leptis Magna, Oea became a colony under Trajan and was probably settled with a corps of legionary veterans. An attractive youthful portrait of Livia graces a bronze of Oea struck during the reign of her son Tiberius.

Oea, AE 25mm
Livia(d. AD 29), struck under Tiberius

The third city of the Tripolis, Sabratha was also known as Abrotonum. It too was a trading post for gold, jewels and ivory. They also supplied Rome with wild animals for its many public entertainments.

Sabratha, AE 24mm
Augustus, 27 BC - AD 14

Zeugitana

When we think of Zeugitana, we think immediately of Carthage. It was, after all, the Roman success against Carthaginian forces that launched it on a five-hundred year quest to dominate the world. The city was so ultimately devastated however, at the close of the Third Punic War, that it never did completely recover its former importance. A Roman colony was established by Lepidus on the old Carthaginian site in 42 BC, and Octavian reinforced that settlement with additional veterans in 28 BC. He also issued coins from the new colony. Carthage became the capital of the province of Zeugitana and in AD 68 was the base from which Clodius Macer launched a brief attempt at becoming emperor. Later in the imperial period, Carthage blossomed as a cultural center and was considered the most important city in Africa—perhaps second or third in the empire.

Carthage, Zeugitana, AE 23mm
Augustus, 27 BC -AD 14

Hippo, Zeugitana, AE 26mm
Tiberius with L. Apronius (proconsul)
ca. AD 18-21

Hippo, Zeugitana, AE 36mm, before AD 2
Augustus with his grandsons Caius and Lucius

Hippo, in Zeugitana, is not a simple matter of identification. There were two cities by that name. Hippo Regius was a coastal city beside the mouth of the Ubus river. It was originally a harbor town of the Carthaginians, passing temporarily into the hands of the Numidian kings after the Second Punic War. From them, it received the epithet Regius or "Royal". It was an important Roman city and boasted one of the largest theaters in Africa. This Hippo was the home of Saint Augustine. The other Hippo was Hippo Diarrhytus or Zaritus (now Biserta), which is also a coastal site, west of Utica. There has been some confusion as to which city certain coins actually belong to. We have not undertaken the arguments here and present the coins simply as Hippo. The most recent scholarship on this subject is in *Roman Provincial Coins.* One of the specimens illustrated here (attributed by RPC to Hippo Regius) is a sestertius-sized bronze with a stunning set of portraits. On the obverse is a "kinder, gentler" Augustus, with an actual smile on his face. On the reverse are his two grandsons, Caius and Lucius. Both of the unfortunate young heirs died prior to their grandfather—leaving him without a successor.

Utica was a port city in what is now Tunisia about thirty miles northwest of Carthage. It supported Rome in the Third Punic War, and was rewarded with additional lands after the fall of Carthage in 146. It then became the capital of the new Roman province of Africa. In 81 BC, the city served as a base for Pompey in his war against the Marians in Africa. It unfortunately supported Pompey once again in 46 when he opposed Caesar. The resulting defeat left Utica suffering from sanctions and deprivations. It was, however, raised to the status of municipium by Octavian in 36 BC. Utica was made a colony in the time of Hadrian and was confirmed by Septimius Severus.

The coins struck at Utica under Augustus and Tiberius are very "Roman" in fabric and appearance, as are virtually all of the coins from Zeugitana during this period.

Utica, Zeugitana, AE 31mm, Tiberius, AD 14-37

Numidia

Numidia was located east of Mauretania and west of the province known simply as Africa or Libya. It was a country of fertile pastures and was famous for its cattle. The Romans defeated the Numidian king Jugurtha in 106 BC and subsequent kings served at the pleasure of Rome.

Juba I, the son of Hiempsal, was an ally (Client King) of Pompey and during the civil war fought against Caesar's forces in Africa. After the defeat at Thapsus, he was forced to commit suicide and thus ended the Numidian kingdom (see facing page). At that time, Numidia was made the Roman province of Africa Nova. During the period from 60 to 46 BC Juba struck silver portrait denarii and a variety of bronze coins. On the reverse of the denarii, and a sestertius-sized bronze, is an important Numidian building which has been called both a temple and the Royal Palace. The smaller bronze coins featured a personification of Africa wearing an elephant-skin headdress, and the reverse motif of a lion walking right. Even in ancient times, the lion was regarded as the "King of Beasts" and this allegorical imagery presents Juba as the king of Africa.

Kings of Numidia, AR denarius
Juba I, 60-46 BC

Kings of Numidia, AE 22
Juba I, 60-46 BC

The settlement of Rusicade was originally established by the Phoenicians, but later became the Roman colony of Colonia Julia Veneria Rusicade. The anonymous bronze illustrated here is assigned to Rusicade by Mazard, and features conjoined heads of the Dioscuri. Its legends are in Punic script, but the existence of many Punic inscriptions on monuments from the Roman period verifies that this is not necessarily an uncommon feature.

Rusicade, AE 29mm, 1st century BC

Mauretania

Juba II was born in Numidia about 50 BC. His father, Juba I, lost his kingdom to Caesar in 46 and the young boy was taken to Rome and paraded in Caesar's Triumph. He was then raised in the Caesarean household and became a close friend of Octavian. He became a very learned scholar and was granted Roman citizenship. Juba was given the kingdom of Numidia, his paternal heritage, by Octavian in 30 BC. Five years later, Numidia was added to the province of Africa and Juba was, in compensation, given the kingdom of Mauretania.

Mauretania, AR denarius
Juba II, 25 BC - AD 23

Mauretania, AR denarius
Cleopatra Selene, wife of Juba I

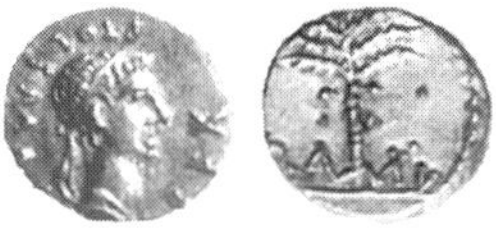

Mauretania, AR denarius
Ptolemy, AD 23-40

He married Cleopatra Selene, the daughter of Cleopatra VII of Egypt, and they had a son named Ptolemy. Juba was well educated and apparently authored many books on historical subjects, which are known only by their mention in Pliny. Among these are a history of Africa, a Roman history and a history of painting. He died a natural death, and was survived by his son Ptolemy who ruled until the time of Caligula.

Juba, Cleopatra and Ptolemy all appear on attractive portrait denarii struck in Mauretania. Those of Cleopatra are rather scarce.

Mauretania, AE 36mm, Juba II, 25 BC - AD 23

Bocchos II, the son of a Mauretanian king of the same name, was confirmed in his position by Octavian. After his death, there was an interregnum of some eight years before the appointment of Juba II as king of Mauretania. The rare specimen illustrated here was apparently struck during that interregnum.

Mauretania, Bocchos II
AE 18mm, 49-33 BC

Lix (or Lixus) was a commercial city on the west coast of Mauretania Tingitana. The obverse of the coin illustrated here depicts an Egyptian-North African deity similar to the Greek god Hephaistos (Roman Vulcan). The reverse shows what seems to be a distyle entrance, with large capitals, most likely part of a templeto the deity honored on this coin.

Lix, Mauretania, AE 27mm
ca. 1st century BC

BIBLIOGRAPHY

The Romans in Africa

Broughton, T.R.S. *The Romanization of Africa Consularis,* Baltimore, 1929.

Mazard, J. *Corpus Nummorum Numidae Mauretaniaeque,* Paris, 1955, (with later supplements in *Libyca*).

Müller, L. *Numismatique de l'Ancienne Afrique,* Copenhagen, 1860-63.

Salzmann, Dieter. "Zur Münzprägung der mauretanischen König Juba II und Ptolemaios", *Mitteilungen Deutsches Archäologisches Institut. Abteilung Madrid,* Heidelberg, 1974 pp. 174-183.

Tameanko, Marvin. "Coins of ancient Mauretania portray a mixture of architectural styles", *The Celator,* Vol. 5, No.12, December, 1991. pp. 14-16.

Zedelius, V. "P. Quinctilius Varus in Achulla", Bonner Jahrbucher 183, 1983, pp. 469-474.

Portraits of Interest

Achulla, Africa, AE 29mm (x1.5)
P. Quinctilius Varus
Proconsul, 8-7 BC

In addition to a wealth of distinctive imagery on the reverses of provincial coins, there are also some important obverse types. Portraits of certain celebrities, usually imperial family members or high officials, appear only on provincial coinage. Also portrayed on provincial coinage are a number of Roman client-kings.

Included in the following section are numismatic portraits of some interesting individuals who do not appear, or appear very rarely, on Roman Imperial issues. The bronze coins from Achulla in Africa illustrated here are illustrative of the Romans whose images will never appear on imperial coinage. They served back to back as Proconsul of Africa—a stepping stone to more important posts. The first, P. Quinctilius Varus, became better known to Roman historians than many who served as emperor. He was commander of the three legions lost to Arminius in the Teutoburger Wald massacre. He took his own life on the battlefield. His replacement at Achulla was L. Volusius Saturninus, another Roman of noble blood whose deeds are buried in the historical record. These two reverse portraits share a common obverse type of Augustus flanked by Caius and Lucius, his two grandsons and designated heirs. They are clearly part of a special issue, which probably commemorated the refounding of the city.

Achulla, Africa, AE 29mm (x1.5)
L. Volusius Saturninus
Proconsul 7-6 BC

The provincial coins of this period provide much of the information that is known about obscure colonies and political changes. Finding a portrait coin of someone like Varus or Saturninus is extremely interesting and exciting—a real treasure for the collector!

If the historians can be trusted, Fulvia was a woman with a heart of stone. She was the wife of Mark Antony at the time of the Triumvirate proscriptions. It was said that after the execution of Cicero, Fulvia had his head brought to her, layed it on her lap and ridiculed the dead orator—then pierced his tongue with a golden needle. The name of the city Eumenea, in Phrygia, was changed to Fulvia in 41 BC on the occasion of Mark Antony's visit. She died the following year.

Fulvia-Eumenea, Phrygia,
AE 18mm, ca. 41-40 BC
Fulvia, wife of Mark Antony

Antony's second wife, Octavia, appears with him on cistophoric tetradrachms of Asia (see page 44). Cleopatra also appears with Antony on a number of coins. Here, she is alone on a Phoenician tetradrachm.

Phoenicia, uncertain mint
AR tetradrachm
Cleopatra VII, died 30 BC

Augustus did not have any male children of his own, and it was considered fortunate that his daughter Julia gave him two grandsons. These young boys were groomed to become emperor from childhood. Strangely, there are very few portrait coins of the children. Caius was the oldest, and one imperial denarius is variously attributed either to him or to Augustus. The young prince does appear, however, on provincial bronze coins—including one struck at Alexandria in Egypt about the year 2 BC. The name Caius (spelled ΓΑΙΟΣ, there isn't a "C" in the Greek alphabet) is clearly inscribed in Greek letters to the left of the portrait. Sadly, the young Caius died in AD 4 at the age of 23, leaving his grandfather without an heir. His younger brother Lucius had died two years earlier.

Alexandria, Egypt
AE 25mm
Caius Caesar, 2-1 BC

Drusilla was one of the infamous three sisters of Caligula. Her brother supposedly seduced her as a teenager—or perhaps the reverse is true—and later

Miletus, Ionia
AE 20mm (x1.5)
Drusilla, died AD 38

Koinon, Galatia
AE 18mm, AD 39-48
Antonia and
Valeria Messalina

Alexandria, Egypt
AR didrachm, AD 42/3
Children of Claudius

Kings of Pontus, (x1.5)
AR drachm, AD 38-64
portrait of Brittanicus

lived with her as his wife. He demanded all sorts of public honors and affirmations of loyalty on her behalf. When she died at the age of 23 , in AD 38, the manifestations of sorrow on the part of Caligula led to her deification. Drusilla appears on the reverse of a sestertius of Caligula along with her sisters Livilla and Agrippina. They did not fare as well as Drusilla in the midst of Caligula's insanity, they were both banished. Drusilla's portrait may be seen on a bronze coin from Miletus in Ionia, struck while she was still alive.

Antonia was the virtuous wife of Drusus and mother of Claudius. Valeria Messalina was the third wife of Claudius. The two appear together on a bronze coin struck in Galatia during his reign as emperor. Given the reputation of Messalina for blatant promiscuity, it seems ironic that Claudius should place her image on this coin along with his mother.

The three children of Claudius were depicted on a small bronze coin attributed to Caesarea Philippi in Phoenicia, and also on a didrachm from Alexandria in Egypt (illustrated here). Claudia Antonia was a child by the second wife of Claudius; Aelia Paetina, Britannicus and Claudia Octavia were children of his third wife, Valeria Messalina. Depictions of minor children other than potential heirs to the throne are rare in ancient coinage.

Brittanicus, the son of Claudius and Messalina, was born in AD 42. He would normally have been first in line for succession, but Agrippina convinced Claudius to adopt her own son, Nero, and give him precedence for the throne. Shortly after Nero's accession, Brittanicus was poisoned. The imperial coins of Brittanicus are very rare and yet provincial bronzes are fairly obtainable. The silver drachm illustrated here was struck under the client king Polemo II.

Claudia Octavia was featured alone on another coin from Alexandria, but this time because she was the wife of Nero. This was almost an incestuous affair because Nero was the son of Agrippina, the fourth wife and niece of Claudius. She was deserted by Nero for Poppaea Sabina. Claudia Octavia was banished to Pandaterial and put to death. This led to widespread public disenchantment and the subsequent narration of her tragedy in one of the works of Seneca.

Poppaea Sabina was a woman of great beauty and less than great morals. She was married to Otho (future emperor) when Nero became enamored with her. She masterminded the dispatch of her husband to a post in Lusitania, the murder of Nero's mother Agrippina and of his wife Claudia Octavia. She then married Nero, and became pregnant, but was killed in 65 by a kick from the emperor.

Statilia Messalina was the third wife of Nero. She was the granddaughter of T. Statilius Taurus, who had been consul in AD 11. Messalina had previously been married to Atticus Vestinus but Nero had him put to death without accusation or trial so that he could marry her. The portrait of Statilia Messalina appears on a small bronze from Ephesus in Ionia.

The imperial coinage of Otho is not particularly rare, in fact a portrait of this emperor can be obtained rather easily. However, the only portraits available in the imperial series are on gold aurei and silver denarii. These are relatively small in module and do not offer a portrait collector much to be excited about. There are no imperial bronze issues of Otho. Fortunately,

Alexandria, Egypt
AR tetradrachm, AD 56/7
Claudia Octavia

Alexandria, Egypt
AR tetradrachm,
Poppaea Sabina

Ephesus, Ionia
AE 19mm (x1.5)
Statilia Messalina

Antioch, Syria
AR tetradrachm
Otho, AD 69

some wonderful large portraits are available in the provincial series. Illustrated here is one from Antioch in Syria which compares quite favorably to the imperial denarii.

Tabae, Caria. AE 20mm
Domitia, AD 82-96

The coins of Domitia, the wife of Domitian, are very rare in the imperial series, but a number of cities in Asia Minor struck bronzes with her portrait. These can usually be obtained at much more modest prices than their imperial counterparts.

Corinth, Greece, AE 43mm
Antinoüs, died AD 130

Few love affairs have been as heralded through the centuries as that of the emperor Hadrian and his consort Antinoüs. The young Bithynian boy accompanied Hadrian on his travels, and met with an untimely end in Egypt where he apparently drowned in the Nile. As with all such human interest stories there is an element of mystique and intrigue that will probably never be resolved. Some modern historians suggest that he was actually murdered. Hadrian was greatly sorrowed at his loss, and the boy was deified. A number of temples were built in his honor, and a series of memorial coins was issued throughout the East following his death.

Pescennius Niger was a popular military figure serving as Governor of Syria at the death of Pertinax. He was proclaimed emperor by his troops and enjoyed support throughout the East. Almost immediately, he came into conflict with Septimius Severus, who managed to take Rome and establish a claim to the purple. Niger was defeated in several engagements in Asia Minor, and fled south. After a final defeat at Issus, the place where Alexander the Great defeated Darius, he fled east. Niger hoped to take refuge among the Parthians, but he was overtaken and was executed on the spot.

Alexandria, AE diobol
Pescennius Niger
AD 193-194

Annia Faustina was a descendant of Marcus Aurelius and became the third wife of Elagabalus in AD 221. She was divorced the same year when he returned to Aquilea Severa, one of his earlier wives. Coins in her name, and with her portrait, were issued at a surprising number of mints in Asia Minor and the Levant considering the brief span of her imperial status.

Sidon, Phoenicia, AE 27mm
Annia Faustina, AD 221
third wife of Elagabalus

Considering how common the imperial coins of Gordian III are, it is surprising that the coins of his wife, Tranquillina, are rare in that series. It has been suggested that this might have been intentional—a reaction to the exceptional power of the Severan matriarchs or perhaps the unpopularity of Julia Mamaea. Strangely, this did not curtail the production of coins in her name throughout the provinces. Perhaps Asia Minor was far enough removed from the issue to be unaffected. Still, it seems like there should be a better explanation. Although provincial coins of Tranquillina may be a bit more expensive than those of some other imperial wives, only because they are not available elsewhere, they are generally not rare.

Side, Pamphylia, AE 26mm
Tranquillina, AD 241-44
wife of Gordian III

Coins of Julius Marinus, on the other hand, are very rare. These coins honoring the father of Philip I seldom are offered for sale and command strong prices when they do appear. Marinus was a relatively minor official in Arabia. He was deified during the reign of his son and a temple was built in his honor at Philippopolis in Arabia Petraea. This city was the only one to issue coins in his name.

Philippolis, Arabia
Julius Marinus, AE 24mm
father of Philip I, AD 244-9

Julia, Phrygia, AE 27mm
Cornelia Supera, AD 253

The coins of Cornelia Supera are rare in either the imperial or provincial series. She was apparently the wife of Aemilian, but is unknown through any literary reference. The coins in her name were struck at Parium in Mysia and Julia in Phrygia. Aemilian rebelled against Trebonianus Gallus and Volusian in AD 253 and came to power when their own troops murdered them. He ruled only three months before being assassinated by a faction of his troops favoring Valerian. Notice the "dimple" on the cheek of Cornelia, a common manufacturing oddity discussed on page 130.

Alexandria,
AE tetradrachm
Zenobia, AD 270/1

Zenobia inherited the Kingdom of Palmyra from her husband Odenathus. She was a remarkable woman with talents in every field of politics and war. She is said to have accompanied her troops on horseback and even to have marched with them afoot. She is also claimed to have had the advantage of being able to outdrink her diplomatic guests without becoming drunk. Still, she is remembered by history as a woman of great beauty, grace and charm.

Her power and success posed a threat to Aurelian, who launched a major campaign against Palmyra, eventually capturing Zenobia and taking her to Rome bound in golden chains. She was paraded in Aurelian's Victory and then given a sumptuous villa where she lived the rest of her life in great comfort.

Alexandria, Egypt (x1.5)
AE 25mm, AD 297/8
Domitius Domitianus

Portraits of Domitius Domitianus were struck both on imperial folles and on Alexandrian denominations. He was a relatively low ranking administrator, who usurped authority during the reign of Diocletian, and controlled Alexandria for about two years. The coins of Domitianus bear the distinction of being the last coins of the provincial series. After his suppression, Diocletian terminated the unique monetary system of Egypt and installed the standard imperial system of denominations.

Client Kings

The history of Rome's expansion is, in large part, a story of confrontation with Hellenistic monarchies. Over a period of nearly two centuries, one monarch after another lost his kingdom to the Roman conquerors. Some negotiated treaties with Rome that recognized them as *amici* or friends of the Roman people. Others were recognized as *socius* as a reward for service rendered. With the death of Cleopatra, and the demise of the Ptolemaic dynasty, the only monarchs left in the Mediterranean world were those who served at the will of the Roman emperor.

The defense of the empire against barbarian incursions required the maintenance of buffer zones on its fringes. From the first century BC through the third century AD, Roman leaders found that popular local figures served a very useful and effective role in administering these zones. Most of these buffer areas were inhabited by people who were nearly barbarian themselves and not very well suited for inclusion in the Roman system of administration.

Caesar and his successors realized the importance of Romanizing these areas, and often brought the sons of these client kings to Rome for a proper education. They then were sent back to their homes as ambassadors of Roman culture. Juba II, the son of a North African king, was raised in the Caesarean household and as a child became a close friend of Octavian. He later was installed by Octavian as King of Numidia and subsequently moved to Mauretania. He served Roman interests in North Africa well. Following his suppression of the pirates in Cilicia, Pompey accepted the deference of Tarcondimotus, a tribal chieftain in the eastern Cilician highlands, and named him Toparch of Cilicia. He was later named king by Antony. This client king, and his sons, served Roman interests for over a half century. In fact, Tarcondimotus lost his life supporting the cause of Antony at Actium. The Kings of Edessa protected the Parthian frontier for a very long time as Roman clients. Even as late as the time of Aurelian, Palmyra was governed by an acknowledged, if sometimes rebellious, client king. Other regions in which client kings retained nominal control during imperial times included the Bosporus, Armenia, Thrace, Cappadocia, Commagene, Judaea and Arabia. Although this is not a comprehensive list of client kings, the next few pages will illustrate the im-

Kings of the Bosporos, AE 26mm
Cotys II, AD 123-132

Kings of the Bosporus,
AE 26mm, , AD 14-38
Tiberius and Aspurgus

Kings of the Bosporus
EL stater, AD 215/6
Rhescouporis II and Caracalla

Kings of Pontus
AR drachm, AD 56/7
Polemo II and Nero

Kings of Thrace
AE 28mm, 11 BC - AD 12
Rhoemetalces I and Augustus

portance of these allies to Rome.

The Kingdom of Pontus was partitioned after the defeat of Mithridates and part went to Polemo I, who established a client king dynasty that lasted until the death of Nero.

Aspurgus married Queen Dynamis and helped to overthrow her former husband Polemo. They ruled jointly over Pontus and the Bosporus until her death in AD 8. From then on he ruled alone in the Bosporus. A long line of kings from this region dependably served Roman interests and the coins struck in their names often included portraits of the emperors to whom they had pledged allegiance. During the Severan period, the Bosporus kings issued a series of electrum staters that offer interesting stylized portraits and are usually obtainable on the market for much less than gold coins of the imperial mints.

Polemo II was a grandson of Polemo I, and ruled for a time over the Bosporus and Pontus. In AD 64, Nero made Pontus a province and Polemo took up residence in Cilicia.

Rhoemetalces I was made King of Thrace by Augustus in 11 BC. He ruled until AD 12 and was succeeded by his son Cotys IV, and his brother Rhescuporis III who shared the kingdom. The latter murdered his nephew seven years later. The bronze illustrated here depicts Rhoemetalces and his wife Pythodoris with their son Cotys IV. On the reverse are conjoined busts of Augustus and Livia.

Olba, Cilicia, AE 20mm
Ajax, AD 10-15

Ajax is titled "High Priest" on the coins of Olba and was governor or toparch of Lalassis and Cennatis as well. Olba was a city in Cilicia Tracheia, said to be founded by Ajax, the son of Teucer. It was at the 3,000 foot level in the foothills above Lamus. He ruled for only five years, and his authority was limited to a small region.

The Armenian client kings are discussed on page 62. One may surmise from the poor quality illustrations, there and here, that coins of these kings tend to be heavily worn and poorly preserved. They are a specialized, but very popular, collecting field. Most are quite rare.

Kings of Armenia, AE 24mm
Tigranes V (with Augustus), AD 6

The client kings of Edessa, who enjoyed a sporadic reign, are interesting for their distinctly Eastern culture and appearance. Like the Armenian kings mentioned above, a section of this volume deals specifically with them. See page 61 for a discussion of the Kings of Edessa.

Kings of Edessa
AE 23mm, AD 242-244
Gordian III and Abgar X

Chalcis too is discussed in a separate section of this volume. See page 73. The rule of Zenodorus was not particularly successful, although he managed to hold his title in spite of civil unrest. The coins of Octavian (later Augustus) and Zenodorus were at one time considered quite rare. They have appeared recently in greater numbers, however, and are obtainable today without too much difficulty.

Kings of Chalkis
AE 20mm, 32/1 BC
Octavian and Zenodoros

Duke of Palmyra
AE tetradrachm, Alexandria
Vabalathus

Vabalathus, the son of Zenobia, was the only Roman client to be given the title of Duke. This unusual concession was heralded on Roman Imperial antoniani which portrayed him along with Aurelian. This was an obvious attempt to placate the ambitious Palmyrene and his mother. The ploy did not work, however, as this coin from Alexandria was struck for Vabalathus as "Emperor". The usurpation could not go unchecked, and Aurelian eventually attacked the Palmyrene kingdom and deposed Zenobia and Vabalathus.

Kings of Judea, AE 26mm
Herod Agrippa II, AD 86/7

Herod the Great did much to Romanize Judea, but no Jewish client king held longer tenure or controlled more area than Agrippa II. His reign lasted nearly 50 years and spanned the First Jewish War. His coins are relatively common, mostly with portraits of the Flavian emperors.

Nabataea, AE 18mm
Aretas IV , 9 BC - AD 40

The Nabataeans were not as closely connected to Rome as the client kingdoms in Asia Minor and the Levant, but following the excursions of Pompey, the Nabataean kings served at least nominally under Roman authority. On the small bronze illustrated here, King Aretas IV is depicted with his queen Shuqailat.

Himyarite, AR unit
Uncertain king , Time of Augustus

The Himyarites, an Arabian tribe, struck enigmatic silver coins during the time of Augustus which bear his portrait and an imitative Athens reverse. They may have been struck under Roman influence.

Understanding Provincial Coins

Byzantion, Thrace, AE 24mm
Time of Domitian
Without Imperial Portrait

From all other classes of numismatics, ancient and modern, we derive the notion that political authority and the striking of coins goes hand in hand. One of the first elements of attribution in any series is the question "Who was this coin struck by?" The answer might be a person, a city, a country, or even a league of cities or countries. In each case, however, the authority to issue coins is clearly defined on the coinage itself. With Roman Provincial coins, the situation is not always so clear. Numismatists have, over the years, tried to apply the general concepts of issuing authority to the provincial series with very little success. To be sure, each coin gives the name of a city, or a council, or at least the mark of an empowered magistrate. But the implication of authority, taken or granted, may be misleading.

Coins which do not bear the portrait of an imperial figure, are often referred to in catalogues as "semi-autonomous", "quasi-autonomous" or "pseudo-autonomous". Don't confuse this word with "anonymous", which means not in any ruler's name. The lack of an imperial portrait has commonly been taken to mean that the issuing city did not require the authority of the emperor to strike coins. It is also widely believed that the right to issue coins was bestowed and revoked for political reasons, i.e. as reward and punishment. Therefore, the lack of coins at one time or another always tends to beg an historical explanation. Kevin Butcher has argued in *Roman Provincial Coins: an introduction to the Greek Imperials,* that this whole notion is a myth. It certainly does not seem sensible that the issuing of coinage would be a purely political reaction. The primary reason for the very existence of coinage has always been economic.

Butcher points out that the "free" cities of Apamea in Syria and Amisus in Pontus issued coins *with* imperial portraits. If autonomy were a reward, one would think that they would have issued only non-portrait types. Also, he explains that some cities who were not "free" issued contemporary coins with *and without* imperial portraits—sometimes with die links between them.

The title AYTONOMOY (autonomous) was indeed a signal honor, and it was clearly given and taken by higher authority. The use of non-portrait motifs on provincial coinage should not, however, be taken as evidence of a related political event. The question of portrait/non-portrait types and their relationship to autonomy is critically reviewed by Ann Johnson in *ANS Museum Notes* 30. It is probably better, as Johnson suggests, to abandon the terms mentioned above and simply use the terms "portrait" and "non-portrait" in describing these types.

The Provincial Koinon

KOINON ΜΑΚΕΔΟΝΩΝ
AE 26mm, AD 238-244
Time of Gordian III

The provincial coinage issued in the name of a district council (KOINON) was not very common at the time of Augustus and the formation of provincial Roman governments. Most cities issued coinage in their own names—either as autonomous or as individual subjects of the emperor or a client king. In fact, the koina never became very widespread in practice or authority. From inscriptions on provincial coins, we know of koina in Macedon and Thessaly in Greece—also on the islands of Lesbos, Crete and Cyprus. The remainder were from the East. They included councils in Bithynia, Pontus, Cilicia and Syria.

In theory, the koinon may be likened to a federation where representatives of each city in the district form an assembly with a democratic voice. In practice, however, they had very limited powers. One of their main functions was the organization of festivals and games in favor of the imperial cult. The allusion to these games is normally seen in the legends or iconography of the coins which they issued. Other typical images are the temple of the koinon or personifications of the Senate (see facing page). One particular temple of note appears on a bronze from the koinon of Galatia at Ancyra. This temple is the monument upon which the famous *Monumentum Ancyranum,* the political defense of Augustan policy, is preserved.

The koina should not be thought of as independent political powers. They were, of course, under Roman control. In fact, the Roman proconsul or provincial governor is sometimes named on these coins.

Koinon Galatia, AE 20mm
Ancyra, 1st century AD
Temple of Roma and Augustus

Tarsus, Cilicia, AE 17mm (x1.5)
Koinon Temple, AD 166-177
KOINOC ΚΙΛΙΚΙΑC

Demos / Boule / Koinoboulion

Although they do not mean exactly the same thing, the *Demos, Boule* and *Koinoboulion* are interrelated. Demos (ΔΗΜΟϹ) is the Greek personification of the people, or more properly, the spirit of the people. It is roughly equivalent to the Roman *Genius*.

Boule (ΒΟΥΛΕ) was a personification of the local senate. Personifications of the boule are fairly standard. As illustrated here, boule of the cities of Hierapolis and Kibyra in Phrygia are nearly identical. The figure is veiled and sometimes appears to be male, sometimes female. The name itself is feminine. An interesting coin from Tios in Bithynia, illustrated below, depicts Demos and Boule in harmony.

The Koinoboulion was a rather unusual personification of the common council or Koinon. It appears as a seated figure dropping a pebble (vote?) into an amphora on coins of Tarsus and Anazarbus.

Tripolis, Caria, AE 26mm
Head of Demos, ca. AD 138-161

Blaundus, Lydia, AE 27mm
Head of Demos, ca. AD 138-161

Hierapolis ***Kibyra***
Phrygian Boule of the late 2nd century

Tarsus, Cilicia, AE 37mm
Caracalla, AD 198-217
Koinoboulion

Tios, Bithynia, AE 32mm
Julia Maesa, died ca. AD 235
Boule and Demos clasping hands

Those Mysterious Indented Coins

Anchialos, Thrace
Gordian III, AD 238-244
AE 39mm Medallion
(note indents in center of obverse and reverse)

Numismatists have for a long time debated the purpose for and cause of certain indents or "dimples" which appear near the center on coins of several provincial mints. They are particularly notable on coins from the Balkan region, but also appear from time to time on coins from Asia Minor and elsewhere. In fact, the phenomenon occurs much earlier on coins struck in Egypt under the Ptolemaic dynasty. Whether there is a correlation of purpose between the two is unknown, but it seems doubtful that there is any direct influence.

Some numismatists have proposed that the marks were caused by a lathe which was used to prepare the planchet prior to striking. Within a particular series, specimens may be found with and without the indents. When present, the indents are not always centered on the flan. The resulting eccentricity would seem awkward to deal with in any kind of a lathe. Complicating the issue even further, the indents do not always line up with each other from obverse to reverse. This completely eliminates the use of any turning device. What then did cause these indents?

Marcianopolis, Moesia Inferior
Caracalla and Julia Domna, AD 198-217

One possibility is that, prior to striking, the planchet surfaces were smoothed with a bow-drill type of apparatus turning a blade or abrasive disk. This theory was advanced by David Sellwood in *Roman Crafts.* In our opinion, the most plausible theory was advanced by Marvin Tameanko (*The Celator,* Letters to the editor, October, 1992, p. 4.). We quote:

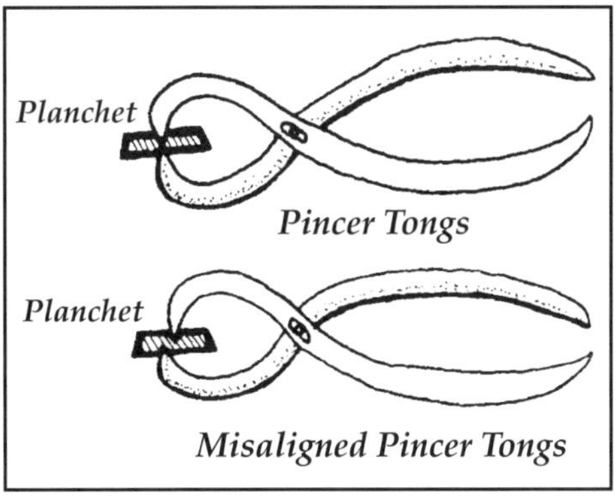

"After studying over 100 such coins in the past years, I can suggest that the dimples were made with a "pincer" type pair of tongs. The pincer's ends were shaped like blunt tips, which made the indentations. The reason the indentations appear off-center on some coins is that the craftsman sometimes gripped the planchet off center with his tongs. The reason some of the dimples do not line up on the obverse and reverse is that some of the pincers jaws were misaligned when they were fabricated, or through wear. The diagram shows how this may have occurred. The "why" for the pincers being used is connected to metallurgical practices in the ancient world. We know that coin planchets were struck when hot, or at least annealed. But how hot is hot? To determine if the coin planchet was hot enough to strike, the craftsman picked up the blank with his pincers. If the tips of the pincers sunk into the surface of the metal, it was hot enough. He then placed the blank onto the lower die in the anvil. If the tips of the pincer did not penetrate the coin, he returned it to the furnace for more heating. If the mint was in a great rush or the pincer operator was tired, lazy or careless, the cool blank was put onto the die, and therefore, no indentations appear in the coin. Some of the coins without dimples which I examined show the typical stress lines in the metal surface and edges which indicate that the coin was not hot enough when struck.

The Neocorate

AE 45mm, Pergamum
Third Neocorate (under Caracalla)
ΠΕΡΓΑΜΗΝΩΝ
ΠΡΩΤΩΝ Γ ΝΕΩΚΟΡΩΝ

Neocorus *(νεωκοροσ)* was a Greek title which designated the individual who had charge of the interior of a temple and looked out for the temple's needs. In Roman times, provincial Greek cities often styled themselves as the neocori *(νεωκοροι)* of the imperial cult. This was an obvious form of flattery, which insinuated the godliness of the emperor and indicated the city's devotion and loyalty. The neocorate of a city was a great and coveted honor, and not one which was presumed arbitrarily. The emperor allowed the bestowing of this right only to cities which had earned the status. Consequently, cities were eager to announce this consideration and usually did so on their coinage. The proclamation of a neocorate on coins was often accompanied by a depiction of the temple.

Originally, it was imperial policy that only one neocorate would be allowed in a city. This rule was later relaxed, and several cities were allowed two or more neocorates. The subsequent awards were depicted on coins by showing two or three temples along with an appropriate inscription. The first neocorate of a city was usually mentioned in the inscription simply as ΝΕΩΚΟΡΩΝ. The second appeared as Β ΝΕΩΚΟΡΩΝ, the third as Γ ΝΕΩΚΟΡΩΝ (e.g. Pergamum).

The importance of the neocorate to citizens of Tarsus is revealed by this bronze medallion. Holed in ancient times, it is apparent that the medallion was worn as a necklace. The position of the hole indicates that the reverse, depicting the second neocorate under Commodus, was the side worn outward, so as to be seen—rather than the image of the emperor it honored!

The approval of a neocorate was usually accompanied by games and festivals. The coins struck for these events often displayed a combination of neocorate and agonistic imagery. Like the number of temples depicted, there also seems to be a correlation between the imagery and the award on some of the "games" issues. Although this may be coincidental, coins bearing the single NEOKOPOC (see illustration above) often have a singular agonistic crown or urn. Those indicating a second or subsequent neocorate have two or more crowns.

Thessalonica, Macedon, AE 27mm
Neocorate under Philip I, AD 244-247

In the case of an alliance coin between Smyrna and Pergamum, the two temples illustrated may allude to the fact that both cities were awarded neocorates under Caracalla. The iconography of neocorate and agonistic references is very complex and not fully understood by most numismatists. It is, however, a wonderful area for study, research and discovery. As we learn more about the interrelationships between these aspects of religion, civic administration and public events, we will undoubtedly be able to unravel some of the underlying symbology that presently escapes us.

Smyrna and Pergamum
Caracalla, AD 198-217

BIBLIOGRAPHY

Portraits / Understanding Provincial Coins

Braund, David. *Rome and the friendly king: the character of the client kingship,* London and New York, 1984.

Cooper Sands, Percy. *The client princes of the Roman Empire under the Republic,* Cambridge, 1908.

Johnston, Ann. "The so-called 'Pseudo-Autonomous' Greek Imperials", *ANS Museum Notes* 30, New York, 1985.

Woodward, A.M. "The neocorate at Aegae and Anazarbus in Cilicia", *Numismatic Chronicle,* London, 1963.

Attributing Roman Provincial Coins

One does not necessarily need to attribute coins in order to collect them. It is possible to rely on the expertise of a dealer or friend for that. However, it is difficult to really appreciate the nature and importance of a coin if one cannot understand all of the details in the coin's design. Furthermore, it is usually to one's advantage economically to be able to attribute coins without the aid of a professional who always charges, in some way, for the service.

The Greek legends tend to discourage many beginning collectors from studying the Roman Provincial series, but this can be overcome. Once a general attribution is made, one can zero in on the particular details of minting time, place and purpose. Like anything else worth doing, learning to attribute Roman Provincial coins will take some effort. And, the information in this book will not make you an expert in attributing these coins. What we intend to do here is to show you the basics of attribution and to help you on your way to understanding how and where to look for the necessary information.

The first thing we will look at is the work of other cataloguers. There are standard references to this series of coins just like there are for Greek or Roman coins. If the reader has been progressing through the earlier volumes of *Ancient Coin Collecting* it will be obvious by now that there are *a lot* of references. The number that one will require depends on the depth to which one explores the information. The old adage "buy the book before you buy the coin" is really not such bad advice. Of course one needs to hold a few ancient coins to become enthralled and motivated, but it is a good idea to set aside part of your collecting budget for reference works in the area of your specialization. The main purpose of *this* book is to help you find that area of specialization more quickly, so you do not unnecessarily invest your time, money and energy in a fruitless search.

Next is a section on reading inscriptions, including the dissection of a coin's legends. We have assembled some of the basic information that you will need to read the Greek inscriptions on provincial coins, and also have shown you where to find more detailed information about reading legends. We have included a table of common titles, with translations, and a list of city names that one is likely to encounter. These are not comprehensive lists, they are provided as a general guide and as a sample of what one might expect to find in the major reference works.

Finally, we have provided information about dating coins, about denominations, and a page of photo enlargement on which to hone your reading skills. After reading this chapter, we hope that you will be able to pick up a provincial coin with a relatively straightforward inscription and identify it to a ruler, a city, and perhaps a date.

The Major Reference Catalogues

David Sear's *Greek Imperial Coins and their values* is a tremendously useful book for the beginner. It cannot, and does not pretend to, list all Provincial coins, nor all of the provincial cities that struck coins for that matter. Still, in one handy reference it includes over 6,000 coin types along with commentary, maps, tables and more. One unique feature of this reference is that the coins are listed by ruler first, and then city. This is a departure from the standard cataloguing system for provincial coins, but a useful complement to catalogues organized by mint. Often, the mint name is obscured, and yet the emperor may be recognized by the portrait. A spin through the coins of that emperor will sometimes result in identification of an otherwise difficult to identify specimen.

The most extensive series of books covering provincial coins is the *British Museum Catalog of Greek Coins.* This 29 volume set covers coins of the Greek world in general, but includes coins of the Roman period. It is not a reference that the beginner would buy, but it is available in many academic and public libraries.

Roman Provincial Coinage is the most recent of the major catalogues. It is a team effort, published jointly by the Bibliothèque National in Paris and the British Museum in London. The first volume (1992) covers coins struck from 44 BC to AD 69. It is unfortunately out of print already, and available only on the secondary market.

For the collector with a healthy library budget, SNG Copenhagen is a very good reference not only to Greek coins, but to Roman Provincial as well. The 43 volume set is available in a seven volume hardbound reprint. Another SNG of great importance to collectors of coins from Asia Minor is the Collection of Hans Von Aulock. The 18 volumes were reprinted in 1987 by the same firm that did the SNG Copenhagen series. The Von Aulock SNG was indexed in a separate volume, which is a tremendous research tool in itself. These are major references for the serious collector and are not inexpensive, even in the reprints. Rounding out the SNG catalogues of interest to provincial coin collectors is SNG Tübingen. The four volumes in print cover Greek and "Greek Imperial" bronze coins from Spain to Ionia. There are also several specialized SNG catalogues covering specific regions. They will be mentioned in the sections to which they pertain.

The catalogue of the Weber Collection includes Greek coins and provincial coins in a three volume reprint of the 1922-29 edition. It is a secondary reference, but contains many otherwise unpublished types. Another catalogue of similar value is the catalogue of the McClean Collection in the Fitzwilliam Museum. It too is available in a three volume reprint. It is usually referred to as Grose, in favor of the cataloguer.

The eight volume catalogue produced by Henri Cohen in the 1890s is primarily a catalogue of Roman Imperial coins, but it also includes the provincial coins with latin legends. Because of this, it is still a useful reference to these issues. It is available in a reprint.

An original *Historia Numorum,* by Barclay Head, is in itself a collectible. No need to worry, it has been reprinted several times. This work, primarily about Greek coins, is also very useful for information about the cities which struck provincial coins.

Another specialized work about Greek coins that is also useful for provincial coins is Anson's *Numismata Graeca* (See bibliography, p. 154). Although a bit outdated, this 13 volume set is still a valuable resource for the attribution of difficult coins.

BIBLIOGRAPHY

Reference Catalogues

BMC. *A Catalogue of Greek Coins in the British Museum,* 29 volumes, London, 1873-1927.

Burnett, Amandry & Ripollès. *Roman Provincial Coins,* London and Paris, 1992.

Cohen, Henri *Description Historique des Monnais frappées sous l'Empire Romain,* Paris 1880-92, reprint, Graz, 1955.

Head, Barclay V. *Historia Numorum,* London, 1911, Durst reprint, 1986.

Lindgren, Henry Clay (Vol I with Frank Kovacs). *Ancient Greek Bronze Coins of Asia Minor and the Levant from the Lindgren Collection,* 2 volumes, San Francisco, 1989-1992.

_____. *Ancient Greek Bronze Coins: European Mints,* San Francisco, 1994.

Sear, David R. *Greek Imperial Coins and their values,* London, 1995.

SNG Copenhagen: The Danish National Museum, 43 volumes, Copenhagen, 1942-77(reprinted in 7 volumes, New Jersey, 1982.)

SNG Tübingen. *Münzsammlung der Universität, Tübingen,* Tübingen, 1981.

SNG Von Aulock: The Collection Hans Von Aulock, 18 volumes, Berlin, 1957-68 (reprinted in 4 volumes, New Jersey, 1987.)

Reading Inscriptions

Reading the legends on Provincial coinage is perhaps the most intimidating and seemingly difficult aspect of attribution. Unfortunately, the attribution of a coin often requires that the legend be read. There are no comprehensive catalogues in this series, and there are literally thousands of unpublished varieties. Therefore, one cannot rely on visually matching a coin with a picture in some book. Aside from the comparatively few colonial coins with Latin inscriptions, the legends are typically written in Greek. Still, they are not as difficult to deal with

Dissection of a Provincial Coin Legend

we find in the exergue:
AUKLCECE
OVHROC
(AY. K. L. CE. CEOVHPOC)
=
Augustus, Caesar
L. Septimius Severus

around the outer edge:
LCEGETACKAVKMAANTWNIN
(L. CE. GETAC K. AV. K.
M. A. ANTWNIN)
=
L. Septimius Geta and
Marcus Aurelius Antoninus

within the wreath:
PROTA• KOINA
ACIAC CMVPNAIWN
=
First State of Asia, Smyrna

around the outer edge:
EPICTRAKLROVFINOVCOFI
(EPI. CTRA. KL.
ROVFINOV COFI)
=
Eponymous Strategos
Claudius Rufinus, Sophist

as one might think. Unlocking the mystery of a Provincial coin inscription is something like working a crossword puzzle. It is usually necessary to identify certain pieces before others become obvious. Like an Imperial Roman coin, the obverse legend of a provincial coin usually includes the titles of the emperor and his name. The titles are often rendered in Greek, but there are few enough of them to commit to memory. The names will become obvious once the Greek to Latin alphabet transitions are made. ΓΕΤΑ, for example, quickly becomes GETA and before long the mind automatically makes these conversions.

GREEK to ENGLISH
alphabet conversion

Α—short *A* like in father --	**A**
Β—similar to English *B* ----	**B**
Γ—similar to English *Gh* --	**G**
Δ—similar to English *Th* --	**D**
Ε—short *E* as in Epic --------	**E**
Η—*E* as in them ------------	**H**
Θ—*Th* as in thing ------------	
Ι—short *I* as in intrigue -----	**I**
Κ—hard *K* sound -----------	**K**
Λ—similar to English *L* -----	**L**
Μ—similar to English *M* -	**M**
Ν—similar to English *N* ---	**N**
Ξ—*X* as in Alexander --------	
Ο—long *O* as in obey ------	**O**
Π—similar to English *P* ----	**P**
Ρ—similar to English *R* ----	**R**
Σ—similar to English *S* -----	**S**
Τ—similar to English *T* ----	**T**
Υ—short *Y* as in abyss -----	**Y**
Φ—similar to English *Ph* ---	**F**
Χ—similar to English *Kh* --	**C**
Ψ—*Ps* as in Terpsichore -----	
Ω—Long *O* sound -----------	
ω—Long *O* sound -----------	
C—Lunate sigma, like *S* ----	**S**
Є—short *E* as in Epic --------	**E**

The alphabet conversion chart to the right lists the most common Greek letter forms found in the provincial era. One can readily see that there are a few letters without equivalents. There is not an "F" for example in the Greek alphabet, but the letter Φ creates the sound of PH which is close enough for most purposes. Likewise, the "X" in Greek may be likened to a "C" in latin. The letters Ω and ω represent forms of "O". Another peculiarity is the ligature. That is, two or more letters tied together to make one. The most familiar to Latin students is the dipthong Æ. Coin inscriptions include several more, which will take a bit of patience.

For those who lack a background in classical languages, don't despair. Many collectors of Provincial coins begin without knowing a word of Greek or Latin. Start with some coins which have very simple short legends and try reading them. Like anything else, it gets easier with practice.

The lunate sigma, which looks like C, may appear interchangeably with Σ, especially in later inscriptions. It has the same effect as the "soft C" in English, as in Censor—with an "S" sound. In Latin, the "C" is hard, like an English "K". On provincial coins we find COL, in Latin, for Colonia—which is pronounced like

Colony in English. We also find CEBASTE, for Sebaste or "Augustus", in which the lunate sigma is pronounced with an S sound. Since there was not a Greek equivalent for the Latin V, the letter B or the dipthong OY was normally substituted. This can cause some initial confusion in reading names like ΟΥΑΛΕΡΙΑΝΟC (Valerian) and ΟΥΟΛΛΥCΙΑΝΟC (Volusian). Another strange one is OTAKICEBHPA (Otaci[lia] Severa).

Fortunately, there are several places where one can find the inscriptions most commonly encountered. Probably the most accessible is David R. Sear's *Greek Imperial Coins and their values.* This indispensable guide, organized by emperor or autonomous city and including representative types from most major mints, includes an appendix listing the provincial coin issuing cities in alphabetical order. Unfortunately, the cities are alphabetized by their Latin names, not their Greek inscriptions. It is therefore necessary to scan through the 25 page list to correlate a Greek inscription with the Latin name. But all is not lost.

In 1903 the French numismatist, A. Florance, published *Tableaux synoptiques des ethniques des villes et peuples grecs.* This very useful work, with a new English language introduction, was republished in 1966 as *Geographic Lexicon of Greek Coin Inscriptions* (Argonaut Publishers, Chicago). It provides an alphabetical listing of cities by their Greek ethnic. This is a great help, but sometimes it is impossible to read the entire inscription and the city name remains obscure. There is still hope.

In 1929, Dr. Severin Icard wrote *Identification des monnaies par la nouvelle méthode des lettres-jalons et des légendes fragmentées: Application de la méthode aux monnaies grecques et aux monnaies gauloises.* Don't let the title turn you away, as it has hundreds or maybe even thousands of other beginners. Argonaut also republished this work (1968) as *Dictionary of Greek Coin Inscriptions*—a somewhat better title for marketing. Icard is the Provincial coin collector's dream come true. It not only lists city ethnics alphabetically, it lists fragments of inscriptions alphabetically as well. Therefore, if you can only read the middle three letters of a word, as often is the case, chances are quite good that you will be able to identify the city—or at least narrow down the possibilities—by using Icard. If you only want to collect coins of one or two provincial cities, Icard will probably not be a great help. But if you want to wade through a pile of unattributed provincials, it will prove invaluable.

Finally, a helpful little book titled *Greek Numismatic Epigraphy,* by John E. Hartmann and George MacDonald (editorial compilation by Argonaut, Chicago, 1969), will give you more than enough information to sink your teeth into.

In case you're not quite ready for Florance, Icard et. al., the following pages include some common abbreviations and terms found on provincial coins. It is not possible in this short space to reproduce the comprehensive lists of Florance and Icard, however the practice coins are selected from cities on our abbreviated list. Once the place names are translated, look for related information in the geographical sections found earlier.

The sample page from Icard, shown below, illustrates the method used to search for inscriptions from fragmentary information. The fragments are arranged alphabetically, in the column to the left. The missing letter or letters may be found in the column to the right. This makes it possible to reconstruct a full city ethnic from only a small fragment of a coin's legend. This is a snap for modern computers, but Icard was indispensable to collectors of the pre-computer era.

SAMPLE PAGE FROM ICARD

ЄMЄ — 140 — E·NA

ЄMЄIA,_NEIOΣ (frag. c.) ; voir ...... N

ЄMЄIA·HPAIA, Argos *Argolidis* ...... N

EMEIOΣ, Alexandria *Aegypti* ...... ZЄYΣ N

ЄMЄCIC, Tium *Bithyniae* ...... N

EMHΣ, Telmessus *Lyciae* ...... TEΛMHΣΣEΩN vel TEΛ

ƎMI vel AЯƎMI (rétrogr. = IMEPA·ION), Himera *Siciliae* ...... ИOI·Aꟼ

EMI (frag. c.) ; voir ...... ϟEΓEϟTAΞIB... vel ϟAΓEϟTAΞIB

EMIΔΩPOY, Artemidorus, rex *Bactrianae* ...... BAΣIΛEΩΣ ANIKHTOY APT

EMINAKO, Eminacus, rex *Thraciae*.

ЄMIC,_MIΔ·OΣ (frag. c.) ; voir ...... APT

ЄMICA_CHNΩN_CΩN, Emisa *Syriae*.

EMI ΣHMA, Ephesus *Ioniae* ...... ΦANOΣ

EMIΣTOKΛEOΣ,_KΛHC (frag. c) ; voir ...... Θ

ЄMICΩN, Emisa *Syriae* ...... MHTPO KOΛ

ЄMICΩNЄΩN, Themisonium *Phrygiae* ...... ⊙

ЄMICΩN KOΛΩNIAC, Emisa *Syriae*.

ЄM MAPKOY HPΩOC TO B, Byzantium *Thraciae* ...... ЄΠI M

ЄMMONIACIA, Magnesia ad Sipylum *Lydiae*.

EMO R REMO, *Gallia* Remi, *br.* B.136 ...... R

ЄMONIA, Perperene *Mysiae* ...... HΓ

ƎMOΠ (rétrogr. = ΠOMEΣ FΣΣM), Poseidonia *Lucaniae* ...... MΣΣƎ.Σ

EMOΣ, Delos, ins. *Cycladum* ...... AΘE O Δ

ЄMOTЄIXЄITΩN, Panemoteichos *Pisidiae* ...... ΠAN

EMOY, Alexander, rex *Epiri* ...... AΛEΞANΔPOY TOY NEOΠTOΛ

EMOY (frag. c.) ; voir ...... EYΓOΛ

ЄMOVPЄΩN,_PIЄΩN, Anemurium *Ciliciae* ...... AN

ЄMOYCIA,_CIΩN, Anthemusia *Mesopotamiae* ...... ANΘ

EM ΠIEPIAI, Seleuceia *Syriae* ...... ΣEΛEYKEΩN TΩN

EM·Π·OPITΩN vel ENΠOPITΩN, Emporium *Hispaniae*.

ƎMYꟼYƎ (rétrogr. = EYPYMEΔO), Selinus *Siciliae* ...... OΔ

ЄMΦЄITHC vel MЄMΦI, Memphytes, nomus *Aegypti* ...... NOMOC M

EMΦOEY NOMOC, Phtemphytes, nomus *Aegypti* ...... ΦΘ

EMΩN,_MΩNOΣ,_MOY (frag. c.); voir ...... ΠOΛ

EN, Enchelli *Illyriae* ; Entella et Enna *Siciliae*.

EN, Mende *Macedoniae* ; Menelaus, rex Salaminis *Cypri* ...... M

EN, Diocaesarae Sepphoris *Galilaeae* ...... TPAIANOC AYTOKPATΩP EΔΩK

E·NAIΩN, Imbros, ins. *Thraciae* ...... AΘ

The following sample page from *Geographic Lexicon of Greek Coin Inscriptions* illustrates the method used by Florance to record inscriptions. The entries are arranged alphabetically. Notice that the regular sigma and the later lunate sigma (which looks like a C) are not segregated. The authority, city and district are arranged in columns to the right.

SAMPLE PAGE FROM FLORANCE

— 82 —

ΣΕΛΥΜΙΥΣ	Auton.	Sillyum	Pamphyliae.
ξΕΝΣΕΡ.	»	Hyria (?)	Campaniae.
CЄΟΥΗ.ΑΝΤωΝ? ΝΙ-ΚΟΠΟΛΙC	Imp.	Nicopolis Emmaus	Palæstinae.
ΣΕΠΦΩΡΗΝΩΝ	»	Sepphoris (Diocaesareia)	Galilaeae.
ΜΕΡ.	Auton.	Ser. . .	Bruttii.
ξΕΡ	»	Seriphos, insula	Cycladum.
CЄΡΔΙΚΗC (ΟΥΛ-ΠΙΑC)	Imp.	Serdica	Thraciae.
CЄΡΔΩΝ	»	»	»
CЄΡЄΙΦΙΩΝ et ΙωΝ	»	Seriphos, insula	Cycladum.
ξΕΡΙ.	Auton.	» »	»
ξΕΡΜΥΛΙΚΟΝ	»	Sermyle	Macedoniae.
CЄΥ (Severiana)	Imp.	Amasia	Ponti.
ξΗ ; ξΗξ	Auton.	Sestus	Chers. Thraciae.
ξΗξΑ ; ξΗξΑΜ	»	Sesamus	Paphlagoniae.
ξΗξΤΙ	»	Sestus	Chers. Thraciae.
CΗCΤΙΩΝ (ou ΤΙωΝ)	Imp.	»	»
ΣΙ	Auton.	Sicinos, insula	Cycladum.
—	»	Sicyon	Sicyoniae.
—	»	Sidon	Phoeniciae.
— (en monogr.)	»	Sigeum	Troadis.
—	»	Sinope	Paphlagoniae.
—	Fédérales.	Sidyma	Lyciae.
CΙΒΙΔΟΥΝΔЄΩΝ	Imp.	Sibidunda	Phrygiae.
ΣΙΒΛΙΑΝΩΝ	»	Siblia	»
ΣΙΓΕ.	Auton.	Sigeium	Troadis.
ΣΙΔ. ; ΣΙΔΗΤΩΝ	»	Side	Pamphyliae.
CΙΔΗΤΩΝ, CΙΔΗC	Imp.	»	»
ΣΙΔΙΝΩΝ	Auton.	Incert.	Italiae.
ΣΙΔΩΝΙΩΝ	»	Sidon	Phoeniciae.
ΣΙΔΩΝΟΣ	Imp.	Sidon	Phoeniciae.
ΣΙΚΕΛΙΑ ; ΣΙΚΕΛΙΩ-ΤΑΝ	Auton.	Syracusae et Alaesa	Siciliae.
ΣΙΚΙ	»	Sicinos, insula	Cycladum.

TITLES AND ABBREVIATIONS

INSCRIPTION	TERM	MEANING
ΑΔ, ad	*(preposition)*	*on, at, by*
ΑΡ, ΑΡΙ, ΑΡΙΣ, ΑΡΙΣΤ	*Aristos*	*Optimus*
ΑΝΕΘΗΚΕΝ	*Anetheken*	*Dedicated (it)*
ΑΝΘΥΠΑΤΟΣ	*Anthepatos*	*Proconsul*
ΑΡΜ, ΑΡΜΕΝΙΑΚΟϹ	*Armeniacus*	*Armeniacus**
ΑΡΧΙΕΡΕΥΣ (ΙΑ)	*Archierus (ia)*	*Chief Priest(ess)*
ΑΡΧΩΝ	*Archon*	*Chief Magistrate*
ΑϹϹΑΡΙΑ	*Assaria*	*monetary unit*
ΑΣΙΑΡΧΗΣ	*Asiarches*	*Asiarch*
ΑΣΥΛΟΥ	*Asylia*	*Inviolable*
ΑΥ. ΑΥΤ, ΑΥΤΟΚΡ	*Autokrator*	*Emperor*
ΑΥΤ, ΑΥΤΟΝΟΜΟΣ	*Autonomous*	*Free*
ΑΥΓ, ΑΥΓΟΥϹΤΟϹ (Α)	*Augustus (a)*	*Augustus (a)*
ΒΑΣΙΛΕΩΣ	*Basileus*	*King*
ΒΡΙΤ, ΒΡΙΤΤΑΝΙΚΟϹ	*Brittanicus*	*Brittanicus**
ΒΟΥΛΗ	*Boule*	*The Senate*
ϹΑΡ, ϹΑΡΜΑΤΙΚΟϹ	*Sarmaticus*	*Sarmaticus**
Ϲ, ϹΕ, ϹΕΒ, ϹΕΒΑΣΤ	*Sebastos (e)*	*Augustus (a)*
ϹΟΦΙ, ΣΟΦΙΣΤΗΣ	*Sophist*	*Educator*
ΔΑΚ, ΔΑΚΙΚ	*Dacicus*	*Dacicus**
ΔΗΜΑΡΧ ΕΞ	*Demarch. Ex.*	*Tr. Pot.*
ΕΝΔΟΞΟΣ	*Endoxos*	*Illustrious*
Ε, ΕΠΙ	*(preposition)*	*On, of*
ΕΤΟΥϹ	*Etoyc*	*Year*
ΕΥ, ΕΥΣ, ΕΥΣΕΒ	*Eusebes*	*Pious*
ΕΥΤΥ, ΕΥΤΥΧΗϹ	*Felix*	*Fortune*
ΦΙΛΗ	*Fili*	*Friend*
ΓΕΡ, ΓΕΡΜ	*Germanicus*	*Germanicus**
ΙΕΡΕΥΣ (Α)	*Iereus (a)*	*Priest(ess)*

ΙΕΡΟC	*Ieros*	*Sacred*
ΙΠΠΙΚΟΣ	*Hippikos*	*Knight*
Κ, ΚΑΙ, ΚΑΙΣ, ΚΑΙCΑΡ	*Caesar*	*Caesar*
ΚΑΙ	*(conjunction)*	*And*
ΚΑΛΛΙΣΤΕ, (K. in AMK)	*Kalliste*	*Most Beautiful*
ΚΟ, ΚΟΙ, ΚΟΙΝΟΝ	*Koinon*	*Council*
ΚΟΛ, ΚΟΛΩΝΙΑ	*Colonia*	*Colony*
ΜΕΓΙΣΤΗ, (M. in AMK)	*Megiste*	*Greatest*
ΜΕΤ, ΜΕΤΡΟ, ΜΕΤΡΟΠΟ	*Metropolis*	*Mother City*
ΝΑΥΑΡΧΙΣ	*Navarchis*	*Imperial Port*
ΝΕΩΚΟΡΟΣ	*Neocorus*	*Temple Keeper*
ΟΒΟΛΟC	*Obolos*	*Unit = 2 Assaria*
ΠΑΡ, ΠΑΡΘ, ΠΑΡΘΙΚΟC	*Parthicus*	*Parthicus**
ΠΠ, ΠΑΤ, ΠΑΤΡ	*Pater Patridos*	*Father of his country*
ΠΡΟΣ	*(preposition)*	*By*
ΠΡΟΤΗ, (A. in AMK)	*Prote*	*First*
ΡΩΜΑΙΩΝ	*Romaion*	*(Of The) Romans*
ΣΑΡ, ΣΑΡΜΑΤΙΚΠΣ	*Sarmaticus*	*Sarmaticus**
Σ, ΣΕ, ΣΕΒ, ΣΕΒΑΣΤ	*Sebastos (e)*	*Augustus (a)*
ΣΤΡΑΤΕΓΟΣ	*Strategos*	*Chief Magistrate*
ΤΑΜΙΑΣ	*Tamias*	*Treasurer*
ΤΕΤΡΑΡΧ, ΤΕΤΡΑΡΧΟΥ	*Tetrarchos*	*Ruler*
ΤΗΣ	*(feminine article)*	*The*
ΤΩ, ΤΩΝ	*(masculine article)*	*The*
ΘΕΟΥ, ΘΕΟΣ, ΘΕΟC	*Theos*	*Divine*
ΧΑΛΚΟΝ	*Chalkon*	*Unit = 1/4 Assaria*
ΥΠΑΤΟC	*Upatos*	*Consul*

* *Title indicating the conqueror of........., as in Armenia, Dacia, etc.*

note: Due to lack of space, or individual preference, die-engravers often used shorter or longer abbreviations, often abbreviating a string of words to a single letter each. Dates may also be found within a legend.

Mint Cities by Province

Aeolis .... *Aegae*
Aeolis .... *Cyme*
Aeolis .... *Elaea*
Aeolis .... *Myrina*
Aeolis .... *Temnus*
Amorgos (Cyclades) . *Aegiale*
Amorgos (Cyclades) . *Minoa*
Arabia Petraea .... *Adraa*
Arabia Petraea .... *Bostra*
Arabia Petraea .... *Charachmoba*
Arabia Petraea .... *Dium*
Arabia Petraea .... *Eboda*
Arabia Petraea .... *Esbus*
Arabia Petraea .... *Gerasa*
Arabia Petraea .... *Medaba*
Arabia Petraea .... *Petra*
Arabia Petraea .... *Philadelphia*
Arabia Petraea .... *Philippopolis*
Arabia Petraea .... *Rabbathmoba*
Attica .... *Athens*
Attica .... *Oropus*
Bithynia .... *Apameia*
Bithynia .... *Bithynium (Claudiopolis)*
Bithynia .... *Caesarea Germanica*
Bithynia .... *Calchedon*
Bithynia .... *Cius*
Bithynia .... *Claudiopolis*
Bithynia .... *Creteia Flaviopolis*
Bithynia .... *Heracleia Pontica*
Bithynia .... *Juliopolis*
Bithynia .... *Nicaea*
Bithynia .... *Nicomedia*
Bithynia .... *Prusa ad Olympum*
Bithynia .... *Prusias ad Hypium*
Bithynia .... *Tium*
Boeotia .... *Thebes*
Boeotia .... *Thespiae*
Bosporus .... *Agrippia Caesarea*
Bpeptoa .... *Tamagra*
Byzacene .... *Achulla*
Byzacene .... *Hadrumetum*
Byzacene .... *Leptis Minor*
Byzacene .... *Thaena*
Byzacene .... *Thapsus*
Byzacene .... *Thysdrus*
Cappadocia .... *Caesarea*
Cappadocia .... *Tyana*
Caria .... *Alabanda*
Caria .... *Alinda*
Caria .... *Amyzon*
Caria .... *Antiochia ad Maeandrum*
Caria .... *Aphrodisias*
Caria .... *Apollonia Salbace*
Caria .... *Attuda*
Caria .... *Bargasa*
Caria .... *Bargylia*
Caria .... *Ceramus*
Caria .... *Cidramus*
Caria .... *Cnidus*
Caria .... *Cys*
Caria .... *Euippe*
Caria .... *Euromus*
Caria .... *Harpasa*
Caria .... *Heracleia Salbace*
Caria .... *Hydisus*
Caria .... *Hyllarima*
Caria .... *Iasus*
Caria .... *Mylasa*
Caria .... *Myndus*
Caria .... *Neopolis ad Harpasum*
Caria .... *Orthosia*
Caria .... *Sebastopolis*
Caria .... *Stratoniceia*
Caria .... *Tabae*
Caria .... *Trapezopolis*
Caria .... *Tymnesus*
Cephallenia .... *Cranii*
Cilicia .... *Adana*
Cilicia .... *Aegeae*
Cilicia .... *Alexandria ad Issum*
Cilicia .... *Anazarbus*
Cilicia .... *Anemurium*
Cilicia .... *Antiochia ad Cragum*
Cilicia .... *Augusta*
Cilicia .... *Carallia*
Cilicia .... *Casae*
Cilicia .... *Celenderis*
Cilicia .... *Cestrus*
Cilicia .... *Claudiopolis*
Cilicia .... *Colybrassus*
Cilicia .... *Coracesium*
Cilicia .... *Coropisus*
Cilicia .... *Corycus*
Cilicia .... *Diocaesarea*
Cilicia .... *Epiphaneia*
Cilicia .... *Flaviopolis*
Cilicia .... *Germanicopolis*
Cilicia .... *Hieropolis Castabala*
Cilicia .... *Iotape*
Cilicia .... *Irenopolis*
Cilicia .... *Isaura Nova*
Cilicia .... *Laerte*
Cilicia .... *Lamus*
Cilicia .... *Lyrbe*
Cilicia .... *Mallus*
Cilicia .... *Mopsus*
Cilicia .... *Myus*
Cilicia .... *Ninica Claudiopolis*
Cilicia .... *Olba*
Cilicia .... *Philadelphia*
Cilicia .... *Pompeiopolis*
Cilicia .... *Seleuceia ad Calycadnum*
Cilicia .... *Selinus*
Cilicia .... *Soli-Pompeiopolis*
Cilicia .... *Syedra*
Cilicia .... *Tarsus*
Cilicia .... *Titiopolis*
Cilicia .... *Zephyrium-Hadrianopolis*
Crete .... *Axus*
Crete .... *Cnossus*

Crete	*Cydonia*
Crete	*Eleutherna*
Crete	*Gortyna*
Crete	*Hierapytna*
Crete	*Lappa*
Crete	*Latus*
Crete	*Lyttus*
Crete	*Polyrhenium*
Cyclades	*Andros*
Cyclades	*Gyaros*
Cyclades	*Ios*
Cyclades	*Melos*
Cyclades	*Myconos*
Cyclades	*Naxos*
Cyclades	*Paros*
Cyclades	*Pholegandros*
Cyclades	*Seriphos*
Cyclades	*Siphnos*
Cyclades	*Syros*
Cyclades	*Tenos*
Cyclades	*Thera*
Egypt	*Alexandria*
Epirus	*Buthrotum*
Epirus	*Cassope*
Epirus	*Nicopolis*
Epirus	*Phoenice*
Euboea	*Carystus*
Euboea	*Chalcis*
Euboea	*Eretria*
Galatia	*Ancyra*
Galatia	*Germa*
Galatia	*Pessinus*
Galatia	*Tavium*
Galilaea	*Diocaesarea-Sepphoris*
Galilaea	*Sepphoris*
Galilaea	*Tiberias*
Gallia	*Bienna*
Gallia	*Cabellio*
Gallia	*Lugdunum*
Gallia	*Nemausus*
Greece	*Corinth*
Hispania	*Abdera*
Hispania	*Acci*
Hispania	*Bilbilis*
Hispania	*Caesaraugusta*
Hispania	*Calagurris*
Hispania	*Carteia*
Hispania	*Carthago Nova*
Hispania	*Cascantum*
Hispania	*Celsa*
Hispania	*Clunia*
Hispania	*Corduba*
Hispania	*Dertosa*
Hispania	*Ebora*
Hispania	*Emerita*
Hispania	*Eracavica*
Hispania	*Graccurris*
Hispania	*Hispalis*
Hispania	*Ilercavonia with Dertosa*
Hispania	*Ilerda*
Hispania	*Illici*
Hispania	*Irippo*
Hispania	*Italica*
Hispania	*Italica*
Hispania	*Julia Traducta*
Hispania	*Laelia*
Hispania	*Oba*
Hispania	*Osca*
Hispania	*Osicerda*
Hispania	*Osset*
Hispania	*Pax Julia*
Hispania	*Saguntum*
Hispania	*Segobriga*
Hispania	*Segovia*
Hispania	*Tarraco*
Hispania	*Turiaso*
Hispania	*Urso*
Illyricum	*Apollonia*
Ionia	*Clazomenae*
Ionia	*Colophon*
Ionia	*Ephesus*
Ionia	*Erythrae*
Ionia	*Lebedus*
Ionia	*Magnesia ad Maeandrum*
Ionia	*Metropolis*
Ionia	*Miletus*
Ionia	*Neapolis*
Ionia	*Phocaea*
Ionia	*Priene*
Ionia	*Smyrna*
Ionia	*Teos*
Ionian Island	*Chios*
Island near Lesbos	*Poroselene*
Island of Attica	*Aegina*
Island of Caria	*Cos*
Island of Cilicia	*Seabaste (Elaeusa-Sebaste)*
Island of Ionia	*Samos*
Island of Thessaly	*Peparethus*
Island of Thrace	*Samothrace*
Island of Thrace	*Thasos*
Island off Caria	*Astypalaea*
Island off Caria	*Rhodus*
Island off Elis	*Zacynthus*
Island off Epirus	*Corcyra*
Island off Troas	*Tenedos*
Italia	*Paestum*
Judaea	*Aelia Capitolina*
Judaea	*Anthedon*
Judaea	*Ascalon*
Judaea	*Eleutheropolis*
Judaea	*Gaza*
Judaea	*Jerusalem*
Judaea	*Nicopolis-Emmaus*
Judaea	*Raphia*
Lemnos	*Hephaestia*
Lesbos	*Eresus*
Lesbos	*Methymna*
Lesbos	*Mytilene*
Locris	*Opus*
Lycaibua	*Hyde*
Lycaonia	*Barata*
Lycaonia	*Dalisandus*
Lycaonia	*Derbe*
Lycaonia	*Iconium*
Lycaonia	*Ilistra*
Lycaonia	*Laodiceia Combusta*

Lycaonia	*Laranda*
Lycaonia	*Lystra*
Lycaonia	*Parlais*
Lycaonia	*Savatra*
Lycia	*Acalisus*
Lycia	*Antiphellus*
Lycia	*Aperlae*
Lycia	*Araxa*
Lycia	*Arneae*
Lycia	*Arycanda*
Lycia	*Balbura*
Lycia	*Bubon*
Lycia	*Candyba*
Lycia	*Choma*
Lycia	*Corydalla*
Lycia	*Cyane*
Lycia	*Gagae*
Lycia	*Limyra*
Lycia	*Masicytes*
Lycia	*Myra*
Lycia	*Olympus*
Lycia	*Patara*
Lycia	*Phaselis*
Lycia	*Phellus*
Lycia	*Podalia*
Lycia	*Rhodiapolis*
Lycia	*Termessus Minor*
Lycia	*Tlos*
Lycia	*Trebenna*
Lydia	*Aninetus*
Lydia	*Apollonieron*
Lydia	*Apollonis*
Lydia	*Attaleia*
Lydia	*Bagis*
Lydia	*Blaundus*
Lydia	*Briula*
Lydia	*Came*
Lydia	*Cibiani (Upper)*
Lydia	*Cilbiani (Lower)*
Lydia	*Daldis*
Lydia	*Dioshieron*
Lydia	*Germe*
Lydia	*Gordus-Julia*
Lydia	*Hierocaesarea*
Lydia	*Hypaepa*
Lydia	*Hyrcanis*
Lydia	*Indi-Stratoniceia*
Lydia	*Maeonia*
Lydia	*Magnesia ad Sipylum*
Lydia	*Mastaura*
Lydia	*Mostene*
Lydia	*Nicaea*
Lydia	*Nysa*
Lydia	*Philadelphia*
Lydia	*Saïtta*
Lydia	*Sala*
Lydia	*Sardes*
Lydia	*Silandus*
Lydia	*Stratoniceia-Hadrianopolis*
Lydia	*Tabala*
Lydia	*Thyatira*
Lydia	*Titacazus*
Lydia	*Tmolus Aureliopolis*
Lydia	*Tomaris*
Lydia	*Tralles*
Lydia	*Tripolis*
Macedon	*Amphipolis*
Macedon	*Beroea*
Macedon	*Cassandreia*
Macedon	*Dium*
Macedon	*Edessa*
Macedon	*Heracleia Sintica*
Macedon	*Pella*
Macedon	*Philippi*
Macedon	*Stobi*
Macedon	*Thessalonica*
Mauretania	*Caesarea*
Mauretania	*Tingis*
Megaris	*Aegosthena*
Megaris	*Megara*
Megaris	*Pagae*
Mesopotamia	*Anthemusia*
Mesopotamia	*Carrhae*
Mesopotamia	*Edessa*
Mesopotamia	*Nisibis*
Mesopotamia	*Rhesaena*
Mesopotamia	*Singara*
Moesia Inferior	*Callatis*
Moesia Inferior	*Dionysopolis*
Moesia Inferior	*Istrus*
Moesia Inferior	*Marcianopolis*
Moesia Inferior	*Nicopolis ad Isturm*
Moesia Inferior	*Tomis*
Moesia Superior	*Viminacium*
Mysia	*Adramyteum*
Mysia	*Apollonia ad Rhyndacum*
Mysia	*Attaea*
Mysia	*Cyzicus*
Mysia	*Hadrianeia*
Mysia	*Hadriani ad Olympum*
Mysia	*Hadrianothera*
Mysia	*Lampsacus*
Mysia	*Miletopolis*
Mysia	*Parium*
Mysia	*Pergamum*
Mysia	*Perperene*
Mysia	*Pitane*
Mysia	*Poemanenon*
Pamphylia	*Aspendus*
Pamphylia	*Attalia*
Pamphylia	*Magydus*
Pamphylia	*Perga*
Pamphylia	*Side*
Pamphylia	*Sillyum*
Paphlagonia	*Abonuteichus*
Paphlagonia	*Amastris*
Paphlagonia	*Germanicopolis*
Paphlagonia	*Ionopolis*
Paphlagonia	*Neoclaudiopolis*
Paphlagonia	*Pompeiopolis (Sebaste)*
Paphlagonia	*Sebaste*
Paphlagonia	*Sinope*
Peloponnesus	*Thuria*
Peloponnesus	*Aegeira*
Peloponnesus	*Aegium*
Peloponnesus	*Argos*

Pisidia	Sibidunda
Pisidia	Termessus Major
Pisidia	Timbriada
Pisidia	Tityassus
Pontus	Amasia
Pontus	Amisus
Pontus	Cerasus
Pontus	Neocaesarea
Pontus	Nicopolis ad Lycum
Pontus	Sebasteia
Pontus	Sebastopolis-Heracleopolis
Pontus	Trapezus
Pontus	Zela
Samaria	Antipatris
Samaria	Caesarea
Samaria	Diospolis-Lydda
Samaria	Joppa
Samaria	Neapolis
Samaria	Nysa-Scythopolis
Samaria	Sebaste
Sarmatia	Olbia
Sarmatia	Tyra
Sicily	Agrigentum
Sicily	Lilybaeum
Sicily	Panormus
Sicily	Segesta
Syria: Chalcidice	Chalcis
Syria: Coele-Syria	Damascus
Syria: Coele-Syria	Demetrias
Syria: Coele-Syria	Heliopolis
Syria: Coele-Syria	Laodiceia ad Libanum
Syria: Coele-Syria	Leucas on the Chrysoroas
Syria: Commagene	Antiochia ad Euphratem
Syria: Commagene	Doliche
Syria: Commagene	Germanicia Caesarea
Syria: Commagene	Samosata
Syria: Commagene	Zeugma
Syria: Cyrrhestica	Cyrrhus
Syria: Cyrrhestica	Hieropolis
Syria: Decapolis	Abila
Syria: Decapolis	Canata or Canatha
Syria: Decapolis	Capitolias
Syria: Decapolis	Gadara
Syria: Decapolis	Pella
Syria: Palmyrene	Palmyra
Syria: Seleucis/Pieria	Antiochia ad Orontem
Syria: Seleucis/Pieria	Emisa
Syria: Seleucis/Pieria	Gabala
Syria: Seleucis/Pieria	Laodiceia ad Mare
Syria: Seleucis/Pieria	Nicopolis Seleucidis
Syria: Seleucis/Pieria	Paltus
Syria: Seleucis/Pieria	Raphanea
Syria: Seleucis/Pieria	Rhosus
Syria: Seleucis/Pieria	Seleuceia Pieria
Syria: Seleucis/Pieria	Apameia
Syria: Trachonitis	Caesarea Panias
Syria: Trachonitis	Gaba
Syrtica	Leptis Magna
Syrtica	Macaraea and Bilan
Syrtica	Sabratha
Syrtica	Oea
Thessaly	Magnetes
Thrace	Abdera
Thrace	Anchialus
Thrace	Apollonia Pontica
Thrace	Augusta Trajana
Thrace	Bizya
Thrace	Byzantium
Thrace	Coela
Thrace	Deultum
Thrace	Elaeus
Thrace	Hadrianopolis
Thrace	Maroneia
Thrace	Mesembria
Thrace	Nicopolis ad Nestum
Thrace	Odessus
Thrace	Pautalia
Thrace	Perinthus
Thrace	Philippopolis
Thrace	Plotinopolis
Thrace	Serdica
Thrace	Sestus
Thrace	Topirus
Thrace	Trajanopolis
Thracian Island	Imbros
Troas	Abnydus
Troas	Alexandria
Troas	Antandrus
Troas	Assus
Troas	Dardanus
Troas	Gargara
Troas	Ilium
Troas	Pionia
Troas	Scepsis
Zeugitana	Carthage
Zeugitana	Clypea
Zeugitana	Hippo Diarrhytus
Zeugitana	Utica

***For a listing of cities sorted in alphabetical order, without regard to province and including Greek ethnics, we recommend David R. Sear's* Greek Imperial Coins and their values.**

Dates and Dating

Many provincial coins bear precise dates of issue. These are normally determined in one of two ways. The *era date* of a city, which is based on the year of its founding, or the *regnal date* of the reigning monarch may be recorded on the coin. In either case we can determine the date of issue if there is an historical record of the particular starting date..

Era dates can be a bit confusing. First of all, there were many different eras by which a city's date might be reckoned. The most common are included in a chart on the following two pages. It will be noticed that some cities have more than one era date. That is because changes in political fortune caused the refounding of certain cities. They typically restarted the numbering on coins issued after the new era date.

Regnal dates are more straightforward, except that a few rulers had more than one regnal date. This could happen if a ruler was driven from power and then regained the throne at some later date after an interruption in the coinage. The only place where this can really be a problem is in the coinage of client kings.

In either the era or regnal dating systems, we find that the year in Roman times does not synchronize with our calendar year today. Consequently, it is necessary to express the year in a split convention like AD 96/7, that is, in the latter part of AD 96 and early part of AD 97, unless we know in precisely which month an event occurred.

The dates may also be recorded in retrograde. This is not normally a problem as far as determining the correct reading because the letters for 10s and 100s are different than those for units. A few provincial coins use Roman numerals for recording the dates.

Those coins that do not bear recorded dates can sometimes be dated by the iconography if it relates to an imperial visit or the construction of a known monument or some other recorded historical event.

GREEK DATES

1	Α	20	Κ	100	Ρ
2	Β	30	Λ	200	Σ
3	Γ	40	Μ	300	Τ
4	Δ	50	Ν	400	Υ
5	Ε	60	Ξ	500	Φ
6	Ϛ	70	Ο	600	Χ
7	Ζ	80	Π	700	Ψ
8	Η	90	Ϙ	800	Ω
9	Θ				
10	Ι				

Greek dates are written in letters, and are read either from right to left or left to right. For example, the year 123 is written ΓΚΡ or ΡΚΓ, depending on the time and place. Since their calendar year did not start on January 1, as ours does, a Greek year will be expressed in overlapping dates like 148/7 BC or AD 147/8.

Era dates

Included in the following chart are the foundation dates of most cities which are known to have dated their coinage to a city era. Certain other cities used regnal dates of the reigning emperor.

City	Province	Era Dates
Abila	Syria	64 BC
Adraa	Arabia Petraea	AD105
Aegeae	Cilicia	47 BC
Alexandria ad Issum	Cilicia	67 BC
Amasia	Pontus	2 BC
Amisus	Pontus	32 BC
Anazarbus	Cilicia	19 BC
Antiochia ad Orontem	Syria	49 BC
		31 BC
Aradus	Phoenicia	259 BC
Ascalon	Judaea	104 BC
		58 BC
Augusta	Cilicia	AD 20
Beroea	Macedon	31 BC
Bostra	Arabia Petraea	AD 105
Botrys	Phoenicia	31 BC
Byblus	Phoenicia	31 BC
Caesarea Panias	Syria	3 BC
Caesarea ad Libanum	Phoenicia	312 BC
Canata *or* Canatha	Syria	64 BC
Capitolias	Syria	AD 97
Cerasus	Pontus	AD 64
Chalcis	Syria	AD 92
Cibyra	Phrygia	84 BC
Cibyra	Phrygia	AD 25
Damascus	Syria	312 BC
Dionysopolis	Phrygia	AD 152
Diospolis-Lydda	Samaria	AD 199
Dium	Arabia Petraea	64 BC
Dora	Phoenicia	64 BC
Eleutheropolis	Judaea	AD 199
Emisa	Syria	312 BC
Epiphaneia	Cilicia	68 BC
Flaviopolis	Cilicia	AD 73
Gaba	Syria	61 BC
Gabala	Syria	47 BC
Gadara	Syria	64 BC
Gaza	Judaea	61 BC
		AD 128

Gerasa	Arabia Petraea	64 BC
Germanicopolis	Paphlagonia	6 BC
Hyrgaleis	Phrygia	84 BC
Irneopolis	Cilicia	AD 52
Koinon of Pontus	Bithynia	AD 64
Laodiceia ad Lycum	Phrygia	AD 123
Laodiceia ad Mare	Syria	48 BC
Leucas on the Chrysoroas	Syria	38 BC
		AD 48
Mallus	Cilicia	68 BC
Medaba	Arabia Petraea	AD 105
Mopsus	Cilicia	68 BC
Neapolis	Samaria	AD 72
Neocaesarea	Pontus	AD 64
Neoclaudiopolis	Paphlagonia	6 BC
Nicopolis ad Lycum	Pontus	AD 64
Nicopolis-Emmaus	Judaea	AD 71
Nysa-Scythopolis	Samaria	64 BC
Orthosia	Phoenicia	312 BC
Paltus	Syria	259 BC
Pella	Syria	64 BC
Pessinus	Galatia	25 BC
Petra	Arabia Petraea	AD 105
Provincia Dacia	Pisidia	AD 246
Ptolemais-Ace	Phoenicia	48 BC
Rabbathmoba	Arabia Petraea	AD 105
Raphia	Judaea	60 BC
Rhosus	Syria	39 BC
Samosata	Syria	AD 71
Sebaste	Samaria	25 BC
Sebasteia	Pontus	2 BC
Sebastopolis-Heracleopolis	Pontus	3 BC
Seleuceia Pieria	Syria	109 BC
		31 BC
Sidon	Phoenicia	111 BC
Sinope	Paphlagonia	70 BC
		45 BC
Soli-Pompeiopolis	Cilicia	66 BC
Tavium	Galatia	25 BC
Tiberias	Galilaea	AD 20
Trapezus	Pontus	AD 64
Tripolis	Phoenicia	312 BC
Tyre	Phoenicia	126 BC
		AD 201
Viminacium	Moesia Superior	AD 239
Zela	Pontus	AD 64
Zephyrium-Hadrianopolis	Cilicia	68 BC

Coins for Reading Practice

A

B

C1 *C2* *C3*

A— Obv: ΑΛΕΞΑΝΔΡΟΥ=Alexander Rev: KOINON/ ΜΑΚΕΔΟΝΩΝ/Β ΝΕΩΚΟ=Koinon of Macedonia, 2nd Neokorate
B= Obv: AY/KAI/M/AURH ANTWNEINOC=Augustus Caesar Marcus Aurelius Antoninus Rev: ΚΥΖΙΚΗ ΝΩΝ/ΝΕ ΩΚΟΡ
C1— ΚΙΒΥΡΑΤΩΝ=Cibyra C2—ΝΙΚΑΙΕΩΝ= Nicaea C3—Philip I

Denominations

One will immediately notice when looking at provincial coins in a collection or sale catalogue that the bronze denominations are usually given simply in millimeters. This is because practically nothing is known about the bronze denominations, at least in the East, or their relationships. Silver coins do not fare a lot better. The Tetradrachm in Ephesus was equal to three denarii, but in Syria it was worth either three or four denarii depending on the reverse type, and in Egypt it was worth only one denarius. Some tetradrachms from Egypt are physically smaller than didrachms from Cappadocia—and worth only half as much. This can be terribly confusing, but the relationship is really important only to students of ancient metallurgy. The silver coins became standardized in the second century and a silver drachm weighed the same as a silver denarius. In fact, some drachms look so much like denarii that one has to look at the inscription to see if it is in Latin or Greek.

There were also attempts to standardize the bronze. At some Roman colonies, Antioch in Pisidia for example, the sestertius was replicated in size and design. Even the imperial mint SC may be found on certain provincial issues which parallel the Roman standard.

On rare occasions, the denomination was included in the coin's legends. But, on the whole, bronze coins followed a very poorly defined standard if any at all. Coins of the same ruler and type, even the same die, will often vary greatly in size and weight. This is due, no doubt, to the fact that the bronze was a token coinage and was tariffed at more than its intrinsic value. Within any particular city, at any particular time, we find the bronzes struck in fractional amounts. Although these too vary in size and weight, the relative proportions can be roughly established. One unit of value that occurred with some frequency was the *assaria.* It is not uncommon to find coins denominated in multiples of the assaria.

Caesarea, AR tridrachm
Gordian III, AD 241/2

Caesarea, AR didrachm
Gordian III, AD 241/2

Caesarea, AR drachm
Tranquillina, AD 241/2

BIBLIOGRAPHY

Attributing Provincial Coins

Anson, Leo. *Numismatica Graeca: Greek Coin Types Classified for Immediate Identification,* 13 Vols. 1910-16, available in reprint.

Florance, A. *Geographic Lexicon of Greek Coin Inscriptions,* Chicago, 1966.

Howgego, C.J. *Greek Imperial Countermarks,* London, 1985.

Icard, Severin. *Dictionary of Greek Coin Inscriptions,* Chicago, 1968.

Münsterberg, Rudolf. *Die beamtennamen auf denn grieschen münzen, geographisch und alphabetisch geordnet,* (Four 1911 Numismatischen Zeitschrift articles) reprinted in Germany, 1985.

Plant, R. *Greek Coin Types and Their Identification,* London, 1979.

Sear, David R. *Greek Coins and Their Values,* London, 1995.

Roman Provincial Iconography

One of the primary attractions to collectors of provincial coinage is the richness of its iconography. Roman Imperial coinage, and even that of the Hellenistic kings that ruled from Thrace to Egypt, is fairly conservative. To be sure, each has its notable types and there is much to be attracted to in each series, but neither approaches the Roman Provincial series in diversity or originality.

Caesarea, Cappadocia
Divus Augustus, AD 33/4
struck under Tiberius

The most remarkable feature of these coins, and the one that attracts many collectors, is the complexity of reverse types. We have included on the following pages a few of the popular themes that collectors tend to enjoy. For example, Architectural types are fairly common and sometimes are very sophisticated. Cultural themes like mythology, art, and literature abound. Also of interest are various public themes like entertainment, transportation and religion. Astrology (Astronomy) was a subject of great interest to the ancients just as it is to us. Many provincial coins bear references to astrological beliefs. Although we have discussed astrological motifs earlier in the section about Roman Egypt, we have included a further discussion here as it pertains to other parts of the empire.

Finally, we should not ignore the portraiture from provincial mints. There is a natural tendency for us to think of the Rome mint as a sort of standard for all others to emulate. This was not always the case. There are coins within the provincial series which far outshine, in terms of artistic execution, anything produced by the Rome mint. Therefore, the portrait collector will find fertile ground here for selecting examples which appeal to one's senses rather than simply to one's historical interest. We have included a very short essay about portraiture, which does not begin to do justice to the topic, but will hopefully spur interest and further consideration.

At the end of this section the reader will find a brief gallery of masterpieces from the world of provincial coinage. These vignettes should adequately illustrate the point that we are attempting to make here. Roman Provincial coins can be beautiful, exciting, intriguing and more.

Portrait Styles

Caracalla from Smyrna

Elagabalus from Kolossai

Because the titulature and formal names of Caracalla and his second cousin Elagabalus are identical, they are often confused, and not only by beginning collectors. Provincial coins are more susceptible to erroneous attribution than imperial coins because the latter often include titles and dates of office that clearly divide the two emperors. Mature portraits of Caracalla are relatively easy to identify, whether on imperial or provincial coinage, because of his distinctive scowl and angular features which convey the image of power. Youthful portraits are, however, another matter. Ann Johnston, in an enlightening discussion on the subject (*ANS Museum Notes* 27, 1982) helps to clear up some of the mystery.

Johnston begins by stating unequivocally that there are no infallible methods for 100% accuracy. Nevertheless, there are some helpful guidelines. First of all, the obverse legend may be totally disregarded. For every rule there are exceptions and they are needlessly confusing. One of the primary factors in identification of the subject is the portrait. As stated above, the mature portraits of Caracalla may be easily assigned. Elagabalus was a teenager during all of his reign, and even the Roman proclivity for enhancing the maturity of young rulers could not age his image beyond that of a young man. Consequently, the portraits of Caracalla at the age of 14 to 18 tend to look quite like those of Elagabalus at the same age.

The Roman historian Cassius Dio explains the probable cause of this familial likeness. In a ploy to gain acceptance for her grandson as a legitimate heir, Julia Maesa reportedly claimed that he had actually been fathered by Caracalla. She apparently succeeded in convincing the troops that there was a likeness at the same age. Maesa was the sister of Julia Domna—making Caracalla her nephew. A liaison between Caracalla and Maesa's daughter, Julia Soaemias, would therefore have been incestuous. That apparently did not weigh too heavily on the troops who acclaimed Elagabalus as emperor. Whether Elagabalus actually looked like Caracalla or not is irrelevent to our purpose of attributing the coinage. The fact is that the youthful portraits which appear on coinage are similar. Even so, Johnston suggests some recognizable differences in the portraits of these two rulers.

Elagabalus was never made to look childish, but rather as more mature than he actually was. Therefore the very youthful portraits may be assigned, like those of full maturity, to Caracalla. Also, Elagabalus chose to appear effiminate whereas Caracalla opted for a very masculine appearance. Dio relates that Elagabalus regularly had his facial hair removed to foster that image. The most distinctive features of Elagabalus, according to Johnston, are "large eyes with heavy lids, full lips, rounded nose and a generally rounded profile, and fairly close cropped hair." The large eyes are, of course, an artistic convention to emphasize the spirituality of the individual—who was himself priest of an Eastern cult. Caracalla, by contrast, was typically portrayed with full cheeks and an upturned nose with indented bridge.

Aside from the portrait itself, there are other factors which may shed light on the attribution. Sometimes it is possible to identify a magistrate through comparison of monograms, and thereby link a subject coin to others of a known series. Unfortunately for the beginner, this requires a rather sophisticated set of references. There are other similar techniques for identification, like analysis of denominations, engraving style, and die linkages between cities, which require good references and are beyond the scope of most newcomers to the field.

One other element of consideration that *is* within the ability of collectors without a reference library is the reverse type. Several types are peculiar to Caracalla, and thereby make an identification to him more certain. Naturally, any pairing with Septimius Severus, Julia Domna or Geta will immediately identify the figure as Caracalla. Likewise, a scene of two or more imperial figures seated or standing together is identifiable. Caracalla reigned with his father and brother for a time, and was often depicted with them, while Elagabalus was sole ruler. Also peculiar to Caracalla were a variety of warlike scenes depicting the emperor with a bound captive. Elagabalus (Heliogabalus) was a sun worshipper, and types depicting the sun, in a chariot for example, are more likely to belong to him than to Caracalla during his early years.

Finally, on certain issues, the surest way to separate the two rulers is by date or city titles. In the case of era dates, they can easily be read and the equivalent AD date worked out. City titles were also bestowed in a very formal way, and the dates of assumption can usually be worked out with a little research. For those who are able to obtain a copy of Johnston's article, a useful appendix, by city, records a variety of coins and their proper attributions.

Ninica-Claudiopolis, Cilicia, AD 235-238
AE 33mm under Maximinus I Thrax
two reverse varieties of the same basic issue portraying Maximus

It is difficult to assess the cause of divergent portrait types in the provincial series. Traditionally, the view has been taken that provincial mints often lacked current models from which to derive the physical features of a new ruler. This may well have been the case when the imperial chamber was entered through a revolving door, but the provinces were not entirely devoid of news and information. With the efficient communication system that the Romans maintained, it seems that provincial mints should have known enough about a new emperor and his family to portray them at representative ages—even if they didn't have immediate access to sculpted or painted models. The two specimens illustrated above depict Maximus, the son of Maximinus I, who was raised to the rank of Caesar when his father was acclaimed emperor in 235. As one can immediately detect, the boy is presented in one example (Reverse A) as a youth of not more than eight or nine years old. In the second example (Reverse B) he is portrayed as a young man, perhaps in his late teens or early twenties. Maximinus had served as governor of Mesopotamia under Severus Alexander, and the age of his son could hardly have been unknown to the Roman bureaucracy in nearby Cilicia. Amazingly, the two reverse types are linked to the same obverse die—so they can't be considered early and late issues of the reign (besides, not even a mighty Caesar could age that much in three years). Did mint officials add a few years to the young prince's image because they had erred early on, or did they advance his maturity for propagandistic purposes?

Architectural Coin Types

The monuments depicted on ancient coins give us a postcard view of the ancient world. Roman Imperial coins tend to give us a glimpse of Rome, but provincial coins take us on a tour of the entire ancient world. Many of the structures that we see on these coins are lost forever. Some may yet be resurrected. In the meantime, we can enjoy their fascination and marvel over their details simply by holding a small piece of metal up to the light.

The Lighthouse of Alexandria one of the Seven Wonders of the Ancient World AE drachm (x1.25), AD 148/9

On a bronze drachm from Alexandria, we see the personification of the city, Alexandria herself, holding a sail before the lighthouse known as the Pharos. This "Wonder of the Ancient World" is long since lost, but we can judge from the several artists' versions of it about what it must have looked like.

The multitude of temples and shrines seen on provincial coins are discussed on the following pages, but one shrine stands out, if for no other reason than its sheer size. That was the mountain called Argaeus, which was a sacred shrine in itself. It appears regularly on coins of Caesarea in Cappadocia, over a lengthy period. On several of the coin types honoring this sacred mountain, it is depicted on an altar—almost as if it were a miniature icon of the holy place. It is not unlikely that such icons were kept in private homes of the region much like religious icons are still kept in private homes today.

Mount Argaeus, Caesarea, Cappadocia, AE 31mm
Macrinus, AD 218

Temples and Shrines

The difference between a temple and a shrine is slight. The former is a place of worship, while the latter is a repository for an object of worship. Therefore, shrines will normally be depicted along with the object of worship, as in the Black Stone of Emesa or the Tyche of Antioch (see under "The Levant"). Temples are the most prevalent architectural motif on provincial coins, and usually the temples represented are specific structures. Some are identifiable and some remain obscure to us, but most of them probably existed at the time the coin was struck. Whether the details of their depiction are accurate or not is another matter. This question is treated at length by Drew-Bear (ANSMN 19).

At Pergamum, in the Fall of AD 214, the emperor Caracalla visited the shrine of Asklepios to entreat the god's healing powers for diseases that had been plaguing him. The success of that visit led to Caracalla's reconstruction of numerous temples at the city. A coin struck in Pergamum at that time depicts Caracalla overlooking a religious ceremony which includes a bull and a priest with a temple (identified as that of Asklepios) in the background. This same motif appears on a coin struck at Tarsus. The Tarsus coin, unfortunately, is not dated—but it would seem logical that it too was issued during Caracalla's passage through Asia Minor. Both of these coins seem to depict an important and widely practiced ceremony called the Bouphonia (see bibliography, Tameanko, *Butting Bulls*). This ceremony was held in honor of Zeus, and involved the leading of bulls to a place in which special grain cakes had been placed. The first bull to kneel and eat the cakes was chosen for the sacrifice—that is, he himself *chose* to be sacrificed. This sacrifice was conducted at seeding time to promote fecundity of the harvest.

Pergamum, Mysia, AE 46mm
Caracalla, AD 214
Temple of Asklepios?

Tarsus, Cilicia, AE 34mm
Caracalla, AD 198-217
Neocorate Temple?

Another identifiable temple appears on a pair of coins struck by Philip the Arab at Heliopolis, or the ancient city of Baalbek. The temple, portrayed in a frontal and side perspective, is that of Jupiter Heliopolitanus, which was built in the first century BC (see Price & Trell, pp. 159-66). In this particular cult, Jupiter was revered as the god of fertility and creation. The worship of this hybrid Roman-Semitic god exemplifies the practical tolerance and adaptability that allowed Roman administration to prosper in the provinces.

Heliopolis, Coele-Syria, AE 28-30mm
Philip I, AD 244-249
Temple of Jupiter Heliopolitanus

One major difference between temples of the Greek style and those of the Roman style is the aspect of enclosure. The Greek temple was basically a free and open structure, with columns surrounding a small sanctuary. As a structure it tended to say "Come In". The Roman temple was exactly the opposite. It was a very protective enclosure, with little outward appeal and practically no accessibility. It tended to say "Keep Out". The temple to the local god Ma, which appears on coins of Neocaesarea in Pontus, exemplifies this Roman architectural approach. Behind the outer columns lies a masonry wall and large doors, which of course are closed. As mentioned above, this Roman assimilation of local deities was commonplace. The Romans did not, however, abandon their engineering and architectural principles.

Neocaesarea, Pontus. AE 30mm
Septimius Severus, yr 146, (AD 209/10)
Temple of Ma / Zeus (Jupiter)

Pergamon, Mysia,
Orichalcum 20mm (x2)
Tiberius, AD 14-37
Temple of Divus Augustus

The gods honored at provincial cities were not entirely Greek or local divinities. The divine emperors were worshipped as well. At Pergamum, for example, a temple to the deified Augustus was erected during the reign of Tiberius. The distyle temple shown on coins of that time reveals a monumental statue of Augustus at the entrance. These temples, usually not too ostentatious, were erected at cities throughout the empire.

The portrayal of a temple dedicated to Melqarth at Tyre, another Phoenician city, was not very complex architecturally. At least the artist who engraved the dies for this issue under Macrinus did not try to include the entire complex with its courtyards and rose bushes. The simple lines of this building, comfortably centered amidst an easily read inscription, suggest that the celator gave the composition some forethought. Melqarth was the Phoenician equivalent of the Greek Herakles and Roman Hercules.

Tyre, Phoenicia, AE 35mm
Macrinus, AD 217-218
Temple of Melqarth

At Byblos, the ancient Gebal of Biblical reference, a temple to Astarte was depicted on a bronze coin of Macrinus. This composition, aside from its interest as a visual documentary, provides an unusual perspective. The courtyard of the temple is drafted in an aerial perspective, while the facade is frontal. Yet another element is in 3/4 perspective. The combination of these views is a bit disfunctional, but it is nevertheless effective in presenting the main features of the site.

Byblos, Phoenicia, AE 27
Macrinus, AD 217-218
Temple of Astarte (Diana)

Emisa (Homs) was a market city on the caravan route through Syria. It was famous for its great temple of El-Gabal (the Sun). The Romans and Greeks referred to this deity as Heliogabalus. Julia Domna was the daughter of a high Priest of the temple by the name of Bassianus. After she married Septimius Severus, the city was given many honors and privileges. The Great Altar of Emisa is depicted on a coin of Domna, illustrated here. The temple also included a shrine which held a meteorite which was worshipped there (see page 72).

Emisa, Syria, AE 26mm
Julia Domna, AD 193-211
The Great Altar of Emisa

The temple of Zeus at Zeugma, on the western bank of the Euphrates in Commagene or northern Syria, is presented in an interesting bird's-eye view. At the entrance to the temple is a peribolos (courtyard) containing a grove of trees. Zeugma means "bridge", and the city took its name from the fact that Alexander the Great crossed the Euphrates at that point on a pontoon bridge made of boats. Trajan built a bridge of stone at the site.

Zeugma, Syria, AE 29mm
Philip I, AD 244-249

The temple on Mount Gerizim is a recurring feature on the coins of Neapolis (modern Nablus) in Samaria. Originally a Samarian temple, it was rebuilt by Hadrian as a temple to Zeus. The temple was situated on a lofty perch, and was reached by a long set of stairs. These are clearly depicted in the coin motif.

There are many other provincial coins with temple motifs, and they make a very interesting topical area to collect. Part of the joy, of course, is in the discovery and imagination of these structures as actual places. Sometimes we can relate these images to actual places visited.

Neapolis, Samaria, AE 25mm
Trebonianus Gallus, AD 251-253

City Views

Nicaea, Bithynia
AE 23mm (x1.5)
Quietus, AD 261-262

The city walls at Nicaea were famous in ancient times and are still an attraction today. The city was built on a flat fertile plain and therefore required substantial walls to defend it against its enemies. A triumphal arch and a pair of large gateways (visible on this coin) were constructed to celebrate the visit of Hadrian to the city. The modern highway at Nicaea (Iznik) still passes through these gates. The coin illustrated here is one of the last provincial coins to be issued at the city.

Augusta Traiana, Thrace
AE 30mm
Caracalla, AD 198-217

There were some seventy cities in the empire named Augusta, and they are often confused with one another. This city was founded by the emperor Trajan, and was located in almost exactly the center of Thrace. The coins of Thrace often depict city walls, as the city was a refuge for landowners and rural workers during times of stress. The walls shown here are unusual in that they depict a large central turret above the closed city doors. This probably served both as an observation tower and as a defense against scaling of the outer turrets.

Amasia, Pontus, AE 35mm
Severus Alexander, AD 226/7

Amasia in Pontus, not to be confused with Amisus on the Black Sea coast, was home to the families of the Pontic kings and a favorite residence of Mithradates the Great. In the year 228 of the Roman city era (AD 226/7) Amasia struck a series of large bronze coins, one of which (illustrated here) featured a wonderful aerial perspective view of the city. The temple at the top of the scene is known to be that of Zeus Stratios.

The Agonistic Coin Types

Heliopolis, Syria, AE 26mm (x1.5)
Gallienus, AD 253-268
Athlete drawing tally from an urn

ΑΓΩΝΗΣ (agones), derived from Agon—the Greek god of the games, was a general term used for the contests held at national festivals. The Greeks had four main festivals, the Olympian, Pythian, Isthmian, and Nemean. Under the Romans, scores of new games with their own titles and purposes were added to the list. The organizers of these games were called ΑΓΩΝΟΘΕΤΑΙ (Agonothetae). In the province of Asia, the presiding magistrates of the sacred games were called ΑΣΙΑΡΧΑΙ (Asiarchae). These titles were very prestigious and the positions were considered a great honor. So great an honor, in fact, that some agonothetae paid the cost of the games out of their own purse.

The *demiourgos,* or chief magistrate of the city, generally presided over these games while the *agonothetae* decided disputes and awarded the prizes to victors. The prizes were not entirely symbolic. Victors at the more important games were awarded a pension and the right of triumphal entrance upon their return home. For this entry, a special temporary opening was made in the city walls.

The holding of games was, in many cases, part of a larger competition between cities vying for special honors and titles. This sort of rivalry is exemplified by the coinage issued at Tarsus and Anazarbus in Cilicia during the Roman period. Jones *(Cities of the Eastern Provinces)* records the celebration at Tarsus of the Epinicia, Olympia, Actia, Coraea, Demetria and games in honor of the emperors like the Augusteia, Hadrianeia, Commodeia and Severeia. At Anazarbus, he lists a rival Epinicia and Olympia, the Sebasmia, Ecumenical games in honor of Hadrian and Decius, and the "Antoniniana, first of the World". Virtually all of these games were propagandized on coinage issued by their host cities. One of the most blatant—and in retrospect ridiculous—examples of propaganda was the introduction of Philadelpheia games during the reign of Septimius Severus. These games were held to honor the "brotherly love" between Caracalla and Geta, the sons of Severus. Of course there was anything but love between them, and Caracalla

Laodiceia, Phrygia, AE 43mm
ca. AD 218-222
ΟΙΚΟΥΜΕΝΙΚΟΙ
(games open to all contestants)

ultimately arranged his brother's murder—literally in the arms of their mother. The games actually survived the murdered brother as Caracalla continued the subterfuge.

The propagandistic value was, of course, not the only reason to issue coinage. It was probably, in most cases, not even the primary reason. These games attracted people from all over the province, just as the Olympic games today attract people from all over the world. Spectators came to watch their favorite athletes compete and to enjoy the festivity of the occasion. In fact, some of these games were declared Ecumenical Games (οικουμενικοι) which meant literally "World Games" and were open to all competitors regardless of their residence.

Travellers to certain of these games were protected by a warrant of safe passage so that they were not molested on their return home. The convergence of these visitors to the games, and the commercial activity inherent in the process, required a substantial increase in the mint output of a host city. These games-related coins commemorated the event, and probably were prized themselves as wonderful souvenirs.

Perinthus, Thrace, AE 41mm
Septimius Severus, AD 193-211
ΦΙΛΑΔΕΛΦΕΙΑ ΠΕΡΙΝΘΙΩΝ
ΝΕΩΚΟΡΩΝ

Games related coins did not always depict athletes or prizes. The Philadelpheia games, for example, were heralded on a bronze coin from Perinthus, where the central motif is a depiction of Herakles performing one of his 12 Labors—the capture of the Erymanthean Boar.

More often than not the games coins did feature imagery of athletes or prizes, sometimes both. The prizes shown on coins include vases, wreaths, and various garlands or crowns.

The reasons for holding games were numerous. The games imitating the Olympian, Nemean, Pythian and Isthmian festivals are fairly obvious. But the list of lesser important games is quite long. The Alexandrean games honored Alexander the Great. The Actian games celebrated Octavian's victory; the Hadrianea, Antonea, Commodea, Severea, Gordianea and probably others, were held in honor of emperors. An entire pantheon of gods were honored at games. Then there were the league games, the games honoring nymphs, and the games named after places where they were held—for whatever reason. The list goes on.

Pergamum, Mysia, AE 41mm
Valerian I, AD 253-260
Γ ΝΕΩΚΟΡΩΝ
Wreath inscribed ΟΛΥΜΠΙΑ

A large bronze coin from Pergamum depicts the acoutrements of the games, with two agonistic "urns" and a wreath on the traditional four-legged table. Beneath are what seem to be prizes or items used in conducting the contests. The purpose of the urns is enigmatic. Some see them as prize crowns which were placed, at least temporarily, on the heads of the victors. Some renderings of the object clearly show a concave base which would be practical for such a purpose. Others see it as a basket or urn. It clearly held palm branches and perhaps other branch-like symbols of victory. This does not obviate its later use as a crown. Whatever the meaning, it clearly is related to victory. The inscription "OLYMPIA" in Greek, within the center of the wreath, identifies these games as part of that cycle.

Another coin from the Olympic Game cycle was struck at Anchialus in Thrace. This coin bears only one agonistic urn and one prize beneath the four-legged table. It is clear that these symbols have very precise meanings, but as of this writing few if any numismatists fully understand them. One exceptional coin from Anazarbus, a city known for its many games and festivals, has *six* such urns on its reverse.

Anchialus, Thrace, AE 28mm
Gordian III, AD 238-244
Olympian Games

An unusual games coin struck for Valerian I at Side in Pamphylia, has on its reverse the depiction of a Roman magistrate receiving a prize crown or urn from Apollo. The identification of the god is assured by a tripod against which he leans. This coin, because of the inscription OMONOIA has been attributed as an alliance coin between Side and Delphi. The basis for this attribution escapes the present writer. It seems clear enough that the scene depicts either Apollo giving a gift of the games (Pythian?) to the city, or the city dedicating the games to Apollo. The word IEPOC (sacred) in the field suggests that the athletes who participated were protected. The term OMONOIA (Concord) is commonly used in the recognition of alliances, but it may in this case signify the name of the games. In other words, an ancient version of the "Friendship Games".

Side, Pamphylia, AE 36mm
IEPOC in field
OMONOIA in exergue
Valerian, AD 253-260

Another coin with the same general motif was struck at Thyateira in Lydia about 50 years earlier. This coin also bears the ethnic of Stratoniceia in Caria. The two cities apparently cooperated in hosting games honoring the emperor Elagabalus. The fact that Apollo presents the prize crown to the city magistrate (perhaps emperor in this case) indicates that the games follow the Pythian program. The abbreviation ΕΠΙ in the inscription indicates the games are Epinician Games, or in other words, games hosted in honor of the emperor's victories.

Thyateira, Lydia, AE 42mm
ΕΠΙ (NEIKIA)
Elagabalus, AD 218-222

Stratoniceia and Thyateira are actually quite distant from each other. It is interesting that they should be involved jointly in this project, and the cooperation probably suggests other common ground. The occurence of these repetitive motifs would suggest that die-engravers followed standard models for depicting certain types of events.

Culture in the Hinterland

The Three Graces, who lived together with the Muses on Mount Olympus, were minor deities and personifications of grace, charm and beauty—everything culturally significant to the Greeks and so admired and envied by the Romans. Their names were Euphrosyne (Joy), Thalia (Bloom) and Aglaia (Brilliance). The three, who are also referred to sometimes as the Charities, were generally represented in Greek and Roman art as three maidens whose hands were linked together. Horace described them as "The sister—Graces, hand in hand, conjoined by love's eternal band." The standard iconography was that of two Graces facing, with the third (in the middle) turned away and modestly covering the others with her arms.

Deultum, Thrace. AE 23mm
Gordian III, AD 238-244
The Three Graces

The Graces do not appear with great regularity on ancient coins, and are consequently popular among collectors. In addition to the lovely specimen from Thrace illustrated here, one will find the Graces on coins of Marcianopolis, Nicaea, Cremna, Perga, Tarsus, Anazarbus and other cities of the East.

Just as an appreciation of Homer is today a mark of erudition, the cultured of Roman society also recognized the greatness of his work. The depiction of scenes from the Iliad is not common on ancient coins, but there are more in the provincial series than anywhere else. It is generally felt by readers of Homer's account that one of the most poignant episodes is the death of Ajax, who committed suicide after humiliating himself before his peers. This passage of the Iliad has provided artists for more than two millennia with a powerful image. At Prusa ad Olympum, in Bithynia, a die engraver froze forever that lonely moment just before Ajax fell on his sword in despair. The important city of Prusas, built by the Bithynian King Prusias, was located on the northern side of Mount Olympus (different from that mentioned above, which was in Thessaly).

Prusa ad Olympum, Bithynia
AE 26mm, AD 198-217
Ajax committing suicide

Germanicopolis, Paphlagonia
AE 29mm
Julia Domna, AD 217
Venus in her bath

The statue of "Venus" crouching in her bath was sculpted by a famous Bithynian artist named Diodalses in the third century BC. It was then, and still is, considered a masterpiece. Of course the subject was known at that time by her Greek name, Aphrodite. The statue was especially admired by the Romans, who made many copies of it. There are a number of surviving Roman reproductions, which are today identified as Venus. The depiction of this famous work of art on a coin of Julia Domna reflects the contemporary appreciation of artistic excellence and also an appreciation of art history. Very few original Greek statues have survived, but fortunately the Romans left us with some idea of the splendor that they inherited from the fallen Hellenistic monarchs.

An appealing bronze from Bizya in Thrace bears an unusual narrative scene. The subject is Kapaneus, a descendant of Proteus, depicted in typical heroic form. The naked warrior with shield and helmet, lunging forward, is a standard image that may be seen on Greek coins of the fourth century and perhaps earlier. It is the pose adopted for Ajax on the Locrian coins and Leuscapsis on those from Magna Graecia. Kapaneus was the hero who helped Polynices in his attempt to recover the throne of Thebes . The story is related in a classic play by Aeschylus called *Seven Against Thebes.* In the play, Kapaneus boasts that not even the gods could keep him from scaling the walls of Thebes. Of course he was rewarded for his impudence by being struck down with a lightning bolt from Zeus. The Greek love of literature was unabated in the provincial period and, in fact, the Romans became very much enamored with Greek culture.

Byzya, Thrace, AE 29mm
Septimius Severus, AD 193-211

Transportation in the Roman Provinces

One of the oldest and most effective forms of transportation known to man is by water. The Romans were much less dependent upon sea transportation than their predecessors, because of the extensive road system that they maintained. Still, the transportation of large quantities of men and material, in the shortest amount of time, required an efficient fleet. The reliance of Romans upon the sea is reflected in a great diversity of nautical types. Some coins simply display ships at sail, others reveal ships at anchor in a harbor, or being loaded. Cities that served the Roman fleet faithfully were honored with special titles and awarded special privileges.

Hadrianopolis, Thrace, AE 24mm
Tranquillina, AD 241-244

Side, Pamphylia, AE 23mm
Salonina, ca. AD 253-268
NAYAPXIC in exergue

Ancient Side was located on the Mediterranean coast, south of the city of Aspendus and at the western end of what is known today as the "Turkish Riviera". It was originally an Aeolian colony and in Roman times, became a prosperous city with a large amphitheater. That it was an important maritime port is attested by the title *Navarchis*—which appears, along with depictions of the Roman fleet, on an impressive bronze coin of Salonina. This term is derived from the word meaning "flagship of the fleet".

Temenothyrae, Phrygia, AE 41mm
Gallienus, AD 253-268

Titanius, the Archierus or High Priest of Temenothyrae in Phrygia was distinguished on a very unusual bronze medallion struck during the reign of Gallienus. A narrative reverse, which includes the priest's name in its inscription, illustrates the effort and precision necessary to transport what appears to be a large cult image to its place of honor. Several attendants carefully steady the form with ropes as it is moved on a two-wheeled cart drawn by a pair of oxen. The apparent strain makes it clear that the object is heavy, and probably carved from stone. One would hope that the road was not too bumpy or the journey too long.

Ephesus, Ionia, AE 32mm
Gordian III, AD 238-244

Another form of surface transportation is depicted on a large bronze from Ephesus in Ionia. This four-wheeled cart has side panels and a canopy, as well as a platform for the driver. It is pulled by two mules. Carts of all types hauled people and materials over the Roman roadways and it was not unusual for them to traverse great distances. Over time, the stone-paved roads took on distinct ruts. These ruts are clearly visible today on any excavated roadway. There is a well known story, perhaps true, that the modern rail system in Britain and the U.S. is derived from that Roman system. As the story goes, the production of cart axels was standardized because of the deep ruts. Axels of sizes other than the standard caused the wheels of a cart to fall into one rut and ride above the other. This caused breakdowns and great discomfort. When the first tramways were built in England, the cars were built from the same forms that were used to make carts. Therefore, they retained the same wheelbase (4 feet, 8.5 inches). These trams evolved into modern trains.

One of the greatest transportation stories of all time is the account of Noah and his Ark. Although the story was known from numerous folk tales, it was translated from the Hebrew Bible into Greek during the reign of Ptolemy II in Egypt. From that time on, it became a literary as well as oral tradition. Remarkably, this story of Noah is the theme of a series of Roman Provincial coins from Apameia in Phrygia. Noah and his wife are portrayed in a floating chest, a pun on the city's name, but there can be no doubt of the allusion. The name ΝΩΕ (Noah) is engraved prominently on the makeshift boat. Why would the Apameans choose this unusual subject for their coinage? Read the fascinating article by Marvin Tameanko listed in the bibliography to this section!

Apameia, Phrygia
AE 34mm
Philip I, AD 244-249

Astrological/Astronomical Types

Perinthus, Thrace, AE 40mm
Severus Alexander, AD 222-235

One thing that the Romans had in common with nearly all of their conquered subjects, was a belief that the affairs of man were guided and controlled by the stars. The depiction of astrological or astronomical motifs, within the art of the entire ancient world, has a long and interesting history. Actually, the two were synonymous in ancient times. It is only in the modern scientific world that we distinguish between the two. It is not surprising that we find astrological images with some frequency on the coinage of the Romans—both imperial and provincial. Sometimes the imagery is specific, as in the case of a personal horoscope. At other times it is commemorative of a notable celestial event. An entire series of astrological coins was struck at Alexandria, and they are discussed earlier in the chapter about Roman Egypt. The phenomenon, however, was widespread.

The bronze medallion from Perinthus, illustrated above, represents a general view of the Cosmos and the acknowledgement of astrological influence. This interpretation, advanced by Catherine C. Lorber *(Treasures of Ancient Coinage: From the Private Collections of American Numismatic Society Members),* accounts for the appearance of the same general motif at various places and times. Similar astrological "wheels", representing the twelve signs of the Zodiac around a central narrative scene, were issued at Sardis in Lydia, Nikaia and Tios in Bithynia, Irenopolis in Cilicia, Ake-Ptolemais and Sidon in Phoenicia, Amastris in Paphlagonia and Alexandria in Egypt.

Sol and Luna are often depicted together in facing poses, side by side, or in profile poses with conjoined heads. A bronze drachm from Alexandria illustrates the typical representation of Sol with a radiate crown and the head of Luna resting on a crescent.

Alexandria, Egypt
Antoninus Pius, AD 141/2
Sol and Luna

Antioch, Syria
AD 55/6, AE 20mm
the Star of Bethlehem

To the modern observer, one of the most important astrological/astronomical events of ancient times was the mysterious Star of Bethlehem. Dr. Michael Molnar, an astronomer at Rutgers University, has performed a detailed analysis of this event, and in a forthcoming book (tentatively titled *Finding the Star of Bethlehem)* has related the "Aries" coins of Antioch directly to the famous star in the East. This coin was issued by the Roman Legate of Syria. For a preliminary article, see *The Celator,* December 1991, pp. 8-12. Also see Molnar's articles about the astrological sign of Augustus on coins (*The Celator,* April 1994) and about comets on the coins of Mithridates the Great and their relationship to the Roman Wars (*The Celator,* June 1997).

One of the most intriguing astrological references in ancient coinage is to the Phrygian deity Mên. This obscure figure, also known as Mensis, or "month" is absent from virtually all of the major dictionaries of mythology. It is the title of a male moon god which appears on several provincial coins. His latin name would be Lunus and he is usually depicted wearing the well known Phrygian felt cap, not unlike Mithras. It would seem, in fact, that there is a close relationship between this deity and the Mithraic Mysteries. The most authoritative book on this subject is *The Origins of the Mithraic Mysteries: Cosmology & Salvation in the Ancient World,* by David Ulansey (Oxford, 1989).

On a coin struck under Gallienus at Sillyeum in Pamphylia, Mên is clearly identified as an astrological figure as he is set amongst a crescent moon and star (the sun). The ancient belief that everything has male and female aspects, is not entirely understood, and just what the role of Mên was as compared to that of Luna is unclear. The worship seems to be centered in Asia Minor.

Sillyeum, Pamphylia
AE 32mm
Gallienus, AD 253-268
Mên on crescent

This unusual deity also appears on provincial coins of Antioch in Pisidia, there too wearing a Phrygian cap and depicted with a crescent moon in the background.

BIBLIOGRAPHY

Roman Provincial Iconography

Casson, Lionel. *Travel in the Ancient World.* Toronto, 1974.

Casson, L. and Martin Price. *Coins, Culture and History in the Ancient World,* Detroit, 1981.

Donaldson, T.L. *Architectura Numismatica: Ancient Architecture on Greek and Roman Coins,* London, 1859 (reprint, Chicago, 1966).

Drew-Bear, Thomas. "Representations of Temples on the Greek Imperial Coinage", *ANS Museum Notes,* 19, New York, 1974.

Gardner, Percy. *The Types of Greek Coins: An Archaeological Essay,* Cambridge, 1883 (reprint, Chicago, 1965).

Handler, S. "Architecture on the Roman Coins of Alexandria", *American Journal of Archaeology,* 1971.

Hill, Philip V. *The Monuments of Ancient Rome as Coin Types,* London, 1989.

Imhoof-Blumer, F. and P. Gardner. *Numismatic Commentary on Pausanius,* London, 1885-1887 (reprint as *Ancient Coins Illustrating Lost Masterpieces of Greek Art,* Chiclago, 1964).

Johnston, Ann. "Caracalla or Elagabalus? A Case of Unnecessarily Mistaken Identity", *ANS Museum Notes,* 27, New York, 1982.

Krzyzanowska, Aleksandra. "Le culte de Mên à Antioche de Pisidie d'après les monnais coloniales", *Mélanges offerts à K. Michalowski, Warsaw,* 1966, pp. 513-521.

Naster, Paul. "Isis Pharia sur les monnaies impériales d'Alexandrie", *Bulletin de la Société Française de Numismatique,* vol. 23, no. 2, 1968, pp. 238-240.

Penn, R.G. *Medicine on Ancient Greek and Roman Coins,* London, 1994.

Price, Martin and Bluma Trell. *Coins and Their Cities: Architecture on the Ancient Coins of Greece, Rome, and Palestine",* London, 1977.

Richter, Gisela M.A. "The origin of verism in Roman portraits", *Journal of Roman Studies,* 1955, pp. 39-46.

Scanlon, Thomas F. *Greek and Roman Athletics, a Bibliography,* Chicago, 1984.

Starr, C.G. "Naval activity in Greek imperial issues", *Swiss Numismatic Review,* 46, 1967, p. 51f.

Trell, Bluma. "The Cult-Image on Temple-Type Coins", *Numismatic Chronicle,* 1964, pp. 241-246.

Tameanko, Marvin. *Architecture and Engineering on Ancient Coins,* Iola, WI, 1998.

Vermeule, Cornelius C. "Roman numismatic art A.D. 200-400", *Numismatic Circular,* vol. 64, 1956 and vol. 65, 1957, London.

Masterpieces of Provincial Coinage

The following section includes a group of enlarged photographs of various Roman Provincial coins that the author believes are exceptional specimens. The selection is not based on any particular criteria, but mainly on visual and emotional appeal. A coin, like the Severus Alexander tetradrachm from Egypt, may be common. The execution of its die is, however, masterful when considered in the context of its time. There are literally hundreds of coins in this series that could match the quality or appeal of coins presented here, and this is not an attempt to present the "best" known. It is simply an opportunity to illustrate the beauty that may be seen on Roman Provincial coins in general.

Masterpieces of Provincial Coinage

Syedra, Cilicia, AE 34mm
Trajan Decius, AD 249-251

The Gymnasiarch was a very important magistrate in provincial cities, and a position of great honor. Even generals and emperors were anxious to hold the title. It was so coveted that the term sometimes lasted only a month—allowing more to share the honor. Although public games were an extremely important part of community life, the Gymnasium was of even greater importance. This was, just as the name implies, a place of exercise and relaxation. It was also a place of education and training for athletes. The role of the Gymnasiarch dates back at least to the laws of Solon, who charged this official with management of the Gymnasium and everything connected with it. He was much like a priest, with specific rituals to perform. He was charged with paying city sponsored trainees and providing the oil which athletes used on their bodies before training or competing. He also organized and managed certain public games. This beautiful bronze from Syedra presents a simple but elegant composition including the athlete's oil basin, a palm branch and two vases—probably containing oils. It alludes to games held under the authority of the Gymnasiarch, who might very well in this case have been the emperor himself.

Masterpieces of Provincial Coinage

Soli-Pompeiopolis, Cilicia, AE 23mm
Time of Domitian, AD 83/4

Cnaeus Pompeius Magnus was one of Rome's most famous and successful generals and statesmen. His military ability was so great that he was saluted Imperator by Sulla at the age of 23. He was very successful in Africa, and Spain, and by sheer good fortune claimed the successful conclusion of the Servile War. In 67 BC, Pompey was commissioned by the Senate to prosecute the war against the pirates of Cilicia. He completely routed the pirates, destroyed their fleet and settled a great many of them at the city of Soli, which was renamed Pompeiopolis. He went on to consolidate Roman power in Cilicia and Syria, leaving behind him a Roman East. Much of this land he left to the administration of local princes who served at the pleasure of Rome. Most of the major cities he made free, but subject to Roman law and arms. Pompey came to an inglorious end at Alexandria in 48 BC while seeking asylum after losing the civil war to Julius Caesar. The exceptional portrait of Pompey on this coin of Soli-Pompeiopolis was struck in the year 149 of the Pompeian era. It reveals a man of determination and stern character. It also reveals a lasting respect in Cilicia for the conqueror that many Romans feared and hated.

Masterpieces of Provincial Coinage

Tarsus, Cilicia, AE 38mm
Maximinus I, AD 235-238

The Judgement of Paris is one of the most famous mythological stories of all time. (For a full account of the story see page 99 of this volume). Surprisingly, as important and popular as it is, depictions of the story on coinage are relatively scarce. This bronze issue from Tarsus is one of the most extraordinary examples that may be seen. It is really an allegorical scene. As Paris presents the golden apple to Aphrodite, the fairest of the goddesses, the entire scene is crowned by the inscription TAPCOY AMK, that is, Tarsus: First, Greatest, most Beautiful.

Tarsus and Anazarbus contended fiercely for this title, both of them claiming it during this period, and they went to extraordinary lengths to support their claim—with elaborate games, imperial visits, neocorate temples and dedications of all sorts.

Masterpieces of Provincial Coinage

Sagalassos, Pisidia, AE 38mm
Gordian III, AD 238-244

Demeter was the mythical Mother Earth (not Earth itself, which was Gaea) . She had a daugher, Persephone, around which an entire series of stories (the Eleusinian Mysteries) evolved. Persephone was abducted by Hades and taken to the nether world. Grief stricken, Demeter searched the world for her abducted daughter. In this search she is often depicted riding in a biga of dragons. This same biga was later given to Triptolemus to aid mankind (see facing page).

In this emotional composition from Sagalassos in Pisidia, Demeter carries a flaming torch to light the sky as she continues her search through the night. The trailing drapery of her garb gives a sense of motion and immediacy to the scene, as does her forward leaning stance. As in all great numismatic compositions, the legend complements rather than detracts from the main narrative elements.

Masterpieces of Provincial Coinage

Hadrianopolis, Thrace, AE 26mm
Caracalla, AD 198-217

Triptolemus was regarded by at least one account as the son of Oceanus and Gaea (Earth). He was the inventor of the plow and of agriculture as well as civilization in general. As a compensation for the accidental death of his son, Demeter gave Triptolemus a chariot with winged dragons and seeds of wheat. He spent his life travelling over the earth sowing this wheat and teaching man the fundamentals of agriculture.

On this bronze from Hadrianopolis in Thrace, a region of agricultural prosperity, Triptolemus is shown travelling over the Earth (Gaea) who receives his gift of grain. It is not only a bold mythological narrative, but a masterful execution of dragons in flight. In the chariot, Triptolemus is holding a cloth sowing bag and casting grain as he crosses the sky.

Masterpieces of Provincial Coinage

Philippopolis, Thrace, AE 37mm
Caracalla, AD 214

The reverse of this provincial bronze from Thrace heralds the celebration of the Pythian Games at Philippopolis in AD 214, honoring the memory of Alexander the Great. It was struck in the name of the *Koinon Thrakon* or "League of Thracian Cities" as the inscription records. Games-related coins were struck at many cities throughout the provinces as a form of civic aggrandizement, but the unusual majesty of this issue might be attributed to the physical presence of the emperor Caracalla, who was in Thrace at that time leading a campaign against the Goths.

The composition of this reverse type is remarkable technically as well as iconographically. The ornate four-legged prize table, in vivid three dimensional perspective, adds an important element of depth and effectively projects the prize (variously described as an urn, basket or a crown) as the central element. The prize itself holds the palm branches of victory and is wrapped in a large banner bearing the name ΠΥΘΙΑ. Beneath the table are other prizes—an amphora, a palm branch and a stack of balls (the favorite game of both Greek and Roman citizens). The Pythian Games, next to the Olympics, were the most important of the main celebrations which rotated on a four year schedule. They were first held at Delphi, originally called Pytho, in the year 586 BC.

Masterpieces of Provincial Coinage

Corinth, Greece, AE 25mm
Lucius Verus, AD 161-169

The mythical heritage of Corinth is related in this extraordinary narrative scene. Atop the Acrocorinth, home of a noted temple of Aphrodite, the winged horse Pegasus takes to flight. At the base of the mountain is the Fountain of Peirene where Pegasus came to drink and rest. The spring feeding this fountain was home to the local nymph of that name. The mythological tale of the birth and adventures of Pegasus is one of great popularity today, and certainly was also in ancient times. The ubiquitous silver staters of Corinth and her colonies, known as the "Colts of Corinth", carried the image of Pegasus to the far corners of the Greek world. The winged horse was also important in Roman mythology and iconography. It was natural therefore to continue this Greek motif on the Roman coinage of Corinth.

Masterpieces of Provincial Coinage

Laodicea, Phrygia , AE 42mm
Caracalla, AD 198-217

The scene on this rare provincial bronze has been described, tentatively, as the emperor Caracalla in a forum. He is depicted speaking to an assembly of citizens from atop a platform. Along the interior walls are armed soldiers standing at attention. In the entryway, a couple converses while attendants or members of the imperial entourage stand idly in the wings. The upper inscription, partly obliterated on this specimen, seems to refer to the Olympian games held at Loadicea. In the exergue is the city ethnic and its neocorate status. The central figure holds a wreath in his right hand, more or less in reserve, as he presents another to one of those assembled below. A group to the left raise their hands in salute. It is a remarkable narrative scene which captures a brief and rare moment in time—an early photograph one might say. Equally remarkable is the celator's adept composition, which exhibits an extraordinary sense of perspective and imagination in a "bird's-eye" view of the proceedings. The importance of this event is made clear by the huge medallic flan provided for this issue and the skill of the artist employed to execute the dies.

Masterpieces of Provincial Coinage

Antioch, AR tetradrachm (x1.5)
Trajan, AD 98-117

Tetradrachms from Antioch vary greatly in their quality of execution, and the collector will find portraits of superb quality followed shortly by inept attempts. The specimen illustrated here is one of the great masterpieces of coinage from that city. The obverse, with its subsidiary eagle gives the viewer a sense of dimension that few compositions can match. The reverse, while more conventional in its approach, is superb in its detail and modelling. The subject, Hercules, is portrayed as a hard powerful figure with thick brows and hard cheek bones. A square jaw and thick neck bolter the impression of strength and invincibility. Unlike the stereotyped reverses that this seris is famous for, this one reveals a celatorial brilliance at work in the province.

Masterpieces of Provincial Coinage

Emisa, AR tetradrachm (x1.5)
Uranius Antoninus, AD 253-254

With the death of Trebonianus Gallus and Volusian, L. Julius Aurelius Sulpicius Severus Uranius Antoninus briefly assumed the purple in Syria. This priest of Emisa had a long name and a short reign. He assembled reasonable support in the region, perhaps including the city of Antioch, but was quickly deposed when Valerian arrived in Syria. During his tenure, Uranius Antoninus issued gold aurei, silver tetradrachms and some bronze coins. The tetradrachm illustrated here shows that he had access to talented engravers and an experienced mint.

The selection of a bridled camel for this reverse type betrays a regional mentality that probably would not have served the hapless ruler well even if he had survived.

Masterpieces of Provincial Coinage

Antioch, Syria, AR tetradrachm (x2)
Commodus, AD 178/9

This tetradrachm was issued at Antioch while the young emperor Commodus was engaged in the Germanic wars with his father, Marcus Aurelius. On the whole, numismatic portraits of Commodus are not very flattering. Only among the gold aurei do we find any hint of emotion, and even then his features are typically hard.

Later in his reign, Commodus succumbed to a megalomania that made him extremely unpopular with the Roman aristocracy. Therefore, a sensitive, almost innocent, portrayal like that seen here could only have originated early in his reign and only at a provincial mint where his popularity had not yet suffered. The celator's skill is immediately evident in this moving portrait and it completely shatters the myth that provincial mints were staffed with less talented engravers.

Masterpieces of Provincial Coinage

Septimius Severus, AD 193-211
Ancyra, Phrygia, AE 27mm

This wonderful portrait of Septimius Severus needs no explanation of its virtues. Nowhere in the myriad issues from Rome does a celator's work exceed the sculptural excellence of this piece. That it was produced in Ancyra, in a remote section of Asia Minor, is all the more remarkable. In the Severan period we see the last examples of fine Roman portraiture, unshackled by the ethereal conventions of spiritualism. Within a fortnight of this coin's issue, the high relief and flambouyant line disappeared. The lively expression gave way to stoic complacency, and the virtuosity of a master engraver was considered out of vogue.

Masterpieces of Provincial Coinage

Severus Alexander, Year 10 (AD 230/31)
Potin tetradrachm, Alexandria, Egypt

The tetradrachms of Roman Egypt are fascinating in their diversity, and rank among the best and the worst of Roman numismatic art. This is a series where the skill of die-engravers at the Alexandria mint varied greatly, even within issues of the same year. At its best, Alexandrian coinage provides some of the most emotional portraiture of the Severan period. At its worst, portrayals of the imperial family become merely representative lifeless cartoons. This tetradrachm of Severus Alexander, a relatively common and inexpensive coin, presents one of the most penetrating visual images of the young emperor's reign. Even the highly touted portraits on imperial mint sestertii do not match the feeling of this work.

Featured on the reverse is a powerful image of the Egyptian lower-world god Serapis—parallel in some respects to the Roman Jupiter and Aesculapius. He wears on his head an ornate modius (a measuring cup for grain) which is a standard attribute of this deity.

Adding to the beauty and charm of some really exceptional portraits from Alexandria is the regular appearance of a natural chocolate brown patina which is unsurpassed in richness. The combination of a superb artist's skill and nature's delicate aging results in an artefact of extraordinary beauty and great emotional appeal.

Masterpieces of Provincial Coinage

Athens, AE 24mm ca. AD 140-175
view of the Acropolis

In about 460 BC, a young sculptor and native of Athens by the name of Pheidias, completed his first of many great works—a colossal bronze statue of Athena. Today, it is commonly referred to as the Athena Promachos. In its own time it was simply known as "the bronze Athena." The epithet Promachos means "champion" or "defender". Pausanius, in his *Description of Greece,* related that the statue of Athena Promachos was financed by spoils from the Greek victory over the Persians at Marathon. It stood northwest of the Parthenon and was the point upon which the Propylaea or entrance gate of the Acropolis was oriented.

The statue represented a standing Athena, helmeted and holding a spear transversely in her right hand. A shield, upon which her left hand rested, reclined against her left leg. According to Pausanius, the statue was so tall that the gilded spear tip and the crest of Athena's helmet could be seen from ships off the point of Cape Sounion some 30 miles away. The statue, therefore, became a landmark for vessels bound for the port of Athens at Piraeus.

The emperor Caligula (37-41 AD) had a penchant, it seems, for the colossal Athena. Not only did he pave with marble the steps of the Propylaea leading up to the Promachos, but actually planned to remove the statue and ship it to Rome. The idea was certainly not original, as Romans had by Caligula's time hauled off tons of art treasures from Greek lands. Aemilius Paullus had carted off some 250 wagon loads of statues, paintings and the like, among which was a smaller bronze Athena also by Pheidias.

Although the ambitions of Caligula were never realized, the task of relocating the great bronze statue was not beyond the resources of Constantine the Great. Having founded his new capital at Constantinople in AD 330, and anxious to stock it with fine works of art, Constantine removed the Promachos from its home of more than 750 years and reinstalled it before the new Roman Senate building on the Bosporus. It remained there until AD 1203, when it was torn down by an angry mob during the Latin invasion of that year.

The view of the Acropolis on this coin, struck during the reign of Antoninus Pius, presents the statue of Athena as a main feature of the composition. Today, we think of the Parthenon as being the most majestic element on that site, but it is clear from this depiction that the ancients thought differently. The greatly exaggerated entrance stairs were, of course, a Roman improvement started by Caligula and completed by Claudius. The prominence of these stairs in the coin motif served as great propaganda—a reminder to the Greeks that the Roman emperor paid due homage to their gods.

Entrance to the Acropolis at Athens

Glossary

Acropolis: The "High City", usually a citadel at the city's highest point.
Actus: Plot of land 120 feet by 120 feet.
Agonistic: Pertaining to the holding of public games and festivals.
Anatolia: The region basically equivalent to modern Turkey. Also referred to as Asia Minor.
Arsacids: Parthian kings of a dynasty named for Arsaces.
Assaria: A bronze denomination used throughout Asia Minor.
Billon: Silver, debased to 50% or less. Coins with less than 10% silver are normally referred to as Potin.
Bouphonia: A sacrifice to Zeus in the form of a specially selected bull.
Ciliciarch: Leader of the Koinon or Council of Cilicia.
Cista: Basket (Cista Mystica was a basket containing a snake, used in cult rituals). The quaestor's money chest was called a cista.
Cistophorus: Bearer of a basket. A denomination of silver coin in Asia named from its origin as a coin bearing a cista in its design.
Citerior: Nearer (in relation to Rome).
Client King: A ruler who served in his own kingdom at the pleasure of, and under terms dictated by, Rome.
Colony: A settlement of Roman citizens or elevation of a provincial city to the special rank afforded citizens.
Conjoined: Placed one before the other in perspective.
Countermark: Mark applied with a punch to validate a coin for issue.
Cult: A system of religious worship or ritual, usually extreme in its beliefs and practices.
Decapolis: Ten cities of Syria formed into a loose confederation by Pompey the Great.
Decennial: Occurring every ten years, as in the renewal of power.
Decennalia: The festival celebrated by Roman emperors upon attaining ten years of rule and accepting the "obligation" to continue their service to the empire for another such term.
Deified: Acknowledged as a god or goddess.
Demiurgos: Highest official of a city.
Demos: The genius or spirit of the people.
Distyle: Two column.
Duovirs: The rule of two magistrates, for example at Corinth.
Dynasty: Rule by bloodline succession, normally involving several generations of a family.
Elagabal: The sun god of a Semitic cult in Emisa, Syria.
Era Date: Dating system based on a city's foundation or refoundation.
Fabric: The "feel" of a coin based on its characteristics of manufacture such as size, weight, thickness, preparation of flan, etc.

Groma: A surveyors staff used to site the lines of an actus.
Hippodrome: Stadium where horse races were held.
Iconography: The imagery and subject of an artistic composition.
Inferior: Lower.
Iugerum: Plot of land equal to two square acti (120 feet by 240 feet).
Julian Calendar: The calendar invented by Julius Caesar.
Koinon: Senate or council (plural = koina).
Legate: Military leader assisting the governor of a province.
Levant: The countries bordering the Eastern Mediterranean.
Limes: Series of defensive fortifications on the German frontier.
Mên: The male equivalent of the moon goddess Luna.
Millennium: Period of one thousand years.
Municipia: A lesser rank than municipium, with limited privileges.
Municipium: The highest level of government bestowed on a city.
Navarchis: Literally, "flagship". An honorific title bestowed on important maritime cities.
Neocorus: The keeper of a temple to the imperial cult.
Nome: An administrative district of Roman Egypt.
Pedias: Smooth, a term applied to the Cilician plains.
Principate: The stage of government created by Octavian in 27 BC which evolved into the Roman Empire.
Pseudo-autonomous: Endowed with limited self government. Also referred to as "semi-autonomous" or "quasi-autonomous".
Quaestor: A civilian official who handled the financial affairs of the province under the authority of the governor.
Regnal Date: Date based on the reign of a ruler, starting at year 1 on the ruler's accession and restarting with the next reign.
Sella: Chair of authority.
Shamash: A sun god of Mesopotamia, still worshipped in Roman times.
Sothic Cycle: An Egyptian astrological cycle of 1461 years.
Superior: Upper.
Tetrarch: A rank inferior to king, similar to Toparch, held by client rulers of Rome.
Tetrastyle: Four column.
Toparch: A form of principate less dignified than king.
Tracheia: Rough, a term applied to the mountainous regions of Cilicia.
Ulterior: Further (in relation to Rome).
Usurper: One who assumed power and rule without duly constituted authority (whatever that might have been).
Vexillum: A legionary standard (plural = vexilla).
Zodiac: A celestial band extending about eight degrees to either side of the "ecliptic" that represents the path of the planets, the moon, and the sun. This band is divided into 12 equal parts, 30 degrees wide, called signs.

BIBLIOGRAPHY

Additional References

Amandry, M. *Le Monnayage des Duovirs Corinthiens,* Paris, 1988.

Adams, J.P. *Logistics of the Roman Imperial Army. Major Campaigns of the Eastern Front in the First Three Centuries A.D.,* PhD Dissertation, Yale University, 1976.

Babelon, E. *Inventaire de la Collection Waddington,* Paris 1897.

Blair, Peter Hunter. *Roman Britain and Early England 55 B.C.-A.D. 871,* London, 1963.

Braund, David C. *Augustus to Nero: A Sourcebook on Roman History 31 BC - AD 68,* Totowa. NJ, 1985.

Butcher, Kevin. *Roman Provincial Coins, an Introduction to the Greek Imperials,* London, 1988.

Duncan-Jones, R. *Money and Government in the Roman Empire,* Cambridge, 1994.

Grant, Michael. *A Guide to the Ancient World: A Dictionary of Classical Place Names,* 1986, H.W. Wilson; Barnes & Noble 1997.

Harl, Kenneth W. *Civic Coins and Civic Politics in the Roman East, A.D. 180-275,* Berkeley, 1987.

Howgego, Christopher. *Ancient History From Coins,* London and New York, 1995.

Jones, A.H.N. *Cities of the Eastern Provinces,* Clarendon Press, Oxford, 1971.

Jones, John Melville. *A Dictionary of Ancient Roman Coins,* London, 1990.

Peters, F.E. *The Harvest of Hellenism,* New York, 1970.

Sellwood, D. *An Introduction to the Coinage of Parthia,* London, 1971.

Shore, Fred B. *Parthian Coins and History: Ten Dragons Against Rome,* Quarryville, PA, 1993.

Stark, Freya. *Rome on the Euphrates,* New York, 1966.

Toynbee, J.M.C. "Greek Imperial Medallions" *Journal of Roman Studies, 34* (1944), pp. 65-73.

Vermeule, Cornelius. *Numismatic Art of the Greek Imperial World, Interactions Between Rome, Greece, Asia Minor, Syria, the Holy Land and Egypt,* Boston, 1986.

Winspear, A.D. and L.K. Geweke. *Augustus and the Reconstruction of Roman Government and Society,* UW Studies in the Social Sciences, No. 24, University of Wisconsin, Madison, 1935.

General Index